THE CHURCH'S PEACE WITNESS

The Church's
Peace Witness

Edited by

Marlin E. Miller
and
Barbara Nelson Gingerich

WILLIAM B. EERDMANS PUBLISHING COMPANY
GRAND RAPIDS, MICHIGAN

Library of Congress Cataloging-in-Publication Data

The church's peace witness / edited by Marlin E. Miller
and Barbara Nelson Gingerich.
        p.   cm.
Includes bibliographical references.
ISBN 0-8028-0555-8 (pbk.)
1. Peace — Religious aspects — Christianity.
I. Miller, Marlin E., 1938-   . II. Gingerich, Barbara Nelson.
BT736.4.C54 1994
261.8'73 — dc20   94-34356
                                        CIP

Contents

CONTENTS

Preface

Saint John's Gospel quotes our Lord in prayer: "I ask not only on behalf of these, but also on behalf of those who will believe in me through their word, that they may all be one. As you, Father, are in me and I am in you, may they also be in us, so that the world may believe that you have sent me" (John 17:20-21, NRSV). The great prayer for unity among his followers has remained a central prayer for Christians through the centuries, a prayer we make our own.

In our time this prayer is expressed in the purpose of the ecumenical movement: "to call the churches to the goal of visible unity in one faith and in one eucharistic fellowship expressed in worship and in common life in Christ, and to advance toward that unity in order that the world may believe" (from the constitution of the World Council of Churches).

We pray, study, and work for unity to bring Christ's message to the world. As we move toward that unity, we already unite in our commitment to preach God's word, to engage in Christian education, and to witness to God's will for justice, peace, and the integrity of creation, grounded in the confession of the triune God. Since the sixteenth-century Reformation, churches have become separated from one another because of their different understandings of the Christian faith handed down by the Apostles and witnessed to in sacred Scripture. Some of these churches — the Mennonites, the Church of the Brethren, the

Society of Friends — are sometimes called the historic peace churches. The witness of these groups is an important contribution to our ecumenical discussion. Reconciliation among our churches is a gospel priority.

We are grateful to the Commission on Faith and Order of the National Council of the Churches of Christ in the U.S.A. for initiating this discussion on the biblical basis of the unity of the church in its peace witness. Their sponsorship is especially fitting because participants in the conversation have come from the Roman Catholic Church, from all the historic peace churches, and from all the member churches of the National Council of Churches.

This volume comes as an invitation to a process of reconciliation, of seeking a common foundation for our understanding of the church and its mission in the world, grounded in Scripture. We hope that this volume, like the Commission on Faith and Order study guide *Confessing One Faith: The Origins, Meaning and Use of the Nicene Creed: Grounds for a Common Witness* (Cincinnati: Forward Movement Publications, 1988), will provide opportunity for Christians to reflect on the faith we share and explore biblical resources for overcoming our divisions.

Our hope is that the Holy Spirit will bless our efforts to find a basis for a common confession of the apostolic faith today. We are grateful for the witness of the historic peace churches. We ask that the Lord may be our guide:

> Lead us, with all our brothers and sisters, toward communion in
> faith, life, and witness, so that, united in one body by the one
> Spirit, we may together witness to the perfect unity of your love.

Archbishop William H. Keeler, President
National Conference of Catholic Bishops

Reverend Gordon L. Sommers, President
*National Council of the Churches of Christ in
the U.S.A.*

Contributors

PAUL N. ANDERSON Assistant Professor of Biblical and Quaker Studies, George Fox College, Newberg, Oregon

DIANNE BERGANT, C.S.A. Professor of Old Testament Studies, Catholic Theological Union, Chicago, Illinois

CHARLES W. BROCKWELL, JR. Director of Continuing Education, Louisville Presbyterian Theological Seminary, Louisville, Kentucky

DONALD F. DURNBAUGH Archivist, Juniata College, Huntingdon, Pennsylvania

JEFFREY GROS, F.S.C. Associate Director, Secretariat for Ecumenical and Interreligious Affairs, National Conference of Catholic Bishops, Washington, D.C.

DAVID G. HUNTER Associate Professor of Theology, University of St. Thomas, St. Paul, Minnesota

RICHARD L. JESKE Pastor, Holy Trinity Lutheran Church, New York, New York

WILLIAM H. KEELER President, National Conference of Catholic Bishops, and Archbishop of Baltimore, Baltimore, Maryland

HOWARD JOHN LOEWEN Academic Dean, Mennonite Brethren Biblical Seminary, Fresno, California

MARLIN E. MILLER President, Associated Mennonite Biblical Seminary, Elkhart, Indiana

BEN C. OLLENBURGER Professor of Biblical Theology, Associated Mennonite Biblical Seminary, Elkhart, Indiana

GORDON L. SOMMERS President, National Council of the Churches of Christ in the U.S.A., and President, Moravian Church in America, Bethlehem, Pennsylvania

1. Introduction

JEFFREY GROS, F.S.C.

Wars and strife fill our memories and daily find their way into our consciousness through the media. All Christians confess that Christ's peace is to transform our lives and that we are to bring Christ's peace into the life of the human family. Yet we are divided into separate churches and sometimes take up arms against each other in the name of our separate nations and even in the name of our separate Christian confessions. How does our common confession of Christ call us to account for our divisions? How does our common vocation in Christ call us to account for differences in how we exercise responsibility in society? How does our common affirmation of the authority of Scripture call us to account for our divided witness in the world? This volume begins a conversation about how Scripture can help us understand the call to reconciliation among the churches, and specifically the call to reconcile in Christ our differences in witness to the world.

A Confessional Study

This volume was produced from careful scholarly research done under the prayer of the Holy Spirit to serve the reconciliation of the churches. It should be read prayerfully while we await the Holy Spirit's reconciling power to heal our divisions. Contributors hope it will enliven Christians' response to the world in which we live and help all who confess Christ to understand that the Christian community, rather than the secular society, should mediate to the world the values for which Christians stand together.[1]

These discussions were undertaken in a context in which the United States is a powerful force in the global human family, individualism dominates American culture, and the values of secular media intrude into Christian consciousness. This book should challenge us to go more deeply into Christ and become a resource for the spiritual sustenance of the Christian community, which is called to be a community of conviction, of resident aliens in this world.[2] Only Christ can invite us to the pilgrimage of reconciliation and common confession in the world, and we have Christ's pledge that the Holy Spirit will sustain us in this quest.

The Commission on Faith and Order of the National Council of the Churches of Christ in the U.S.A. offers this text as a contribution to the international conversation among the churches in their quest for unity and common witness. As the commission's 1988-91 *Program of Studies* suggests,

> In assisting the churches in their pilgrimage to full, visible unity as the Gospel of Jesus Christ would have it, it is first necessary to understand the Apostolic claims of the churches involved in the discussion, and the confessional issues as they endure to this day that keep the churches separated.
>
> Some churches have been characterized as sectarian and separatist by others. However, the claim of those churches [that] present a radical critique of society, the church's involvement with the state, and Christian engagement with violent defense of the state is that they are doing nothing more nor less than . . . preserving the Christian Faith once delivered to the Apostles. This claim must be tested against the testimony of Scripture and Christian history together in common scholar-

---

1. Thaddeus Horgan, ed., *Apostolic Faith in America* (Grand Rapids: Eerdmans, for the Commission on Faith and Order, National Council of the Churches of Christ in the U.S.A., 1988).

2. Myron S. Augsburger, *The Peacemaker* (Nashville: Abingdon, 1987); Stanley Hauerwas and William H. Willimon, *Resident Aliens: Life in the Christian Colony* (Nashville: Abingdon, 1989). A key document for this discussion is the statement by Douglas Gwyn, George Hunsinger, Eugene F. Roop, and John Howard Yoder, *A Declaration on Peace: In God's People the World's Renewal Has Begun. A Contribution to Ecumenical Dialogue Sponsored by Church of the Brethren, Fellowship of Reconciliation, Mennonite Central Committee, and Friends General Conference* (Scottdale: Herald, 1991).

ship among Christians from the heretofore divided Christian churches. For the churches this ethical dimension dividing Christians from confessing a common Apostolic Faith is central, like the trinitarian, sacramental and church order differences that keep Christians apart. A common understanding of these ecclesiological issues is a necessary prelude to their resolution.

Advances in Biblical scholarship, the transformation of society, the shifting focus of the relationship of all churches to the civil society, and developments in the social ethical understanding of the churches' peace witness make for a new context. Hope that a broader understanding of the implications of Gospel order for peace witness seems to be warranted at this time within the Christian community because some churches [that] originally condemned the peace church position have developed an understanding of religious liberty, the centrality of personal faith, the role of pacifism among the legitimate Christian ethical options, and the urgency of an evangelical witness for peace in the present historical context. Such changes may lead to a revision of judgments made centuries ago about those issues underlying both peace witness and church responsibilities regarding social and political strife and oppression. Common Biblical and historical scholarship and reflection on the contemporary context of the Church may lead to more common affirmations on the nature of the church and what is demanded by the Apostolic Faith than have been possible in previous history. These findings will undoubtedly lead to better common understandings and provide a theological basis for deeper collaboration.[3]

This volume is best read in the spirit in which it was written. Orthodox, Protestant, and Roman Catholic churches and historic peace churches (Mennonite, Brethren, and Quaker) have provided scholars to work on this study. These churches are all called, by their biblical faith and this contribution to its exposition, to deeper communion with each other. It is hoped, too, that this study will lead church bodies to act in ways that deepen their commitment to each other. All who confess faith in the God revealed in Jesus Christ by the power of the Holy Spirit are invited to reflect on this study, according to their interest and station in life, asking what God is doing in the world and what Christ is calling the church to do. Interchurch groups can best explore these concerns

3. *The Program of Studies 1988-1991 of the Commission on Faith & Order* (New York: Commission on Faith and Order/NCCCUSA, n.d.), 12.

together before Christ and the Scriptures, experiencing one another's commitment to Christ, as well as the diversity of our convictions.

At the Canberra assembly of the World Council of Churches (1991), a vision of God's call to unity was articulated:

> The purpose of God according to Holy Scripture is to gather the whole of creation under the Lordship of Christ Jesus in whom, by the power of the Holy Spirit, all are brought into communion with God (Eph. 1). The Church is the foretaste of this communion with God and with one another. The grace of our Lord Jesus Christ, the love of God and the communion of the Holy Spirit enable the one Church to live as sign of the reign of God and servant of the reconciliation with God, promised and provided for the whole creation. The purpose of the Church is to unite people with Christ in the power of the Spirit, to manifest communion in prayer and action and thus to point to the fullness of communion with God, humanity and the whole creation in the glory of the kingdom.[4]

Historical Background

Through the centuries churches have developed different ways of relating to the society in which they live. Some participate fully, at times even claiming to be the cultural and ethical guarantors of social stability. Some churches have relied on the state to enforce their beliefs and impose their ethical values on the whole society. Other Christians have withdrawn, been excluded, or stood in criticism of the society in which they live, and they have suffered and died for their convictions. Through much of our history, these different approaches to the relation between church and society have deeply divided Christians. Even now examples of all these ways of understanding church, peace, and society exist. And in the United States, although all churches here affirm religious liberty, these differences remain church-dividing issues.

During the Reformation and in the centuries that followed it, the role of the church in society was deeply controverted. The sixteenth-century Anabaptists did not recognize the Reformed, Lutheran, and Roman Catholic churches as true churches of Jesus Christ. Their male-

---

4. "The Unity of the Church as *Koinonia* Gift and Calling (Canberra 1991)," *Ecumenical Trends* 22:6 (June, 1993), 5/85.

diction was not only returned in kind, but was enforced by state-authorized violence. The martyrdoms and recriminations of those times no longer persist, thanks be to God. Between the descendants of those who persecuted and the descendants of those who were persecuted, there is at least tolerance. Yet if full communion is to be restored, the unfinished ecumenical work must be done. The memories of those persecutions must be healed, and proper attention given to the diversity of gifts that exist among these divided Christians. Discernment is needed to determine the tolerable limits of diversity within the one gospel affirmation and the mutual corrections that will enable Christians to give authentic witness to Christ in today's world.

Renewed biblical scholarship, the general Christian affirmation of religious liberty, and the escalating violence of modern society all establish a new context in which we can explore the confessional and biblical bases for Christian response to violence in its many forms.[5] Christians need to enunciate together their shared responsibility: to be loyal to the faith once delivered to the apostles and to provide a theological and practical foundation for a future in which the church serves as an appropriate instrument of God's purposes in the world. It was fidelity to different perceptions of the apostolic faith that initially divided the churches. It may be common exploration of biblical and historical sources of that faith that will help us transcend our historical differences and lead us to respond together to God's call to reconciliation and a common witness in the world.

The path taken in this volume continues the journey the churches have begun, under the initiative of the World Council of Churches, "Towards the Common Expression of the Apostolic Faith Today."[6] As

---

5. Jürgen Moltmann, *The Way of Jesus Christ: Christology in Messianic Dimensions,* tr. Margaret Kohl (San Francisco: Harper, 1990), 32:

> The more the European churches free themselves today from their ancient role as established or state churches, the more the Christian congregations find themselves in contradiction to the ideologies and conditions of power that sustain the empires and the "redeemer nations" in which they exist; the more they open themselves for Israel and Jewish existence; and the more acutely they suffer, together with the Jews, for the sake of God's righteousness and justice, over the unredeemed condition of the world.

6. Hans-Georg Link, ed., *Apostolic Faith Today: A Handbook for Study* (Faith and Order Paper 124; Geneva: World Council of Churches, 1985).

the churches seek communion in one faith, in fidelity to Christ, they are seeking to reconcile past confessional divisions as well as contemporary formulations of doctrinal differences. The world council has provided a resource, *Confessing One Faith,* to serve the churches in this healing process.[7] In the United States, the national council has provided a study guide[8] and several studies[9] in support of this process.

The historic peace churches have also provided important confessional testimony to the demanding character of this witness *(martyria)*.[10] In these studies a unique caution about creedal language has come from the Friends, and the familial style of the Brethren has placed doctrinal affirmations in an appropriate communal context, while a Mennonite approach to history has encouraged a fresh look at the fourth-century context of Nicene-Constantinopolitan creedal developments.[11] This conversation is indebted to earlier conversations.[12] Marlin E.

7. *Confessing One Faith: Towards an Ecumenical Explication of the Apostolic Faith as Expressed in the Nicene-Constantinopolitan Creed (381)* (Faith and Order Paper 140; Geneva: World Council of Churches, 1987).

8. *Confessing One Faith: The Origins, Meaning and Use of the Nicene Creed: Grounds for a Common Witness, A Guide for Ecumenical Study* (Cincinnati: Forward Movement, for the Commission on Faith and Order, National Council of the Churches of Christ in the U.S.A., 1988).

9. S. Mark Heim, "Gender and Creed: Confessing a Common Faith," *Christian Century* 102:13 (April 17, 1985), 379-81; Theodore Stylianopoulos and S. Mark Heim, eds., *Spirit of Truth: Ecumenical Perspectives on the Holy Spirit: Papers of the Holy Spirit Consultation, Oct. 24-25, 1985, Brookline, Mass.* (Brookline: Holy Cross Orthodox, 1986); Paul Fries and Tiran Nersoyan, *Christ in East and West* (Macon: Mercer University, 1987); David T. Shannon and Gayraud S. Wilmore, eds., *Black Witness to the Apostolic Faith* (Grand Rapids: Eerdmans, for the Commission on Faith and Order, National Council of the Churches of Christ in the U.S.A., 1988).

10. Howard John Loewen, *One Lord, One Church, One Hope and One God: Mennonite Confessions of Faith in North America: An Introduction* (Elkhart: Institute of Mennonite Studies, 1985).

11. S. Mark Heim, ed., *Faith to Creed: Ecumenical Perspectives on the Affirmation of the Apostolic Faith in the Fourth Century* (Grand Rapids: Eerdmans, for the Commission on Faith and Order, National Council of the Churches of Christ in the U.S.A., 1991).

12. Donald F. Durnbaugh, ed., *On Earth Peace: Discussions on War/Peace Issues between Friends, Mennonites, Brethren, and European Churches, 1935-75* (Elgin: Brethren, 1978); Hans Georg vom Berg, Henk Kossen, Larry Miller, and Lukas Vischer, eds., *Mennonites and Reformed in Dialogue* (Studies from the World Alliance of Reformed Churches 7; Geneva: World Alliance of Reformed Churches, 1986); *Les Entretiens Luthero-Mennonites. Resultats du colloque de Strasbourg, 1981-1984, avec une préface de Pierre Widmer et une présentation de Marc Lienhard* (Montbéliard: Christ Seul, 1984).

Miller's essay in this volume, "Toward Acknowledging Together the Apostolic Character of the Church's Peace Witness," documents some promising European discussions of the subject.[13]

The Present

This volume attempts to build on these earlier conversations, and bring to the confessional explorations the church-dividing issue of the relationship between church and society raised at the Reformation by the Anabaptist churches.[14] The book begins with a background chapter on the uses of Scripture in various North American church documents from the 1980s on the topic of peace, which confess Christian faith and attempt to spell out its implications for Christian witness to society in the contemporary situation. Then follows the biblical core of the book, with interpretations of the Hebrew Scriptures by Ben C. Ollenburger and Dianne Bergant, C.S.A., and of the New Testament by Paul N. Anderson and Richard L. Jeske. These essays give fresh perspectives on the themes of peace and church and invite us to elaborate further the biblical basis for a common ecclesiology and to define its implications for the church's participation in society. Other important studies on ecclesiology and on the church's peace witness have contributed to this process of exploration.[15] The essays here, rather than concluding the process, may generate

13. See also Viggo Mortensen, ed., *War, Confession and Conciliarity: What Does "Just War" in the Augsburg Confession Mean Today?* (Hannover: Lutherisches Verlagshaus, 1993); Ross T. Bender and Alan P. F. Sell, eds., *Baptism, Peace, and the State in the Reformed and Mennonite Traditions* (Waterloo: Wilfrid Laurier University, 1991).

14. Richard J. Mouw and John H. Yoder, "Evangelical Ethics and the Anabaptist-Reformed Dialogue," *The Journal of Religious Ethics* 17:2 (Fall, 1989), 121-37; John H. Yoder, "Reformed Versus Anabaptist Social Strategies: An Inadequate Typology," *Theological Students Fellowship Bulletin* 8:5 (May-June, 1985), 2-7; Richard Mouw, "Abandoning the Typology: A Reformed Assist," *Theological Students Fellowship Bulletin* 8:5 (May-June, 1985): 7-10.

15. See Paul Sevier Minear, *Images of the Church in the New Testament* (Philadelphia: Westminster, 1960); Raymond E. Brown, *The Church the Apostles Left Behind* (New York: Paulist, 1984); Perry B. Yoder and Willard M. Swartley, eds., *The Meaning of Peace: Biblical Studies* (Louisville: Westminster/John Knox, 1992); Ulrich Mauser, *The Gospel of Peace: A Scriptural Message for Today's World* (Louisville: Westminster/John Knox, 1992); Willard M. Swartley, ed., *Essays on Biblical Interpretation: Anabaptist-Mennonite Perspectives* (Elkhart: Institute of Mennonite Studies, 1984); Wil-

more scholarship and so move us toward the agreement needed for reconciliation. It is hoped that Marlin Miller's essay and the "Summary Statement of the Consultation on the Apostolic Faith and the Church's Peace Witness" will encourage further exploration and contribute to the worldwide discussion of what Christian confession requires today.

Though we may come to a common mind or identify more clearly where we still differ about the biblical witness, prescriptural and post-biblical developments are also part of our Christian heritage. In fact, many churches believe that the Holy Spirit was active in the church before the canon of Scripture was defined and that the Spirit continues to protect the church in truth in its subsequent development.[16] The historical chapter by David G. Hunter deals with trajectories in church and peace in the period before Constantine. The chapter contributed by Donald F. Durnbaugh and Charles W. Brockwell, Jr., deals with an additional historical case, that of the origins of the historic peace churches in the sixteenth, seventeenth, and eighteenth centuries, and of the polarizations and condemnations of those times.

The Canberra assembly of the World Council of Churches became entangled in the discussion of what the church's peace witness requires and the level of agreement that does or does not exist among our churches.[17] In the context of discussion of a resolution on the war in the Persian Gulf region, an amendment was introduced and passed that called into question the classical just war position of some of the churches. The prohibition on Christian participation in war was modified from the floor to indicate that such participation might be permissible in Third-World wars of liberation, for example. However, much confusion remained. After a lunch break the assembly rescinded the amendment. But the discussion had brought into focus the impor-

---

lard M. Swartley, ed., *The Love of Enemy and Nonretaliation in the New Testament* (Louisville: Westminster/John Knox, 1992).

16. "Montreal 1963: Scripture, Tradition and Traditions, from the Report of Section II," in Link, *Apostolic Faith Today*, 79-83.

17. Michael Kinnamon, ed., *Signs of the Spirit: Official Report, Seventh Assembly, Canberra, Australia, 7-20 February 1991* (Grand Rapids: Eerdmans, 1991), 203. The text of the amendment, proposed by the (now) General Secretary of the World Council of Churches, Rev. Dr. Konrad Raiser, reads: "We call upon [the churches] to give up any theological or moral justification of the use of military power, be it in war or through other forms of oppressive security systems, and to become public advocates of a just peace" (203).

tance of being in conversation about the confessional basis for our positions on peace, unity, and Christian witness in the world. The measured biblical, historical, and confessional study undertaken here in this volume may make a contribution to our understanding of this urgent question in ecumenical life.

The Canberra assembly made such a contribution in its statement on unity, "The Church as *Koinonia:* Gift and Calling," which was clear about the importance of agreement on common mission and witness:

> The unity of the Church to which we are called is a *koinonia* given and expressed in the common confession of apostolic faith; a common sacramental life entered by the one baptism and celebrated together in one eucharistic fellowship; a common life in which members and ministries are mutually recognized and reconciled; and a common mission witnessing to all people to the gospel of God's grace and serving the whole of creation. The goal of the search for full communion is realized when all the churches are able to recognize in one another the one, holy, catholic and apostolic church in its fullness. This full communion will be expressed on the local and universal levels through conciliar forms of life and action. In such communion churches are bound in all aspects of their life together at all levels in confessing the one faith and engaging in worship and witness, deliberation and action.[18]

Today we are more civil with one another about our divisions, but our full communion in Christ still lies ahead. Likewise, our pluralistic society contributes to differences in our approaches to public order, social witness, and issues of global responsibility for justice, peace, and the integrity of creation. Christians are called to study and work in greater faithfulness to Christ and to Christ's mission in the world. It is hoped that this study will help us do so.

---

18. "The Unity of the Church" (n. 4 above), 5/85. This text goes on to challenge the churches "to recommit themselves to work for justice, peace and the integrity of creation, linking more closely the search for sacramental communion of the Church with the struggles for justice and peace" (6/86).

A Biblical Study

Much biblical work has been done on issues of unity and of the church's calling to peace in society.[19] The vision of unity held out to the churches by ecumenical conversations is one of full community (communion, fellowship, *koinonia*) in a "Conciliar Communion," with common faith, common sacraments, and common decision making for the glory of God and the renewal of the human community.[20] The biblical issues are not unrelated to the sacramental and decision-making questions, as has been shown in the ecumenical study of baptism[21] and ministry.[22] Indeed, as the churches around the world recently responded to the *Baptism, Eucharist, and Ministry* document of the world council, differing views of Scripture and understandings of tradition were identified for wider study.[23] For this reason it is important to keep in mind the church-uniting intent and method used by the authors of the biblical exploration.

The approach to Scripture attempts to present old but persisting difficulties in a new light, under the word of God. Since 1952 the method proposed by the World Council of Churches and widely used in multi-lateral and bilateral conversations is to focus on Christ and to submit the church-dividing doctrinal formulations and styles of church life to the best of modern biblical scholarship. Teams of biblical scholars drawn from the divided churches explore the sources of Christian faith using the best scientific tools and speak to the churches in fidelity to their

19. Dale W. Brown, *Biblical Pacifism: A Peace Church Perspective* (Elgin: Brethren, 1986); Ellen Flesseman-van Leer, ed., *The Bible: Its Authority and Interpretation in the Ecumenical Movement* (Faith and Order Paper 99; Geneva: World Council of Churches, 1980).

20. Kinnamon, *Signs of the Spirit*, 172; see also 96-108.

21. *Baptism, Eucharist, and Ministry* (Faith and Order Paper 11; Geneva: World Council of Churches, 1982); Merle D. Strege, ed., *Baptism and Church: A Believers' Church Vision,* Papers Presented at the Seventh Conference on the Believers' Church, Anderson School of Theology, Anderson, Indiana, June 5-8, 1984 (Grand Rapids: Sagamore, 1986); David S. Russell, "The Ecumenical Role of Baptists," in Franklin H. Littell, ed., *A Half Century of Religious Dialogue: 1939-1989* (Lewiston: Mellen, 1989), 112-31.

22. John H. Yoder, *The Fullness of Christ: Paul's Revolutionary Vision of Universal Ministry* (Elgin: Brethren, 1987); David B. Eller, ed., *Servants of the Word: Ministry in the Believers' Church* (Elgin: Brethren, 1990), 185-96; Melanie May, ed., *For All the Saints* (Elgin: Brethren, 1990).

23. *Baptism, Eucharist and Ministry 1982-1990: Report on the Process and Responses* (Faith and Order Paper 149; Geneva: World Council of Churches, 1990).

traditions' uses of Scripture and history. In this way the churches are called to renewal in light of the Christian revelation and to healing historical divisions in light of the best understanding of that revelation that can be formulated, together, in our time.

The Lutheran-Catholic dialogue has made useful contributions to this method in studies prepared as the basis for convergence and consensus around issues that have divided these churches.[24] In these studies, the development of particular themes or motifs is traced through the biblical books, as these emerge from what is judged to be the oldest witness, through the most recent biblical formulations of the New Testament. Such study witnesses both to the pluralism within the Scriptures and to the development of the church.

In this volume both the Hebrew Scriptures and the New Testament are examined. Both testaments contribute to our understanding of the people of God and their relationship to the societies in which they lived. Both testaments are resources for our churches in matters of ecclesiology, ethics, and societal involvement. Obviously, the essays in this volume do not exhaust the possibilities for laying the foundation for a common ecclesiology or a common witness in society.

While the writers have attempted to provide expositions in tune with the best biblical scholarship available and to be attentive to the traditional uses of Scripture in their churches, they have also taken care to present the material so it is accessible not only for adult study but for classroom use as well. Scholarly detail is provided in footnotes to enable further exploration. This study is to be seen in the context of the wide literature contributing to the reconciliation of the churches, as this chapter's notes indicate.

---

24. Raymond E. Brown, Karl P. Donfried, and John Reumann, eds., *Peter in the New Testament: A Collaborative Assessment by Protestant and Roman Catholic Scholars* (Minneapolis: Augsburg, and New York: Paulist, 1973); Raymond E. Brown, Karl P. Donfried, Joseph A. Fitzmyer, and John Reumann, eds., *Mary in the New Testament: A Collaborative Assessment by Protestant and Roman Catholic Scholars* (Philadelphia: Fortress, and New York: Paulist, 1978); John Reumann, *Righteousness in the New Testament: "Justification" in the United States Lutheran-Catholic Dialogue* (Philadelphia: Fortress, and New York: Paulist, 1982).

The Vision of Unity

This specialized study may well lead the churches to further explorations of issues of justice and peace witness, such as following up with case studies on the early history of the church and the divergent interpretations of the church's role in society noted in David Hunter's essay. Within the united church of the first millennium, the formulations of Augustine in the West, his "just war" approach and *The City of God*, provided the basis for views held in common until the time of the Reformation. In the East, in the Byzantine Empire, in the Middle East, and later in the Slavic world, a different understanding of the relationship between church and state developed. But these differing views were not divisive during those centuries. Our understanding of the roots of modern conflicts can be increased by common studies of these developments, and we may gain an appreciation for the opportunities we face.

Modern historical scholarship has made an important contribution to the ecumenical movement in its investigation of the history of exegesis. Scholars can trace both the variety and the convergence of interpretation over the centuries and identify the continuing role of ancient exegetical debates in modern discussions. Because the biblical text sets certain limits to interpretation and poses the same questions to readers in different ages, one can discover how the ongoing conversation with the biblical text influences theological deliberation.[25]

The condemnations of the sixteenth century still stand as a burden on our corporate memory, though at present they are largely unused. Some ancient condemnations between East and West have been lifted.[26]

---

25. In the case of the church's peace witness, certain texts (e.g., Matt. 5:38-42; Rom. 13:1-4; Luke 3:14; 1 Pet. 2:13-14; John 18:36; and Acts 5:29) have set the agenda for discussion, and studying the history of their interpretation provides opportunities for understanding church-dividing issues. The commentaries and sermons by ancient church theologians as diverse as Augustine, Origen, John Chrysostom, and Cyril of Alexandria; the glosses and collations of the early medieval church; the comments on the decretals; and the most influential commentators of the High Middle Ages all contain portions of the debate on these and other key texts and set the stage for divisions of the sixteenth century and beyond. Uncovering the common exegetical tradition and identifying the continuing hermeneutical debate on these texts may assist present exegetical work and ecumenical endeavor.

26. E. J. Stormon, S.J., ed., *Towards the Healing of Schism: The Sees of Rome and Constantinople: Public Statements and Correspondence between the Holy See and the Ecumenical Patriarchate, 1958-1984* (Ecumenical Documents, vol. III; New York: Paulist, 1987).

Proposals have been made for lifting the mutual condemnations from the Reformation era.[27] However, Roman Catholic, Protestant, and Orthodox divergences from Anabaptist, Quaker, and Brethren Christians may require more soul-searching before acts of common confession and reversals of rejection become possible.

This study is meant to move us toward common confession. We must also heed the gospel call to find those graced moments when we can witness together in the world, with authority, to the truth of revelation. The study of authority and the quest for common structures for decision making are delicate issues in the ecumenical movement, and convergences on these matters are proposed to the churches only slowly and cautiously. Still, conversation on these issues is vital. The elements of personal, communal, and collegial decision making have been proposed to the churches as essential to exercising a common authority under the gospel. The historic peace churches should have a significant voice in these conversations, especially in American culture.

The personal dimension of authority in the churches is familiar to those churches that have ministers entrusted with the stewardship and exercise of *episcope* on behalf of the community. Although there is no uniformity among the churches in how bishops exercise their ministry in the midst of the whole people of God, there is growing convergence on its importance in the discussion. Likewise, collegial forms of decision making are familiar to American Christians, since their democratic structures of secular government have come from the Reformed churches, Presbyterian and Congregational, which affirm ordered assemblies in which the Holy Spirit mediates the wisdom of the community through duly designated representatives. However, important lessons on communal discernment can be learned from the decision-making styles of Quaker, Mennonite, and Brethren communities. In a church united under Christ's headship, all believers' gifts are to be used. As we seek to be attentive to the Spirit's guidance in making decisions together, we cannot be satisfied until we find ways to be accountable together to the one revelation of God in Jesus Christ.

As we continue to discuss ways of deciding and acting together, the historic peace church heritage and insights, theology and experience,

---

27. Karl Lehmann and Wolfhart Pannenberg, eds., *The Condemnations of the Reformation Era, Do They Still Divide?*, tr. Margaret Kohl (Minneapolis: Fortress Press, 1990).

will be a rich resource. The centrality of discipline, ethics, and appreciation for the Holy Spirit's presence in the gathered community can only enrich our common quest for God's will in the church's exercise of authority.

Conclusion

Christians agree that our divisions are sinful and that God calls us to unity, but we do not yet see clearly the way to unity. In our prayer and study, the Holy Spirit will disclose to us how we are to move forward. The ecumenical movement has made proposals that make the vision of unity more concrete and explicit. This study is offered in the hope that it will make a modest contribution to this great work of grace that God has given to the church. May the summary statement's recommendations and the biblical and historical studies contribute to our pilgrimage toward communion in faith, life, and witness.

2. An Analysis of the Use of Scripture in the Churches' Documents on Peace

HOWARD JOHN LOEWEN

Introduction: The Use of Scripture
as an Ecumenical Point of Contact

The documents on peace selected for analysis here represent the major Christian confessional traditions: Orthodox, Catholic, and Protestant. Except for the Orthodox statement (the work of an international group), they are expressive of these traditions in the North American context. Nine of the eleven are Protestant. The statements are listed here, preceded by the abbreviated church name that will be used throughout this paper (for more information see the select bibliography at the end of this volume):

Baptist "American Baptist Policy Statement on Peace." Adopted by the General Board of the American Baptist Churches, 1985.

Catholic National Conference of Catholic Bishops. *The Challenge of Peace: God's Promise and Our Response, A Pastoral Letter on War and Peace.* Washington, D.C.: United States Catholic Conference, 1983.

Episcopal *To Make Peace: The Reports of the Joint Commissions on Peace*

15

of the General Convention of the Episcopal Church. Cincinnati: Forward Movement Publications, 1988.

Evangelical   *Guidelines: Peace, Freedom, and Security Studies.* National Association of Evangelicals, 1986.

HPC (Historic Peace Churches)   Douglas Gwyn, George Hunsinger, Eugene F. Roop, and John Howard Yoder. *A Declaration on Peace: In God's People the World's Renewal Has Begun. A Contribution to Ecumenical Dialogue Sponsored by Church of the Brethren, Fellowship of Reconciliation, Mennonite Central Committee, and Friends General Conference.* Scottdale, Pa.: Herald Press, 1991.

Lutheran   *Lutheran Church in America Social Statements: Peace and Politics.* Adopted by the Twelfth Biennial Convention of the Lutheran Church in America, 1984.

Methodist   The United Methodist Council of Bishops. *In Defense of Creation: The Nuclear Crisis and a Just Peace.* Nashville: Graded Press, 1986.

Orthodox   "Orthodox Perspectives on Justice and Peace." In *Justice, Peace and the Integrity of Creation: Insights from Orthodoxy,* edited by Gennadios Limouris, 16-27. Geneva: WCC Publications, 1990.

Presbyterian   The United Presbyterian Church in the United States of America. *Peacemaking: The Believers' Calling.* New York: The General Assembly of the United Presbyterian Church in the United States of America, 1980.

Reformed   "Christian Faith and the Nuclear Arms Race: A Reformed Perspective." A Report from the Theological Commission, General Synod, 1980.

UCC (United Church of Christ)   The Peace Theology Development Team. *A Just Peace Church.* Edited by Susan B. Thistlethwaite. New York: United Church Press, 1986.

16

All these documents have been produced in the 1980s by these church bodies or their representatives. They reflect a concentrated effort by Christian churches to express their convictions about increasing national and international problems of peace and justice. Though they unite in giving expression to a vision of peace, they reveal different assumptions about the shape of that vision and its implementation. Each assumes that the goal and process of achieving greater unity is a worthy one, but the question remains whether the Christian vision and virtue of peace can achieve confessional status among these church bodies sufficient to establish it as a point of genuine unity among world Christians.

The purpose of this study is to analyze the use of Scripture in the churches' documents on peace. The task is threefold:

1. To analyze the nature of the scriptural appeal each document makes: What texts are used and how are they used? (Section I)
2. To determine each document's use of Scripture in the structure of the theological argument: What is the relationship between Scripture and theological reflection? (Section II)
3. To identify the ecclesial and moral implications of each statement's theological formulation as informed by Scripture: What is the relation between the theology informed by Scripture and the church's social-ethical agenda in the contemporary situation? (Section III)

The goal is to understand more fully each tradition's use of Scripture, and to see more clearly, from a hermeneutical and theological perspective, what are the points of convergence and divergence among these statements on the issues of peace and justice.

I. The Nature of the Scriptural Appeals

Our analysis of the use of Scripture in these documents begins by identifying the particular texts to which each statement appeals and from which it draws its theological warrants. The question of *how* Scripture is used must from the outset engage us in the question of *what* scriptural texts are being used. The tables accompanying this study present the actual use of Scripture from a variety of perspectives and provide a data base for observations and conclusions throughout the paper. Using this scriptural data base we may attend to the primary task of assessing the theological use of Scripture in these peace documents.

Scripture can be employed in theological reflection in at least three major ways: narrative, conceptual, and expressive. The *narrative* approach views Scripture as the story of God's salvific action through agents or in creation. It issues in a hermeneutic of identification in which the stories of Scripture ground theological formulations. The *conceptual* approach uses Scripture as a source of doctrinal statements about God, people, and the world. It issues in a hermeneutic of translation in which the statements of Scripture serve as the logical background for theological proposals. The *expressive* approach views Scripture in terms of God's presence (or absence) in existential events. It issues in a hermeneutic of expression in which Scripture is used symbolically in theological proposals to evoke authentic existence.

Narrative Use of Scripture

The narrative use of Scripture is found most prominently in the Presbyterian, Methodist, and HPC documents.

The Presbyterian statement, *Peacemaking: The Believers' Calling*, for the most part uses this first approach, with some use of the third approach, and less of the second. It employs Scripture primarily to identify the biblical understanding of peace and to support a life of peacemaking. In its use of Scripture it gives priority to the scriptural motifs of kingdom, love, reconciliation, image of God, justice, and freedom, united under the central biblical motif of *shalom*, identified with the reconciling love of Jesus Christ for the world. It attempts to minimize the gap between then and now and to relate the biblical themes directly to contemporary issues, particularly to the nuclear crisis.

The Presbyterian document cites nineteen books of the Bible with a total of thirty-nine references, almost equally divided between Old and New Testaments. In order of frequency, the Psalms, Isaiah, Jeremiah, Matthew, Luke, and Colossians are the most quoted books. Jer. 6:13-14; Ps. 85:8, 10; and Col. 1:19-22 are the high frequency texts.

The Methodist document, *In Defense of Creation*, claims with Methodist founder John Wesley that the Scriptures are the ultimate source of knowledge and authority, and begins with a section on biblical foundations. It gives priority to Scripture over all post-biblical traditions. It sees the biblical account of God's involvement in creation and history as standing in judgment over the conflicting voices of Christian tradi-

18

tions. It affirms a transcendent biblical vision and assumes continuity between the biblical generations and our own. The central organizing biblical motif is the *shalom* of God's good creation, understood as an ongoing process in which a fallen and endangered earth and its people are being redeemed and restored.

The Methodist document cites fourteen books of the Bible with a total of twenty-eight references, the majority from the New Testament. In order of frequency, John, Isaiah, Matthew, Colossians, Ezekiel, Romans, and Ephesians are the most quoted books. Col. 1:19-20 and Matt. 5:9 are the high frequency texts.

More than any other statement, the HPC document, *A Declaration on Peace*, uses a narrative hermeneutic. On that basis it develops a doxological theology and a characterological ethic which are to guide the church in the world today. It makes no appeal to general moral principles or to technical information about weapons and strategy, but instead attempts to draw believers into the force-field of the biblical story of redemption. It uses one mode of discourse, biblical theology, because the Bible is common to all Christian communions. A hermeneutic of peoplehood is assumed more than explicitly articulated. Thus the HPC book translates and interprets the biblical narrative in its own terms through the priestly, prophetic, sapiential, and royal servanthood motifs. These four facets of the nature and mission of God's people are embodied, fulfilled, and universalized in the life, death, resurrection, and ascension of Jesus Christ and in the pouring out of the Spirit on all flesh. The central organizing biblical motif is reconciliation.

The HPC statement cites twenty-six books of the Bible in a total of ninety-eight references, almost two-thirds of them from the New Testament. In order of frequency, Hebrews, Genesis, Isaiah, 1 Corinthians, Proverbs, and Matthew are the most cited books. The most extensive scriptural citations are of the primal history of Genesis (focusing more on the fall and redemption than on creation texts), the wisdom tradition as reflected in Proverbs and Paul (1 Cor. 1:18–3:3), the prophetic messianic texts of Isaiah, the Sermon on the Mount (Matt. 5:9, 11), John, and, most frequently, the Hebrews texts about Christ's high-priestly atoning work (Heb. 9:11, 12, 14, 22). The latter give the document a strong christological grounding. The use of Scripture in this document is extensive, a wide range of texts is represented, and Scripture is treated as the exclusive source and norm for theological reflection on war and peace. Scripture does not function as background or foreground for theological reflection. Rather, it presents the foundational reality into which the faithful body is invited. The biblical narrative is the story about the church; the two are inseparable.

Conceptual Use of Scripture

The conceptual use of Scripture is found more prominently in the Catholic, Baptist, Evangelical, Episcopal, and Reformed documents.

The Catholic document, *The Challenge of Peace,* is a prime example of a conceptual use of Scripture. The statement develops a biblical theology of peace, grounding the task of peacemaking in the biblical vision of the kingdom of God, and making that task central in the ministry of the church. Bible texts are cited to articulate this vision of peace. The Catholic text gives significant attention to the conceptual content of Scripture relating to peace. It gives even more attention to the conceptual content of tradition, but this is tempered by appeals to the prophetic biblical vision in which the tradition has its origin. The church has a primary status as a bearer of the vision of *shalom,* and is not just a community conformed to it. The Catholic document exhibits a hermeneutic of translation, the church's translation of the tradition, significantly informed by the scriptural vision and also by the contemporary nuclear crisis. Scripture provides the background for a moral and theological critique of nuclear war.

The Catholic document cites twenty-one books of the Bible in a total of sixty-six references, with well over half from the New Testament. In order of frequency, Matthew, Luke, John, Isaiah, Jeremiah, and Ephesians are the most quoted books. John 20, Matthew 5, and Luke 6 are the most frequently cited chapters. There are no references to the creation theology of Genesis. The most frequent references from the Old Testament are to the major prophets Isaiah, Jeremiah, and Ezekiel. The most extensive New Testament references are to the Gospels, particularly to Matthew and Luke, but also to John (John 20:19-29; Matt. 5:3-10, 39-42, 44-48; Luke 6:27-31, 37). In its biblical section the Catholic statement draws heavily from the prophetic messianic tradition, which narrates God's intervention in history. Subsequent sections of the statement appeal more directly to tradition, especially to creation theology, to construct theological and ethical proposals. Scripture seems to inform the ensuing theological and ethical reflection in a general way. Its meaning is assumed more than interpreted. Tradition and reason are the context for understanding the content of Scripture more than in most of the other documents.

The "American Baptist Policy Statement on Peace" makes direct appeals to scriptural texts, establishing some context in the story of Israel, but more in the life of Jesus. Overall it cites texts more in conjunction with general themes (creation and sin, for example) than as part of the biblical story. Thus it tends to use Scripture as a source of principles, with some patterning from the life and ministry of Jesus. It exhibits an evocative use of Scripture at the beginning, citing two texts as pronouncements. Generally speaking, the statement attempts, albeit briefly, to interpret Scripture and not just assume it. It manifests an ideational use of Scripture, where key theological themes (creation, sin, peace and justice, forgiveness and reconciliation) are developed and centered around the theme of *shalom.* It displays a hermeneutic of translation in which scriptural teaching and the church tradition on war and peace serve as background for an application of policy and principles, followed by a social-scientific analysis of the contemporary situation.

The Baptist document cites eleven books of the Bible with a total of sixteen references, two-thirds from the New Testament. In order of frequency, Matthew, James, and Ephesians are the most quoted books. Jas. 4:1-2, 4 and Eph. 2:12, 14ff. are the high frequency texts. Of all the peace documents, the Baptist statement contains the fewest Scripture references.

Peace, Freedom and Security Studies, the National Association of Evangelicals statement, is the only document that identifies the infallible authority of Scripture as a fundamental reference point. The evangelical statement approaches Scripture as a source of principles, and lists six. For the most part, the meaning of biblical texts is assumed; the content and meaning of principles are clarified by quoting Bible texts at length more than by interpreting these texts. The document exhibits an ideational discrimen: The central theme is love toward God and neighbor and reconciliation with God and among people. The document highlights the role of law and political community in promoting reconciliation among people, developing this theme against the backdrop of the fundamental issues of peace, justice (understood in terms of human dignity), freedom, and security and from the perspective of the United States' presumed inescapable moral responsibilities in the world. The evangelical document's hermeneutic is a combination of translation and

21

expression. Scripture is used both descriptively and evocatively to provide warrants for the document's agenda.

The evangelical document cites twelve books of the Bible in a total of twenty-three references, about two-thirds from the New Testament. In order of frequency, Matthew, Isaiah, and Luke are the most quoted books. Matthew 5 and Luke 10 are the high frequency chapters.

The argument of the Episcopal statement on peace, *To Make Peace,* centers generally around two Scripture passages: Matt. 22:21 ("Render therefore to Caesar the things that are Caesar's and to God the things that are God's"; see also Rom. 13:1-12) and Matt. 6:44 ("Love your enemies"). The first passage is interpreted to mean that the role of the Christian is "to support the state when it performs its God-given tasks and to seek to reform it when it fails in those tasks" (8). The writers then apply Jesus' injunction to love one's enemies to the international arena, suggesting that, even when engaged in war, Christians must love the enemies against whom they are fighting. The word "enemy" is understood to refer to individuals more than to a corporate entity.

The Episcopal statement cites eight books of the Bible in a total of thirty-five references, all but six from the New Testament. In order of frequency, Matthew, Luke, and Romans are the most quoted books, while four references are also made to the prophetic writings. Matthew 6 and 22, and Romans 13 are the most frequently cited chapters. A laudable attempt is made to interpret these difficult passages, particularly Jesus' words in Matthew, which the writers suggest are not merely instructions to pay taxes: They are a command for the Christian to place God at the center of every decision, including decisions about investments, foreign policy, and paying taxes. In interpreting Romans 13, the writers encourage readers to avoid the temptation to separate the secular (including the state) from the sacred, and they point out that "the incarnation abolished this separation permanently for the Christian community" (8).

Christian Faith and the Nuclear Arms Race: A Reformed Perspective centers its argument around Pauline passages that refer to the powers and principalities (Rom. 8:38-39; 1 Cor. 2:8; 15:24-25; Eph. 1:20-21; 2:1-2; 6:12; Col. 1:16; 2:15). The basic assertion is that people in the United States have adopted a false religion, in which nuclear arms have become the object of worship. This has led to a reliance on weapons that provide the illusion of security. Furthermore, we have adopted a false morality, in which we are able to justify the notion of destroying millions of innocent people and much of the earth's resources. The state becomes our false god, the ultimate object of our allegiance. The document's interpretation of passages about the principalities and powers removes them from the esoteric realm of angels, spirits, and demons. Rather, they are seen to be "superhuman, transpersonal realities that condition earthly life through the corporate order, structure, organization, and domination which they impose" (6). Mere human fear and pride are insufficient to account for the evil compulsion toward world annihilation; we must recognize the power and influence of evil forces alive in our world. At the same time, we must not lose hope. Christ has overcome these powers and, either before or after a nuclear holocaust, will tame them.

The Reformed document cites seventeen books of the Bible in a total of fifty-five references, half of them from Paul's letters. In order of frequency, Ephesians, Colossians, Isaiah, Romans, Matthew, and 1 Corinthians are the most quoted books, with Ephesians 6 and Colossians 2 being the most frequently cited chapters. In addition to Paul's letters, the statement focuses on the prophets, who urge reliance on God rather than on armaments and who name justice, righteousness, faith, and obedience as conditions for national security.

Expressive Use of Scripture

The expressive use of Scripture is found most prominently in the Orthodox, Lutheran, and UCC documents.

Orthodox Perspectives on Justice and Peace reflects a firm belief in the authority of Scripture, though its explicit appeal to Scripture texts is minimal. The major background papers for this statement quote Scripture more than any of the peace documents studied here. These essays, which elaborate on the critical themes of the Orthodox document, cite thirty-seven books of the Bible in a total of 276 references, almost half of them from the Old Testament. In order of frequency, Genesis, Romans, Isaiah, Psalms, and Matthew are the most quoted books. Genesis 1 and Romans 8 are the high frequency chapters.

The few texts cited in the Orthodox document proper provide warrants for the synergy theology of the Orthodox tradition. Synergy motifs used include Paul's descriptions of Christians as servants of God (Rom. 6:22) and coworkers with God (1 Cor. 3:9), Peter's description of the fundamental character of the church as God's royal priesthood and holy nation (1 Pet. 2:9), and the link between peace and justice found in

1 Clement. These texts illustrate the bond between christology and ecclesiology in Orthodox tradition. The appeal to Scripture is made in the context of holy tradition and the prayers of the church. Together Scripture and tradition are cited as the primary sources that "give to each of us the right orientation and the concrete guidelines and ideals for our lives" (par. 27). It is the Orthodox Christian's personal response to the demands of justice and peace that is focal for this statement.

In the Orthodox document Scripture has evocative and integrative power; with holy tradition and the prayers of the church it is the revelation of God as it is experienced in the life of the church, a resource in addressing the contemporary demands of peace and justice. Its nature and function can only be defined and understood within the context of Christian life and spirituality, whose sole source is the church, ontologically identified as the body of Christ. The fact that all the texts except one appear in the section on "Orthodox Christians responding to the demands of justice and peace" evidences a more expressivist use of Scripture, which evokes authentic existence. Here Scripture is used to point to the ideal possibilities of Christian existence in the world today. In the Orthodox document Scripture does not have an epistemological or interpretive function independent of holy tradition and the Holy Spirit at work in the contemporary situation. Its use is governed by the central theological motif of "the awareness of God's active love and presence in history for the salvation of the world"; "The experience of the saving presence of God's love for us, his creatures, has provided us with understandings which have been articulated theologically in the teaching, creeds and affirmations of faith in the church" (par. 13).

The Lutheran document, *Peace and Politics,* selects Scripture texts to undergird the theme of celebrating in hope the peace of God's reconciliation. Its strongest statements are about the church as a sign of the peace of God's reign in a broken world. This peace is a present possession expressed through love of enemies. It is a gift that the world cannot know. The Lutheran document denies the possibility of our establishing permanent peace, but encourages all to persist in the politics of peace, looking forward to the coming of the reign of God. Scripture is used largely to evoke and express hope in the face of the nuclear crisis. The Lutheran document is unique in integrating a wide variety of biblical references in its theological as well as practical material.

The Lutheran document cites twenty-one books of the Bible with a total of sixty references, about two-thirds from the New Testament.

In order of frequency, Romans, Genesis, Matthew, Luke, Psalms, Isaiah, and John are the most quoted books. Romans 13 is the most frequently cited chapter. In its use of biblical texts the Lutheran statement refers to the early narratives of Genesis that deal with the fall and with sin. For a biblical creation theology it draws more heavily on the Psalms than on Genesis. It appeals to the prophetic messianic tradition of Isaiah and Micah. The greatest number of New Testament references are from Romans, in keeping with Lutheran tradition. But the statement also includes a number of Gospel references, particularly from Matthew and Luke, but also from John.

The UCC document, *A Just Peace Church,* exhibits a conviction that the biblical vision of *shalom* is authoritative for us today. The statement describes both the biblical vision and its meaning for current peace and justice issues. Although the document reflects a narrative hermeneutic, its use of Scripture is more fundamentally expressivist. Its structure reinforces a hermeneutic of integration, which assumes the primacy of the biblical vision but relates it directly to the most troubling moral issue of our day. It quotes Scripture texts at length to evoke an integrative response of peace and justice. *Shalom* in this statement is just peace, a vision directly challenging the church today. More than any other document, this one avoids making a single style normative; it effectively weaves together the Bible, history, and contemporary analysis.

Biblical citations come from various sources, with broad representation from the Prophets, Writings, Gospels, Epistles, and, to a lesser extent, the Law. The document does not refer to Acts or Revelation. It cites eighteen books of the Bible with a total of fifty-nine references, almost half from the Old Testament. In order of frequency, Jeremiah, Matthew, Ephesians, Isaiah, Ezekiel, and Hebrews are the most quoted books. Matthew 5, Ephesians 2, and Hebrews 1 are the most frequently cited chapters.

II. The Structure of the Theological Arguments

In the previous section we identified the types of scriptural appeal in each church's peace document by noting what scriptural texts are used and how they (and Scripture as a whole) generally function within a narrative, conceptual, or expressive framework. Now we take up the task of understanding the use of Scripture in the churches' peace documents from another perspective: Into what broader theological argument is Scripture taken, and how is Scripture related to the structure of that argument? The structure of the theological argument can be formulated in terms of Scripture (theology as *biblical knowledge*), tradition (theology as *ecclesial doctrine*), or contemporary world (theology as *moral reflection*).

Scripture: Theology as Biblical Knowledge

The peace documents that make their theological argument more in terms of Scripture (theology as biblical knowledge) are the UCC, Baptist, and HPC documents.

The UCC document promotes a just peace rooted in the biblical vision of *shalom* as the starting point and regulative concept for Christian faith in our day. It grounds this theological vision in a doctrine of God as a friend with whom we are to have a covenantal relationship of equality, security, unity, justice, and power. This is the eschatological reign of God toward which we are drawn through promise. It is inseparably connected to Jesus' revelations about power, freedom, and relationships with other people and with God, as well as to the Spirit, who nurtures, sustains, and strengthens us to resist the forces of evil. The UCC document promotes a positive view of the state. The state's role is not only to exert force but also to create conditions of love and justice. God's involvement in history as well as creation is the basis for pursuing *shalom*, not out of fear but out of love for justice. The church can make a positive contribution to public policy by asserting this perspective and acting in accordance with it. Thus the UCC document provides a theological grounding for alternative forms of society.

The biblical concept of *shalom* provides the organizing center for theological reflection on the doctrines of creation, sin, Christ, Spirit, church, church and state, and hope. The church as a liturgical community gives expression to this vision. Through biblically grounded theology, historical reasoning, and extensive sociopolitical and moral analyses of the current situation, the UCC document brings this biblical vision of *shalom* to bear on a world at a crossroads. The document does not appeal to the West's tradition of moral philosophy or analyze issues using philosophical categories. In fact, it offers a critique of the moral tradition of the Enlightenment. It contends that we are at a new moment in history because of the arms race, the interest in disarmament, and the new commitment to justice. This historic situation calls for a fresh theological response, a new model of just peace. One cannot effectively appeal to tradition when new voices are emerging whose story the tradition has not yet incorporated. Although the UCC document rehearses the classical pacifist, just war, and crusade positions, it advocates moving beyond these to a new paradigm.

The Baptist document is divided into four sections, each shorter than the previous one: biblical/theological basis, historical overview, situation analysis, policy/principles. The biblical/theological section begins with two peace texts (John 14:2 and Matt. 5:9) and then grounds peace in a theology of creation fundamentally moving toward *shalom*, God's intention for creation. From creation the document moves to sin as covetous want, to be distinguished from a legitimate desire for justice. Citing Jas. 4:2, it identifies sin as the root cause of the lack of peace, the move against God and others rather than with them in truth and love. Later the Baptist document identifies this as dehumanization and contrasts it with the human dignity that *shalom* brings. The central mission of Israel was to help create *shalom*, peace understood in active and positive terms, inseparably joined with justice and liberty. The Old Testament concept of *shalom* is linked to the New Testament, in which salvation and the reign of God are understood christologically, as in the summary of Jesus' ministry in Luke 4.

The document then moves to the theme of dehumanizing violence, identifying its many faces and the walls that separate. The church is to be a peacemaker in this fragmented, violent world, nurturing a vision of peace and justice, giving voice to hope. The Baptist document gathers up key motifs in the biblical story (creation, sin, justice, violence) that relate to the central theme of *shalom* and weaves in biblical texts as substance and support. Although it cites the just war theory as the most prevalent position among American Baptists, it identifies current criticisms and conflicting interpretations of the just war tradition, especially with regard to nuclear war. It recalls Baptists' roles in movements noted for seeking peace and justice and names such well-known Baptist leaders as Harry Emerson Fosdick and Martin Luther King, Jr.

Similarly, the HPC document does not appeal to traditional teaching or to contemporary circumstances as much as to the biblical vision understood in terms of four interrelated metaphors which, it says, should inform believers in matters of war and peace. This vision is grounded broadly in the biblical narrative and reflects a biblical theology of the eschatological reign of God in Jesus Christ manifested through the people of God in a violent world. The church as the body of Christ is to model provisionally a new peaceable world; in God's people the world's renewal begins. The argument in broad outline is that Christ assumed and transformed the traditional Israelite roles of priest, prophet, sage, and royal servant, reconciling the world to God in his crucifixion. Christians are to practice reconciliation, a sacrifice of thanks and praise consistent with the way of the cross. This is a spiritual worship. Thus doxology becomes an important theological category in this statement, which relies heavily on Hebrews for its interpretation of the priestly character of Jesus' life and death. It expresses a *shalom* vision for the people of God, grounded in God's reign manifest in and through Jesus Christ. The primary theological categories giving shape to its theological ethic are christological and ecclesiological. The central biblical motif uniting the themes of creation, fall, redemption, ecclesiology, and eschatology is reconciliation.

The HPC peace statement seeks to transcend classical confessional divisions on matters of war and peace, using biblical-theological formulations to locate a common ground on which Christians may be able to stand together. The effort to bridge between various traditions is most evident in its articulation of the doctrine of the atonement. The appeal is not to historical, philosophical, political, or technical reasoning, but to a vision of peace described by using the four metaphors and functions — prophet, priest, king, sage — grounded in the biblical narrative. The statement attempts to draw the contemporary believer, and the church, into the force-field of the biblical story of redemption. A hermeneutic of peoplehood is assumed more than it is explicitly articulated. Since the document assumes significant continuity between the biblical vision and the contemporary situation, the need for appeal to tradition is minimal. The discontinuity in *A Declaration on Peace* is not between then and now (which would necessitate an appeal to tradition, reason, or experience), but between this age and the age to come.

Tradition: Theology as Ecclesial Doctrine

The peace statements that make their theological argument more in terms of tradition (theology as ecclesial doctrine) are the Orthodox, Catholic, evangelical, and Episcopal documents.

The Orthodox document draws on the heart of Orthodox tradition and teachings. It includes general references to the church's teachings, creeds, and affirmations, citing a handful of Scripture texts and one post-apostolic writing. External references are few. The presenting problem of the Orthodox document is a world in search of justice and peace, faced with environmental, social, and spiritual crises. This fundamental problem is defined using an interdisciplinary social-ethical analysis. The statement does not so much appeal directly to biblical, historical, philosophical, or political reasoning as set forth — on the basis of holy tradition — a theological vision of a peaceful and just world being created by God's sacramental love and presence in history. This eschatological vision for the salvation and restoration of the world in Christ and the church encompasses all of life.

The theological basis of this *shalom* is the creative activity of the triune God. Sin inhibits its realization. Christ, in his death and resurrection, is the divine-human standard by which the restoration of justice and peace must be measured. Through his death, Christ in principle destroyed the power of sin and death, the primary causes of injustice, and made eternal peace through his resurrection. This restoration is the liberation of the human heart, which is to be filled with the prayer of the Holy Spirit. Through this process we regain full communion with God and so participate in the mystery of the cross and resurrection. This renewal in Christ and communion with the Holy Spirit is the basis for the true establishment of justice and peace. The church, Christ's body, recapitulates what has happened in Christ. The church is an ontological-sacramental unity, an extension of Christ in space and time. Through it the gospel of peace and justice can address all dimensions of human existence and thus render judgment on the world. Human participation in the justice and peace of Christ is a continuous spiritual struggle in this era of ideological secularization and radical apostasy.

The structure and substance of the argument ground justice and peace in a theology of restoration and recapitulation. Christology, anthropology, and ecclesiology are inextricably linked. The document emphasizes the being of the believer and the church in God, Christ, and the Spirit. The believers' communion with God is the basis for restoration. Out of that eschatological participation in the new creation, the church — in ontological unity with Christ and through the power of the Spirit — works together with God in God's economy *(oikonomia)*, realizing the eschatological vision of justice and peace in all of life. The document emphasizes God's presence and activity in the world, through the Spirit, and believers' synergistic participation.

The Catholic document is a blend of biblical, theological, political, and philosophical reflection on contemporary warfare. Its theological formulations are grounded in two basic convictions: the transcendence of God and the dignity of the human person. The document begins with a sketch of the biblical vision of war and of peace as a gift from God manifested in the church and ultimately extended to all creation. It then explores how peace can be sought in a sinful world, in which the kingdom is only partially present. Because the reign of God is not fully realized, Catholic Christians make moral choices for the kingdom in the real world in the framework of the just war tradition, which establishes a strong presumption against making war. Having delineated guiding religious principles and perspectives, biblical and traditional, the statement turns to "War and Peace in the Modern World: Problems and Principles," and examines the new moment in which we live and the role of religious leaders in public debate. It then articulates a position against the use of nuclear weaponry, and exposes the inadequacy of deterrence policies. A third section argues that a positive vision of peace is central to Catholic teaching and makes specific proposals for building peace and constructing a world order in which two superpowers and ideologies converge to reflect the fact of global interdependence and to create the necessary conditions for a just world order. The final section is a pastoral challenge recommending spiritual formation for peace and against all kinds of human violence.

The core of the Catholic document's theological argument is a detailed articulation of the nature and meaning of the just war tradition in the context of the contemporary nuclear crisis. This argument is preceded by a description of the biblical *shalom* vision and followed by an examination of the present political and pastoral implications of just war theory. At the center is a strong appeal to natural law, used as a framework for rethinking issues of war and peace in light of the political and moral realities of the nuclear age and of a biblical theology of peace. The just war tradition stands between these two poles, the eschatological vision of a peaceful kingdom and the present historical reality, as a hermeneutical and moral norm guiding the church's response in this crisis moment.

Thus the Catholic document is a thorough application of just war theory to the nuclear situation. Its interpretation of just war ends with support for nuclear pacifism. No longer an adequate approach to assure a lasting peace, deterrence is at best a transitional strategy. Peace must finally be founded on mutual trust and security. This belief derives from the biblical emphasis on covenant fidelity and trust.

If one examines the document in terms of its appeals to the classical sources of authority, Scripture, tradition, and the teaching office, one sees that the first, Scripture, receives new emphasis as the source of the peace vision that must inform the traditional understanding. The second, tradition, is the strongest instrument of authority in shaping the categories and the content of the argument. The third, the teaching office, is assumed in the very form and function of this pastoral letter. The way the first and the second sources are related is both new and ambiguous.

In sum, the primary theological categories of the Catholic document are shaped by a biblical-theological vision, but are more primarily drawn from natural law tradition and the just war ethic rooted in Catholic teaching and applied to the political and moral complexities of the nuclear age. One important category, the church, its nature and mission, though not identified explicitly, permeates the document. The statement displays a strong sense of the church's responsibility to and for the world. The church is seen as a unique instrument of the kingdom of God in history, and peace is one of the signs of the kingdom. A pastoral community of moral discourse, it provides guidance in a violent world; its unity has implications for all creation. A second category, the preservation of creation, is identified most clearly in the statement's repeated emphasis on human survival and on saving the world from nuclear holocaust. It is also expressed in the document's emphasis on the unity of the human family, a unity deriving from the creation of all of us by God. The goal of world order is grounded in this theological truth of classical Catholic teaching. The document makes no reference to scriptural creation texts.

The evangelical document establishes theological foundations in the initial sections, to clarify the history and purpose of its guidelines, and in the succeeding sections, to spell out current obstacles to and political understandings of peace, freedom, and security. Policy goals, program objectives, assessment criteria, and administrative arrangements follow. The central theological motifs are governed by an overriding agenda: the American evangelical community's duty to promote democratic values, especially the sanctity and dignity of the individual person, seen as a core biblical insight. A link between peace, human rights, and freedom is assumed if not demonstrated. The connection between peace and justice, though noted, is not treated as self-evident.

Peace, freedom, and security are the central motifs around which the first principles of biblical teaching about humanity, sin, society, the task of the church, and God's will are organized. According to the evangelical document, the church's primary work is spiritual, to worship and glorify God and to make disciples. Beyond this, evangelicals are called to love their neighbors, serving the world in the ministry of reconciliation between God and human beings and among human beings. Law and political community (especially democratic institutions) are important instruments of this reconciliation among people. This work nurtures a future more congruent with the values of the kingdom of God, though the coming of the kingdom in its fullness is a divine work, not a human work.

The statement acknowledges a plurality of views regarding war and peace, while favoring the just war tradition. It recognizes that eighteenth- and nineteenth-century evangelicalism was more politically involved, and holds up that period as an ideal. Although it calls American evangelical churches to greater historical awareness, the document itself does not include much historical material. Its theological proposal is grounded in a body of theological doctrine expressive of an expansive conservative evangelical tradition.

The Episcopal statement draws heavily on the just war tradition. It looks at scripture texts enjoining Christians to render to Caesar and to God what is due each of them and to love our enemies. The writers then trace the history of the church's experience of war from early Christian pacifism to the Constantinian settlement in 313 C.E., when the church was no longer a persecuted minority and became linked to the state. The Christian community then found it necessary to provide biblically based teaching for the state on maintaining peace, order, and justice in a world of conflict, disorder, and injustice. This led to the gradual development and systematization of the tradition of justifiable war, which has remained the dominant framework for moral discernment about war and peace for the Episcopal Church.

The document asks whether just war criteria have continuing validity in the contemporary international situation, in which nuclear annihilation of the natural order is possible. While the Episcopal Church believes this tradition has continuing relevance, the document provides additional guidelines, recognizing that the current situation is unique in human history:

1. It is the responsibility of the church to remain informed about public policy and to participate in national debate, especially on "the life and death questions of war, its justification, its conduct, and participation in it" (15). The dichotomy between sacred and secular is false; God is the God of all, including the political arena.
2. It is a fallacy that more military might means more security for a nation. Our technological age tempts us to allow technology rather than morality to determine military strategy. The result is a "mad momentum"; the arms race takes on a life of its own.
3. It is naive to believe that nuclear weapons create a stable deterrent; weapons that are built will in time be employed.
4. Nuclear war would result in intentional and indiscriminate destruction of millions of innocent lives. "Such strategies go beyond the bounds of even the most severe interpretation of 'love your enemies'" (15).

Contemporary World: Theology as Practical Reflection

The peace documents that make their theological argument more in terms of the contemporary world are the Lutheran, Presbyterian, Methodist, and Reformed documents.

The Lutheran document affirms that peace is the promise of God and that the peace of God's reign infinitely surpasses the peace of creation. It appeals to the biblical *shalom* vision in the context of the contemporary eschatological community of the Spirit. It understands the peace of God as a present possession, a gift not of this world, the result of our justification by faith in Jesus Christ. The emphasis is on hope in the midst of suffering as we await the eschatological reign of God. Thus peace as God's promise is anchored in creation and to a lesser extent in redemption texts. The eschatological note is strong; creation awaits redemption. The root of war is sin, the willful rejection of God's lordship, and worship of the creature rather than the Creator.

The strongest statements in the Lutheran document deal with the eschatological nature of the church as a sign of the peace of God's reign in a broken world. Its mission is cast in terms of proclaiming the Word. The gospel declares reconciliation and propels us into political steward-

33

ship. It mandates the specifically Christian duty to love enemies. This contributes to survival and well-being on earth. Thus the Lutheran document has a dominant emphasis on God's activity in creation and a correspondingly strong link between political peace and creation theology. A theology of providence is complemented by a theology of preservation grounded in God's continuing "yes" to creation. Politics is an expression of God's yes; in politics people participate in God's work, protecting and caring for the common life. Peace is the goal of politics, and God the Creator is present in the politics of peace. However, temporal peace, the work of God's preservation through politics, is distinguished from peace with God in Christ, a priceless gift of the reign of God. Political stewardship is seen as a vocation for all Christians, especially since the beginning of the nuclear age, a critical moment in history in which the practice of politics is undergoing profound change.

The main theological motifs governing the Presbyterian document can be summarized as follows: Peacemaking in all our relationships is to be grounded in the reign of God, in our worship of God, and in the great commandment embodied in Jesus Christ and his church: Love God and love your neighbor as yourself. Humanity, the bearer of the image of God, is the instrument of redemption. This redeemed human community is to be characterized by justice, freedom, and compassionate order. The document begins with a christological statement concerning Christ's lordship over history and over the people of God. The body of Christ needs to identify with the poor and respond in obedience to the Prince of Peace. It must live with integrity, have a global perspective, and link security with justice. Accordingly, the second section of the document promotes active involvement in peacemaking at multiple levels.

The third section of the Presbyterian document deals with the new global reality and with theological-ethical bases for peacemaking and for policymaking. It reaffirms the lordship of Christ over church and world and calls us to be loyal to him in the context of a new global reality. The statement's focus is not on principles but on Americans' changing awareness of global interdependence (replacing a sense of national self-sufficiency) and of unsolved economic and human problems. In the face of these desperate problems, the "arms stampede," which contributes to them by aiding repression, by bringing us close to self-destruction, and by wasting resources, is decried as immoral, even demonic. The document challenges the ability of the nation-state to provide security and probes the real causes of war—hunger, poverty, and inequality—behind the symptoms. It appeals to the human spirit, to our intuitive sense of decency and repulsion, stressing the spiritual-moral urgency of peacemaking. It appeals to tradition only negatively, declaring the just war tradition inadequate to the nuclear age. The document repeatedly identifies peacemaking as the central responsibility of the church in the modern world. It is at the heart of our life in Christ.

The longest section in the Presbyterian document addresses U.S. foreign policy. The three value assumptions of U.S. foreign policy—national interest, national security, and national power—are placed within the new global context of interdependence and measured by a new set of criteria: justice, freedom, and compassionate order. The old values are obsolete in the current global situation. In this new situation, Christian morality requires that our preoccupation with self-interest be replaced by a greater focus on the interests of others and the world. A public and political policy invigorated by hope in the reign of God will result in engagement in particular political struggles in which greater approximations of justice can be achieved.

The Methodist document attempts to recover the depth and breadth of the scriptural understanding of creation, God's action in history, the world of nations, and human destiny. It affirms the transcendent biblical vision of *shalom* in creation, covenant, and community as God's will and way, standing in judgment particularly on the idolatry of nationalism. *Shalom* is the heart of God and the law of creation. It entails justice, but leaves judgment and vengeance to God. The wisdom of *shalom* breaks with the conventional wisdom, which seeks security by military means.

The Methodist statement traces its theology of *shalom* through all four dimensions of the Wesleyan Quadrilateral: scripture, tradition, reason, and experience. Claiming with Wesley that the Bible is the ultimate source of knowledge and authority, it begins with biblical foundations. After restating this biblical and theological tradition, it calls for contemporary commitment, even recognizing the inadequacy of tradition in the present situation. It states that while the threefold division of pacifism, just war, and crusade never fully reflected the diversity of Christian views, this way of casting the alternatives is particularly outmoded and inadequate for clarifying the ethical dilemmas of the nuclear arms race. Consequently the Methodist document does not, to any significant extent, employ traditional moral theories except to sketch them "in briefest outline before addressing the central nuclear issues and proposing a new and more varied ethical spectrum" (30). Accordingly, most of the document deals with the nuclear challenge to faith. It articulates policies that best express principles of peacemaking and calls the United Methodist Church to be an alternative community in the world.

The Reformed document begins by reflecting on the contemporary situation. It pleads for Christians to wake up to the destructive power of the superpowers' stockpiling of nuclear arms. Many statistics describe the quantity as well as the kind of weapons available to these nations and their power to destroy both humanity and the earth itself. Then the statement uses Scripture to support the belief that continuing the arms race is both foolish and contrary to the will of God, who desires that our ultimate allegiance be directed toward God and that we find our security in right relationship with God rather than in weapons of destruction. The document also examines church tradition, including the teachings on war and peace of the church fathers, of just war theorists, and of the Reformers. The document contends that "nuclear war and the preparations for it violate every code by which historical Christianity has determined a war to be just" (5). Christians are called to positive acts of commitment to God's will for *shalom,* such as seeking to eradicate diseases, alleviate world hunger, and harness solar energy. Further, the people of God are urged to pray for the world, and for political and military leaders.

III. Development of Ecclesial and Moral Implications

We have analyzed the nature of the scriptural appeal and looked at how Scripture is used in the structure of the theological argument in each church's peace document. Now we will identify ecclesial and moral implications of the theological proposal in each statement, and examine the relationship of Scripture to the social-ethical agenda of each document. We will use the familiar labels for three standard approaches to ethics as our grid in this section: *characterological, deontological,* and *teleological.* The first sees ethics and the motivation for morality in terms primarily of the formation of character in community; it employs a narrative hermeneutic. The second approach emphasizes divine commands, eternal principles, or ethical duties as guiding moral behavior and moral decision making. It relies on a more conceptual hermeneutic.

The third approach is oriented primarily toward the consequences or goals of our decisions and practices, and it uses Scripture to express and evoke action. In our analysis, we will also note the peace documents' use of various styles of ethical reflection, such as prophetic, legal, sapiential, apocalyptic, and sacramental.

Characterological Orientation

The peace statements that most display a characterological orientation are the Orthodox, UCC, and HPC documents.

The moral and ecclesial implications in the Orthodox statement should be seen in terms of the threefold structure of the document: the world searching for justice and peace, the response of faith in the face of injustice and threats to peace, and Orthodox Christians responding to the demands of justice and peace. The document begins with an analysis of contemporary issues of justice and peace, especially environmental problems, the arms race, Christian participation in war, economic injustice, injustice in social institutions, and the threat of nuclear war. It explains why the tradition has not developed a just war theory and identifies basic Orthodox theological affirmations bearing on justice and peace. It then recommends various levels of response to peace and justice issues. The practical application in the third section attaches the theological tradition to the recommendations of the policy statement.

The three sections are interconnected: The first provides a clear social-ethical context, the second brings the text of Orthodox theology to bear on it, and the third develops key areas of response based on the main themes of the second. The statement examines moral responses in the areas of personal life, ecclesial life, and outreach to the world: Christians are to be peacemakers with God at personal, ecclesial, and global levels. Personal peacemaking is grounded sacramentally in Christ and the church, thus ensuring our contact with the source of divine peace. The sacramental life is characterized by repentance, humility, self-denial, constant vigilance, and alertness to the personal and social injustices around us. There is an imperative for justice and peace in our ecclesial life, not just in the world. Church leaders are to give guidance, but the church should also draw on the expertise of its members in all fields and disciplines and should use its many structures to bring peace and justice. Thus, the church lives for the world, not only for itself, and acts ecumenically, with other Christian bodies, to promote justice and peace, especially in response to the world's most urgent problem, the nuclear threat.

The document stresses that "our most precious resource in the face of such terrible problems is the awareness of God's active love and presence in history for the salvation of the world" (20). This is the central point of contact between the first section and the second, in which a theological vision is developed. The third section then points to the synergetic response the church must make in the face of injustice and threats to peace. From this we conclude that the connection between theological premises and moral implications is made in terms of a characterological ethic. This ethic calls Christians to be involved in primary spheres of activity (personal, ecclesial, global) in which the believer and the church live out of the peacemaking ethos arising from communion with God in Christian community.

Within this characterological orientation, the Orthodox document uses several styles of ethical reflection: legal (in its appeal to Orthodox tradition and teaching), prophetic (in presenting the problem of the contemporary world situation and describing how Orthodox faith and life relate to this fundamental issue), apocalyptic (in calling for the purity of the church in situations of radical apostasy), wisdom (in emphasizing the importance of knowledge and insight for those dealing with our technical and social mechanisms, but also in claiming the existence of a universal human need to address injustice and violence), and sacramental (implied in its central biblical motif of the presence of God's love in the world, particularly through Christ and through the church, which is understood mystically and sacramentally). These styles of ethical reflection vary in their uses of Scripture, as the statement deals evenhandedly with three areas: the contemporary situation of injustice and threats to peace, the biblical-theological tradition informing justice and peace, and practical responses to the demands of justice and peace.

More than any other, the UCC document avoids making any style of ethical reflection normative, but selects citations from a variety of biblical sources: Law, Prophets, Writings, Gospels, Epistles. The evidence of the Scripture references indicates that this document makes broader use of styles of ethical reflection than most. It employs heavily the prophetic (see references to the prophets and Jesus), yet places that emphasis in the context of a New Testament concept of the liturgical community (see references to John 14–17 and Ephesians), which the just church must be today. Likewise, it employs extensively the wisdom mode and to a lesser degree the apocalyptic. It uses the legal style in sketching out a biblical theology of just peace for the church to model.

It uses texts sometimes in a biblical context and sometimes in a contemporary context and sometimes in a mixture of the two. This fact makes it difficult to determine which ethical orientation predominates. As is the case with most of the other documents, the UCC statement could show more explicitly how the biblical materials inform the policy recommendations. Yet it does weave ecclesial and moral dimensions into its biblical-theological section. In spelling out moral implications, the document applies the challenge of the just peace vision to the church structurally and to Christians personally. It stresses the characterological aspects of peacemaking. Just peace is understood as the presence and interrelation of friendship, justice, and common security from violence.

The HPC document's strong appeal to the nature and mission of the church as God's people is its basis for rejecting Christian participation in any war. The people of God must embody now the peace of Christ in order for the church to become the sacrament of salvation for the world. Thus the HPC statement primarily uses biblical-theological resources to articulate a spiritual-ethical vision that is to form our private and public conduct in war and peace. The specifics of this conduct are not developed in the statement. Rather it develops a theological model that transcends traditional denominational theological premises, a model from which ethical warrants are drawn and in light of which public policy may be addressed.

Its starting point is not a contemporary nuclear crisis but a biblical vision that should inform believers in matters of war and peace. This vision is broadly based in the biblical narrative and constitutes a brief biblical theology of the eschatological reign of God in Jesus Christ through the people of God in a violent world. The paradigmatic language is that of witness, which corresponds to the church's role as prophet. Accordingly, the document articulates the meaning of the biblical account in terms of Scripture as story. The appeal is not to traditional teaching or to the contemporary situation but to the biblical vision understood in terms of priestly, prophetic, sapiential, and royal servanthood themes. There is no technical information about weapons and strategy or any appeal to general moral principles. Little place is given to contemporary social or political analysis. The statement does not use instrumental pragmatism as a form of reasoning; where wisdom is extolled it is the wisdom of the cross, in tension with the wisdom of the world.

In the HPC statement the connection between theological premises and ethical implications is related to its narrative hermeneutic and characterological ethic. The statement is not a code of rules or a pragmatic response to a current situation. It is a body of working biblical-theological insights that one appropriates through a spiritual character-formation process, rather than through pragmatic decision making. It assumes that the task of theology is more than thinking or even doing; a way of being, of living out of the ethos of the biblical *shalom* vision. As a result the HPC statement easily incorporates several styles of ethical reflection (prophetic, legal, wisdom, apocalyptic) in its four sections analyzing the priestly, prophetic, discerning, and royal servant roles of Israel, Christ, and the church. It does so without making sharp distinctions between the text then and the context now, instead articulating a unitive vision. Because it emphasizes the biblical witness rather than contemporary analysis, some may argue that it is integrated vertically but not horizontally.

Deontological Orientation

The peace statements that display a more deontological orientation are the Catholic, evangelical, and Episcopal statements.

The Catholic bishops' statement draws on the Catholic Church's classical teachings as they are expressed in contemporary sources. Vatican II's *Pastoral Constitution on the Church in the Modern World* is one main guide. No direct appeal is made to the classical Thomistic theological arguments or to Aristotelian philosophy. Thus, no one philosophical or ethical theory governs the moral arguments. A deontological approach predominates, but with some attention to ends or consequences in its specific and concrete response to the nuclear threat. Much space is given to historical, social, and political analysis. Informed by tradition and contemporary analyses, the church applies universally binding moral principles and judgments to specific public policy.

The argument is interwoven with fine points of realistic political reasoning. It contends for a moral and political conception of international common good, a vision of global interdependence in the nuclear age. It distinguishes between universal moral principles and their various applications. The line from the articulation of moral principles to their application is clearer and tighter than the line from the underlying biblical-theological premises to the moral principles. Although the last section (which deals with spiritual formation as a central challenge) displays a characterological ethic, the categories and structure of the theological argument in the document as a whole are shaped by just war tradition, both in deontological and in teleological terms.

The relationship of Scripture to moral implications is indirect at best. Although the statement more than most previous Catholic documents incorporates prophetic and even apocalyptic styles of ethical reflection (the latter in dealing with the massive destructive potential of nuclear weapons), it continues to rely heavily on legal and sapiential modes. It continues deontological use of the theological tradition and moral law, and employs teleological arguments extensively in its attempt to relate the biblical vision to the modern world.

The evangelical document, even more than the Catholic statement, uses a decisionist approach to ethics to develop the moral implications of its vision, displaying both deontological and teleological orientations. This is evident in its primary use of legal and sapiential styles of ethical reflection, rather than prophetic, apocalyptic, or sacramental styles (though the statement alludes to the importance of worship of God). It makes strong formal claims about scriptural authority, but its appeal to Scripture is general and provides little content for the broad ethical themes it names. Moreover, it does not show clearly how the biblical material relates to the policy recommendations. Its moral implications are spelled out particularly in the last three sections, on policy goals, program objectives, and assessment criteria. At core they direct American evangelicals to promote peace, freedom, and security through law and political community, both nationally and internationally.

In keeping with its conceptual use of Scripture, the Episcopal statement points to the divine commands of Matthew 22:21 (give to God and Caesar what you owe each) and Matthew 6:44 (love your enemies) to guide Christian behavior. The document charges that the U.S. government has crossed the line between military strength adequate to ensure national security and excessive investment of resources in weapons of mass destruction. The result is self-defeating and idolatrous: We are less secure and we now worship the weapons and technology we have made.

Both domestic and international implications are spelled out, each in terms of the dicta of Matthew 22:21 and 6:44. On the domestic front,

continued military expansion will lead to an inflationary economy, rob
the nation of its natural resources, result in the neglect of basic human
needs because of continued cutting of government social service programs, lead to the breakdown of the family, and contribute to the debil-
itation of both the human psyche (due to fear and insecurity) and ethical
sensitivities. We must attend to these dangers if we are to render to God
the things that are God's. When addressing international affairs, the
document adopts a community hermeneutic, calling Christians in the
U.S. to look at the world from God's perspective. We must see the world
as one, recognizing that our country's decisions affect the whole. We
have the power to influence other nations for good or ill, so we must
seize the opportunity to contribute to world peace.

The move from Scripture to ethical implications is indirect here.
While alluding to these two main texts, the argument rests mainly on
reason. It uses teleological reasoning in its projection of the results of
continued stockpiling of nuclear weapons. Attention to other peace issues (e.g., care for the poor or for the environment) is minimal.

Teleological Orientation

A more teleological orientation is seen in the Lutheran, Presbyterian,
Methodist, Baptist, and Reformed peace documents.

The Lutheran document generally recognizes the role of natural
law, divine law embedded in the created order. Apparently the advent
of total war has led to a natural law demand (i.e., one based on common
sense) that aggressive war be outlawed, not just legally restrained. The
document is politically oriented and provides theological warrants for
involvement in keeping peace, building peace, and making peace. The
church is to be a community of political and moral discourse equipping
people for responsible action in the world for the sake of the neighbor.
The statement moves from theological affirmations to ethical judgment
not so much by a straight line of moral reasoning as by a shift from
apologetic to kerygmatic theology, from theological reflection to
homiletical expression. In its use of Scripture it places prophetic and
wisdom styles side by side. The contemporary context is in the foreground.

The Presbyterian document makes no explicit use of categories of
moral philosophy. Its ethic is more teleological and characterological

than deontological, with an appeal to Christians to pursue *shalom* in the midst of today's crises. In drawing out the moral implications of this mandate, the statement develops a theological and ethical framework from which criteria are derived that challenge the increasing dependence of U.S. foreign policy on an amoral realism. A lengthy political analysis is apparently vital to bringing a biblical-theological perspective to bear on decision making in the nuclear age. Likewise, the statement details the global economic situation and the impact of the arms race on it in order to inspire a new initiative in biblical peacemaking.

Although the Presbyterian document avoids making a single style normative, it cites or alludes to biblical texts from most parts of the canon, with fewest from the books of the Law. It relies heavily on the Old Testament prophets, reinforced by the prophetic dimensions of Jesus' ministry. It avoids prooftexting and generally gives some specific content when it appeals to broad ethical themes in Scripture (*shalom*, love, reconciliation). Its reference to the image of God might have been more directly grounded in the biblical text. The wisdom style also figures prominently in the commonsense critical analysis of the present situation. Accordingly, an appendix lists many recommendations for the church's peacemaking witness, and a study guide helps Christians address peace issues at several levels.

The Methodist document does not use philosophical categories in its analysis or draw out ethical implications of general moral principles, though it does describe a new ethical spectrum for addressing nuclear issues. It engages in lengthy analyses of national and global political and economic situations to make the case for a just peace that counters status quo thinking on the deterrent use of nuclear arms. East-west and north-south conflicts get some attention. The statement articulates policies that best express principles of peacemaking and calls United Methodists to be an alternative community in the world. This call is grounded in the biblical vision of *shalom*, which is distinctively combined with a teleological ethic. A wisdom style of ethical reflection is used, along with prophetic and hints of apocalyptic styles.

The Baptist document analyzes the contemporary scene in terms of tensions between the U.S. and the USSR. It cites data on the effects of the arms race, on effects of superpower intervention in other countries' and regions' affairs, and on international economic inequities. It discusses the interplay between these military and economic factors (especially the inflationary nature of military spending), cites the problem of human rights violations around the world, and names the unprecedented crises the world faces. It identifies principles that are to guide American Baptist involvement in peace and justice issues. These guidelines are grounded theologically, with supporting insights drawn from anthropological, ecclesiological, ecumenical, political, and ecological realms. Prophetic and wisdom styles of ethical reflection predominate. The Baptist document has the fewest biblical quotations and cites the fewest biblical books. Some theological content is present in its appeal to the broad ethical theme of *shalom*.

The Reformed statement uses Scripture to convince people to act now to prevent nuclear war. It employs logic to urge Christians to wake up to the effects on humanity and on the earth of stockpiling nuclear weapons. It reminds us that God has given the principalities and powers temporary authority, but Christ has defeated these forces and is in ultimate control. Christians are not to be paralyzed by fear, but are constrained to work toward *shalom* in the world, because even if human foolishness results in a nuclear holocaust, Christians can live in the hope that this is in God's plan and that God provides salvation for us. A deontological orientation is also evident in the paper in its emphasis on giving allegiance to God rather than seeking security from weapons. This document includes a practical discussion guide with quotations on nuclear weapons and war and Scripture citations on Christian response. Questions for discussion prompt student reflection and action.

Conclusion: The Church Peace Documents as an Opportunity for Ecumenical Conversation

Our goal has been to see the nature of each document's appeal to Scripture, the use of Scripture in each statement's theological argument, and the use of Scripture in developing the moral and ecclesial implications of each statement's peace position. We conclude now with points of interest, convergence, divergence, and concern derived from our analysis of these statements. Our hope is that this listing may facilitate ecumenical conversation on the character of the church's peace witness.

Points of Interest

A Scripture frequency analysis of each statement places the peace documents in this order: HPC (98 Scripture references), Catholic (66), Lutheran (60), UCC (59), Reformed (55), Presbyterian (39), Episcopal (35), Methodist (28), evangelical (23), Baptist (16), Orthodox (4, with 276 references in supporting documents).

The most frequently cited books of the Bible in all of the statements combined are Matthew (79), Romans (67), and Isaiah (66), followed by Genesis (57), Luke and John (43 each), and Psalms (40).

Matthew, Romans, Isaiah, and Luke are the only books of the Bible cited in all of the statements.

The most frequently quoted book of the Bible in each statement is: Genesis (Orthodox), Psalms and Isaiah (Presbyterian), Jeremiah (UCC), Matthew (Baptist, Episcopal, evangelical), Matthew and Luke (Catholic), John (Methodist), Romans (Lutheran), Ephesians (Reformed), and Hebrews (HPC).

The chapter of the Bible most frequently cited in each of the documents is: Genesis 1 (Orthodox), Jeremiah 6 (Presbyterian), Matthew 5 (evangelical, UCC), Matthew 22 (Episcopal), John 20 (Catholic and Methodist), Romans 13 (Lutheran), Ephesians 6 and Colossians 2 (Reformed), Hebrews 9 (HPC), James 4 (Baptist).

The most frequently cited chapters of the Bible in the combined statements are, in order of frequency, Genesis 1, Matthew 5, Romans 8, Psalm 72, John 14, Isaiah 2, and Romans 13.

Points of Convergence

The presenting problem in most of these documents is east-west tension, and particularly the nuclear arms race between the U.S. and the Soviet Union. Most also attend to the related issue of north-south economic disparity. The peace documents converge around these interrelated peace and justice issues.

The documents manifest an increased sensitivity to the destructiveness of war, increased attention to methods of warfare, and increased awareness of the social, economic, and spiritual consequences of preparing for war.

Each statement grounds the vision of peace in the eschatological reign of God as expressed in the biblical narrative, though the way that language is appropriated in subsequent theological argument and ethical discernment varies. The statements display a growing recognition that the reign of God and this world are not simply mixed together in the present, but are distinguished aeonically, with God's reign being *already* realized but *not yet* fully so. The question is whether the *already* is too contaminated by the *not yet* to prevent our living out of the new reality.

Each statement appeals prominently to prophetic and gospel traditions, as well as to Paul, in its use of Scripture (see the high frequency of references to Isaiah, Matthew, Luke, and Romans).

Most of the statements signal the importance of ecclesiology in developing and promoting their vision of peace, though they vary in their assessment of how and how much the church can influence the world through church structures.

Although most statements see the contemporary situation presenting challenges that traditional categories cannot adequately address, each statement sees an ongoing need for tradition to inform present theological and ethical effort, while itself being translated and reformulated in light of new situations.

Each statement addresses the present situation concretely — some more practically and politically, some more biblically and theologically. All assume that the church has responsibility in the political sphere, though they differ about the grounds for involvement and the shape of this involvement. Most espouse nuclear pacifism, reject nuclear deterrence policy, and are concerned about economic injustice. However, the UCC and HPC documents do not dwell on the threat of nuclear holocaust, and the evangelical and Lutheran statements accept the nuclear deterrence policy.

Each statement affirms that peace is a central biblical motif and an integral part of Christian discipleship and that nonviolent management of conflict (national and international) is basic to genuine political security.

In these statements the vision of justice and peace is extended to include the preservation of creation. No longer is the sole concern the destruction of human life. This is especially the case in the Methodist document.

These statements have a common pastoral concern for the praxis of peacemaking and attend to people's frustrations, fears, and hopes. This perspective is beginning to inform the church's scriptural reflection and work, eclipsing the old just war vs. pacifism debate, which has often become reductionistic.

All the statements start with Christian diagnosis of the human condition in all its brokenness; all agree that Old Testament *shalom* includes justice; all affirm that Christ, through his resurrection, brought a new order of peace and reconciliation; all agree that Jesus never resorted to violence in his own defense; and all agree that it is the duty of God's people to witness to a new peaceable kingdom.

Points of Divergence

This vision of God's peaceful reign is grounded in different ways: in the transcendence of God, in the presence of God, in the providence of God, in the triune God, in God as friend, in creation and its preservation, in prophetic justice, in reconciliation in Jesus Christ, in redemptive embodiment in the church, or in eschatological hope.

Some statements display the belief that eschatological peace can be manifested now in the community of God's people, but not so much in the broader world. Others emphasize more the possibility of that peace being extended through the church to the rest of the world. Others relativize present possibilities, emphasizing instead the fulfillment of the reign of God in the future and challenging us to live with hope in the midst of ambiguity in this evil world.

The Presbyterian, Methodist, HPC, Episcopal, and Reformed documents reflect a narrative hermeneutic; the Catholic, Baptist, and evangelical documents a conceptual hermeneutic; and the Orthodox, Lutheran, and UCC documents an expressivist hermeneutic.

The UCC, Baptist, and HPC documents approach peace theology more in terms of Scripture (biblical knowledge); the Orthodox, Catholic, evangelical, and Episcopal documents more in terms of tradition (ecclesial doctrine); and the Lutheran, Presbyterian, Methodist, and Reformed documents more in terms of the contemporary world (practical reflection).

The Orthodox, UCC, and HPC statements develop moral and ecclesial implications using a more characterological approach; the Catholic, evangelical, and Episcopal use a more deontological approach; and the Lutheran, Presbyterian, Methodist, Baptist, and Reformed statements use a more teleological approach.

Some of these statements stress the churchly vision of peaceful witness to the world, others the global vision of a united humanity, and others the Christian vocation of stewardship and responsibility in and for the world.

Some of the statements reject all justification of war; most of them reject all use of nuclear weapons, including their use as deterrents.

Some of the statements focus more on spiritual formation and moral choices in the world, whereas others emphasize more stewardship and practical involvement on the part of the church and individual Christians in the world.

The UCC and HPC statements, more than the others, place the issue of peace and justice in a liturgical and doxological context.

Some of the statements (Catholic and Episcopal) have the faithful and the civil authorities as their audience; for others (Methodist, Baptist) the church, as denomination, is the main audience; still others are trans-denominational in character (HPC, evangelical).

Points of Concern

This study has dealt with hermeneutical rather than doctrinal questions: We have sought to understand how Scripture is used in the churches' documents to provide warrants for beliefs and morals with regard to global issues of justice and peace. The churches must continue to work toward a hermeneutic that integrates the biblical vision of peace more clearly, consistently, and convincingly into its sacramental life, its doctrines, and its morals. We welcome both the narrowing of the hermeneutical gap between biblical vision and contemporary reality on issues of justice and peace and the priority given to Scripture over post-biblical traditions. A continuing concern is the church's tendency to forsake the hermeneutical primacy of the biblical vision of justice and peace for the realisms of contemporary culture. While the statements differ little regarding the content of the biblical narrative, they still differ about the relevance of Scripture for Christians today.

For the churches, embracing the apostolic faith does not mean making a single confession. It means, rather, having a common hermeneutic. The main confessional traditions now have different hermeneutics. But we have seen significant convergences in the midst of divergences. All assume that the goal and process of achieving greater unity is, qualitatively speaking, a worthy one. The world's Christians face the challenge to give the biblical vision and virtue of peace a confessional status among us sufficient to establish it as a focal point for our unity. This might mean placing peace issues in a more liturgical and doxological context, as seen in the UCC and HPC documents.

These documents suggest that a new paradigm is emerging for the churches' thinking about war, peace, and justice. New realities call forth this change in paradigms: new weapons, north-south and east-west conflicts, global interdependence, apocalyptic despair, the Vietnam War, and now the collapse of communism and the advent of the second Russian revolution. These new realities encourage us to relativize three traditional preoccupations: individual conscience regarding killing, self-defense, and rational (just war) calculations regarding war. Instead these church documents emphasize a nonviolence that works aggressively for peace with justice in our relationship with God, with our neighbors, and with the earth. This peace vision requires analysis of the nature and functions of the state and of the church's relationship to government, an analysis that goes beyond attempts to define the limits of permissible violence. We need a biblical theology of the state, and a consequent ethical analysis of the priorities, modes, and limits of Christian participation in the state.

In the 1990s the international situation is dramatically different from that of the 1980s, when these peace statements were written. The global upheavals of the past several years create more than ever a kairotic moment in which Christian communions can move toward greater confessional unity about issues of peace and justice. The church would be remiss if it failed to seize this opportunity to advance its commitment to the apostolic faith and Christian peace witness.

TABLE I: ALL SCRIPTURE REFERENCES
IN EACH STATEMENT

Table I lists all Scripture references found in each church peace statement. The references appear in canonical order. Some chapters and verses appear more than once in the listing because a reference was noted each time a text was cited in a statement. The total number of scriptural references for each book is given in brackets at the end of each listing.

BAPTIST
  Gen. 1:26-29 [1]
  Lev. 25:8ff. [1]
  Prov. 29:18 [1]
  Isa. 2:4 [1]
  Mic. 6:8 [1]
  Matt. 5:9; 25:21ff.; 28:19-20 [3]
  Luke 4:16-21 [1]
  John 14:2 [1]
  Rom. 13 [1]
  Eph. 2:12, 14ff. [2]
  Jas. 4; 4:1-2, 2 [3]

CATHOLIC
  Lev. 26:3-16, 12 [2]
  Deut. 1:30; 20:4 [2]
  Josh. 2:24 [1]
  Judg. 3:28 [1]
  Ps. 85:10-11 [1]
  Isa. 2:4; 7:1-9; 30:1-4; 32:15-20; 42:2-3 [5]
  Jer. 6:14; 8:10-12; 37:10 [3]
  Ezek. 13:16; 37:26 [2]
  Mic. 4:3 [1]
  Matt. 4:17; 5:3-10, 39-42, 44-48; 6:14-15; 8:5-13; 10:34; 12:18-21, 34; 18:21-22; 21:12-17; 28:16-20 [12]
  Mark 1:15; 11:25 [2]
  Luke 6:27-28, 29-31, 37; 11:4; 12:32; 14:31; 17:3-4, 20-21; 22:35-38, 51; 23:34; 24:44-53 [12]
  John 3:13-25; 4:19-26, 46-53; 14:27; 15:12; 20:19, 19-29, 20, 26 [9]
  Rom. 5:1-22; 8:36-39 [2]

50

2 Cor. 5:19-20 [1]
Gal. 3:13, 28 [2]
Eph. 1:10; 2:13-22; 6:10-17 [3]
Col. 1:19-20, 20 [2]
1 Thess. 5:8-9 [1]
Heb. 4:12 [1]
Rev. 17:14 [1]

EPISCOPAL
Isa. 31:1 [1]
Prophets, Prophets, Prophets, Prophets [4]
Amos 3:3 [1]
Matt. 5; 5:9; 6:44, 44, 44; 7:24-30, 28; 15:12-28; 22:15-22, 21, 21, 21; 27:54
    [13]
Mark 12:13-17; 15:39; 25:14-30 [3]
Luke 6:17-49, 27; 7:1-10; 20:20-26; 23:47 [5]
Gospels [1]
Acts [1]
Rom. 12; 12:18; 13:6, 6, 9-10 [5]
1 Cor. 12 [1]

EVANGELICAL
Lev. 19:17-18 [1]
Deut. 32:35 [1]
Prov. 18:17; 24:11-12 [2]
Isa. 2:4; 11:6, 9 [3]
Jer. 6:14 [1]
Matt. 5:9, 38-39, 43-44, 48; 22:37-39; 28:18-20 [6]
Luke 10:25-27, 29-37; 19:13 [3]
John 14:27 [1]
Rom. 12:19 [1]
2 Cor. 5:18-20 [1]
Gal. 6:9-10 [1]
Rev. 21:1, 4 [2]

HPC
Gen. 1-2; 3; 4; 6; 6:5-13; 9; 11; 12:1-3 [8]
Num. 11:29 [1]
Deut. 18:15ff. [1]

51

2 Sam. 7:5, 12, 18-29 [3]
Pss. 2:7; 72:23; 89 [3]
Prov. 8; 8-9; 19:11; 20:17, 20; 21:6-7; 22:8 [7]
Isa. 2; 2:4b; 9; 10; 11; 29:14; 44:24–45:7; 52–53 [8]
Joel 2:28–3:21; 3:11 [2]
Amos 8:4-10 [1]
Mic. 4 [1]
Zech. 9:10 [1]
Matt. 4:1-11, 36; 5:9, 9, 11; 10:16, 18 [7]
Mark 10:42f., 45 [2]
Luke 2:46-47; 6:27; 7:35; 11 [4]
John 11:20; 16:33; 18:37-38, 37-38; 19; 19:2 [6]
Acts 21:9ff. [1]
Rom. 5:5-10; 12:1-2; 13:1, 3f. [4]
1 Cor. 1:18, 25; 1:18–3:3; 3:18–4:3; 4:12-13; 11:5; 12:29; 14:3 [8]
2 Cor. 5:18-19; 11:3 [2]
Gal. 3:27-28 [1]
Eph. 3:9f., 10 [2]
Phil. 1:29; 3:7-9, 10-11 [3]
Col. 1:24; 1:24–2:8 [2]
Heb. 1:1-3; 2; 2:9; 4:15; 6:6; 7:27; 9:11, 12, 14, 22; 10:18; 11:1; 13:12-13 [13]
1 Pet. 2:9, 13ff., 23-24; 4:13-14 [4]
Rev. 5:9-10, 12; 21:2-4 [3]

LUTHERAN

Gen. 1:3; 3:9, 21; 4:9, 14-15 [5]
Exod. 21:24 [1]
Lev. 19:18 [1]
Deut. 32:35 [1]
Pss. 10:17-18; 68:5; 72:1-14; 82:1-3 [4]
Isa. 1:17; 2:2-4; 11:6-9, 9 [4]
Hos. 11:8-9 [1]
Mic. 4:1-3, 4, 6-8 [3]
Matt. 5:9, 44; 24:6; 26:52; 28:19-20 [5]
Luke 2:10-14; 3:14; 6:20-23; 7:22; 10:8-9 [5]
John 14:27, 27; 17:5; 20:21 [4]
Acts 19:8; 20:25 [2]
Rom. 1:28-32; 2:15; 4; 5:1, 10; 8:18-25; 12:1-2, 19; 13:2-3, 4, 4, 7, 8; 16:16
   [14]

1 Cor. 15:18-26 [1]
2 Cor. 5:18-19, 18-19 [2]
Gal. 3:28; 6:16 [2]
Eph. 2:14-16 [1]
Col. 1:20 [1]
Heb. 4:9-10 [1]
1 Pet. 2:13-14 [1]
Rev. 21:3-4 [1]

METHODIST
Deut. 32:35 [1]
Isa. 32:16-18; 40-66; 48:18; 54:10 [4]
Jer. 29:7 [1]
Ezek. 37:26; Ezekiel [2]
Hos. 10:13-14 [1]
Matt. 5; 5:9; Matthew [3]
Luke 19:41-44 [1]
John 3:16; 14:27; 20:19, 20, 26 [5]
Rom. 5:1-2; 8:36-39 [2]
2 Cor. 5:17-20 [1]
Eph. 2:14-19; 6:11-12 [2]
Col. 1:19-20, 20; 2:15 [3]
Jas. 3:17-18 [1]
Rev. 7 [1]

ORTHODOX
Gen. 1; 1; 1–2; 1:1, 1, 1-2, 2, 4a, 4, 10, 12, 18, 25, 26ff., 26ff., 26-28, 26-28,
    26-30, 27, 27, 28, 28, 28, 28, 31; 2:5, 7, 8, 8, 15, 18, 20, 21-22; 3:8, 12-13,
    15, 18, 18; 8:21-22; 30:33, 33; 49:10 [42]
Deut. 15:9 [1]
1 Kgs. 22:19-23 [1]
Pss. 8:6ff.; 24:1, 1; 29:10-11; 33:6; 45:4, 6-7a; 72:1, 2-4, 3, 3, 6, 7, 7, 7, 8, 15-
    17, 16; 85:10; 93:1; 96:1, 10; 97:1-2 [23]
Isa. 1:17-23; 2:4, 4, 4; 6:1-7, 11; 9; 9:7; 11; 11:5ff.; 21:6-8; 26:12; 30:15ff.;
    32:16-17, 17; 42:5, 59; 48:18; 52:7; 54:9-10; 55:12; 59:8; 60:17; 66:12;
    deutero-Isaiah; trito-Isaiah [26]
Jer. 8:15, 15; 12:12; 14:13-14; 16:5; 23:17, 18, 22; 33:6 [9]
Lam. 5:11 [1]
Ezek. 7:25-27; 39:10, 10, 10 [4]

Hos. 1:7; 14:4 [2]
Amos 5:21; Amos [2]
Mic. 4:4; 5:4 [2]
Hab. 1:3; 2:3 [2]
Haggai [1]
Zech. 4:11-14; 6:12-14; 8:16, 19; 9:7, 9-10, 10; Zechariah (2) [9]
Mal. 2:5-6 [1]
2 Macc. 7:28, 28 [2]
Matt. 4:1ff.; 5:9, 14-16, 35-37, 48; 10:34; 11:28-30; 13:8; 18; 22; 23:8; 24:45-
    51; 25; 25:14-30, 35-37; 28:10 [16]
Mark 2:21-22; 4:8 [2]
Luke 2:14; 8:8; 12:41-48, 51; 14:27; 16:33 [6]
John 1:1-12, 3, 3; 3:16-17; 6:26ff.; 14:27, 27, 27; 16:33 [9]
Acts 1:6, 8, 8, 8, 8; 2:47, 47, 47, 47; 17:24-31; 22:20 [11]
Rom. 1:19-20, 21; 2:14-15; 3:10-20, 23-24; 5:1, 5; 6:4, 22; 8:2, 6, 17, 18-24,
    18-25, 19-22, 19-25, 21, 22, 22; 11:36, 36; 12; 12:4, 5; 14:17, 19; 15:13;
    16:1, 20 [29]
1 Cor. 1:23; 3:9; 4:1-2; 5:6, 8; 7:31; 8:6, 6; 11:11; 12:4-7; 13:12-13; 15:20-28,
    24-28 [12]
2 Cor. 3:17, 18; 4:4, 4; 5:17 [5]
Gal. 3:28, 28; 4:4-7, 26; 5:1, 5 [5]
Eph. 1:10; 2:12, 14, 14-15, 14-17; 4:4, 24; 6:15, 17 [9]
Phil. 2:13, 13 [2]
Col. 1:14-17, 15, 15, 16, 19-20, 20, 23; 2:8, 15; 3:15 [10]
1 Thess. 5:8-9, 23 [2]
1 Tim. 5:9-10 [1]
Titus 1:2; 3:5 [2]
Heb. 1:2, 3ff.; 2:10; 3:1; 10:23 [5]
Jas. 1:17; 5:4 [2]
1 Pet. 2:9, 9; 3:7; 4:10 [4]
2 Pet. 1:2-11, 4 [2]
1 John 1:1-4; 3:1; 4:8, 8; 5:4 [5]
Rev. 1:3, 5; 2:13; 3:14; 17:6; 21; 21:10; 22:17, 17-20 [9]

PRESBYTERIAN
Exod. 20:3 [1]
Pss. 34:14; 37:11; 85:8, 10, 10 [5]
Isa. 2:4; 9:5-6; 53:5; 54:10-17; Isaiah [5]
Jer. 6:13, 14, 14, 14 [4]

Ezek. 13:1-16 [1]
Amos [1]
Zech. 8:12 [1]
Matt. 10:34; 22:37-39; 25:31-46 [3]
Mark 8:34 [1]
Luke 2:14; 13:29; 19:41 [3]
John 10:10; 14:27 [2]
Rom. 14:19 [1]
1 Cor. 13:13 [1]
2 Cor. 5:18f. [1]
Eph. 2:14-17; 4:1-16 [2]
Col. 1:19-22, 19-22, 20 [3]
Heb. 13:20f. [1]
Jas. 3:16f. [1]
1 John 4:11, 21 [2]

REFORMED

Exod. 15:11; 20:13 [2]
Lev. 25:18, 18 [2]
Pss. 34:14; 37:3, 3 [3]
Eccles. 4:2-3 [1]
Isa. 31:1, 1; 32; 32 [4]
Jer. 23:6, 6; 33:16 [3]
Ezek. 34:27, 27 [2]
Matt. 5:39, 39-45; 26:52, 67 [4]
Luke 19:37-46 [1]
John 14:27; 16:33 [2]
Acts 5:29 [1]
Rom. 1:25; 5:1-11; 8:31, 38f.; 13:1 [5]
1 Cor. 2:8, 8; 15:24ff., 24 [4]
Eph. 1:10, 10, 20ff.; 2:1ff., 13-22; 3:10; 6:10-18, 12, 12, 12 [10]
Col. 1:15-17, 16; 2:13-15, 13-15, 15, 15; 4:8 [7]
Heb. 6:5 [1]
Rev. 13; 13:4; Revelation [3]

UCC

Gen. 2:1-4a [1]
Num. 6:26 [1]
Ps. 85:10-11 [1]

55

Isa. 11:6-8; 39:8; 41:8; 52:7; Isaiah [5]
Jer. 6:13-14, 14; 7:1-10; 8:11; 22:15-16; 31:29-30, 34 [8]
Ezek. 13:10, 16; 18:2; 34:25-29; 37:26 [5]
Hos. 1:9; 2:18-20; 10:13-14 [3]
Amos 6:1-6 [1]
Mic. 4:4 [1]
Matt. 5:9, 9, 13-14, 13-14, 19; 11:19; 15:1-20 [7]
Mark 10:42-44 [1]
Luke 4:18-19; 19:42 [2]
John 14; 14:16; 15:13; 17:15-18 [4]
Rom. 8:35f.; 10:15; 14:19 [3]
1 Cor. 3:16-17; 6:19; 12:12, 27 [4]
2 Cor. 4:7 [1]
Eph. 1:14; 2; 2:14, 14, 14; 5:16; 6:15 [7]
Heb. 1:1, 13, 16; 11:13, 16 [5]

TABLE II: FREQUENCY OF REFERENCES TO BOOKS
OF THE BIBLE IN EACH STATEMENT

Table II lists the number of times a book of the Bible is cited in each document. The total number of texts cited in each peace statement is given at the end of this table.

	BAPT	CATH	EPIS	EVAN	HPC	LUTH	METH	ORTH	PRES	REF	UCC
Gen.	1				8	5		42			1
Exod.						1			1	2	
Lev.	1	2		1		1				2	
Num.					1						1
Deut.		2		1	1	1	1	1			
Josh.		1									
Judg.		1									
2 Sam.					3						
1 Kgs.								1			
Ps.		1			3	4		23	5	3	1
Prov.	1			2	7						
Eccles.									1		
Isa.	1	5	1	3	8	4	4	26	5	4	5
Jer.		3		1			1	9	4	3	7
Lam.								1			
Ezek.		2					2	4	1	2	5
Hos.						1	1	2			3
Joel					2						
Amos			1		1			2	1		1
Mic.	1	1			1	3		2			1
Hab.								2			
Hag.								1			
Zech.					1			9	1		
Mal.								1			
2 Macc.								2			
Matt.	3	12	13	6	7	5	3	16	3	4	7
Mark		2	3	2				2	1		1
Luke	1	12	5	3	4	5	1	6	3	1	2
John	1	9		1	6	4	5	9	2	2	4
Acts			1		1	2		11		1	
Rom.	1	2	5	1	4	14	2	29	1	5	3

	BAPT	CATH	EPIS	EVAN	HPC	LUTH	METH	ORTH	PRES	REF	UCC
1 Cor.			1		8	1		12	1	4	4
2 Cor.		1		1	2	2	1	5	1		1
Gal.		2		1	1	2		5			
Eph.	2	3			2	1	2	9	2	10	7
Phil.					3			2			
Col.		2			2	1	3	10	3	7	
1 Thess.		1						2			
1 Tim.								1			
Titus								2			
Heb.		1			13	1		5	1	1	5
Jas.	3						1	2	1		
1 Pet.					4	1		4			
2 Pet.								2			
1 John								5	2		
Rev.		1		2	3	1	1	9		3	
TOTALS	16	66	30	23	98	60	28	276	39	55	59

Books not cited in any statement are: Ruth, 1 Samuel, 2 Kings, 1 Chronicles, 2 Chronicles, Ezra, Nehemiah, Esther, Job, Song of Solomon, Daniel, Obadiah, Jonah, Nahum, Zephaniah, 2 Thessalonians, 2 Timothy, Philemon, 2 John, 3 John, and Jude.

TABLE III: FREQUENCY WITH WHICH BOOKS OF THE BIBLE ARE CITED IN THE STATEMENTS TAKEN TOGETHER

This table indicates the frequency with which each book of the Bible is cited in the statements cumulatively. Books are listed in canonical order in the left column, and in order of frequency of total citations in the right column.

Canonical order		Order of frequency	
Gen.	57	Matt.	79
Exod.	4	Rom.	67
Lev.	7	Isa.	66
Num.	2	Gen.	57
Deut.	7	Luke	43
Josh.	1	John	43
Judg.	1	Ps.	40
2 Sam.	3	Eph.	38
1 Kgs.	1	1 Cor.	31
Ps.	40	Jer.	28
Prov.	10	Col.	28
Eccles.	1	Heb.	27
Isa.	66	Rev.	20
Jer.	28	Ezek.	16
Lam.	1	Acts	16
Ezek.	16	2 Cor.	14
Hos.	7	Zech.	11
Joel	2	Mark	11
Amos	6	Gal.	11
Mic.	9	Prov.	10
Hab.	2	Mic.	9
Hag.	1	1 Pet.	9
Zech.	11	Lev.	7
Mal.	1	Deut.	7
2 Macc.	2	Hos.	7
Matt.	79	Jas.	7
Mark	11	1 John	7
Luke	43	Amos	6
John	43	Phil.	5
Acts	16	Exod.	4

Romans	67	2 Sam.	3
1 Cor.	31	1 Thess.	3
2 Cor.	14	Num.	2
Gal.	11	Joel	2
Eph.	38	Hab.	2
Phil.	5	2 Macc.	2
Col.	28	Titus	2
1 Thess.	3	2 Pet.	2
1 Tim.	1	Joshua	1
Titus	2	Judg.	1
Heb.	27	1 Kgs.	1
Jas.	7	Eccles.	1
1 Pet.	9	Lam.	1
2 Pet.	2	Hag.	1
1 John	7	Mal.	1
Rev.	20	1 Tim.	1

TABLE IV: BOOKS OF THE BIBLE MOST FREQUENTLY QUOTED IN EACH STATEMENT

This table shows what books of the Bible are quoted most frequently in each statement. The books are listed in descending order of frequency. Books with the same number of citations in a statement are grouped together.

BAPT	CATH	EPIS	EVAN	HPC	LUTH	METH	ORTH	PRES	REF	UCC
Matt.	Matt.	Matt.	Matt.	Heb.	Rom.	John	Gen.	Ps.	Eph.	Jer.
Jas.	Luke							Isa.		Matt.
										Eph.
Eph.	John	Luke	Isa.	Gen.	Gen.	Isa.	Rom.	Jer.	Col.	Isa.
		Rom.	Luke	Isa.	Matt.					Ezek.
				1 Cor.	Luke					Heb.
Isa.	Isa.	Mark	Prov.	Prov.	Ps.	Matt.	Isa.	Matt.	Rom.	John
Mic.		Rev.		Matt.	Isa.	Col.		Luke		1 Cor.
Luke					John			Col.		
John										
Rom.										
	Jer.	Isa.		John	Mic.	Ezek.	Ps.	John	Isa.	Hos.
	Eph.	Amos				Rom.		Eph.	Matt.	Rom.
		Acts				Eph.		1 John	1 Cor.	
		1 Cor.								
				Luke			Matt.	Ps.		
				Rom.				Jer.		
				1 Pet.				Rev.		
							1 Cor.			
							Acts			
							Col.			

TABLE V: NUMBER OF STATEMENTS IN WHICH MOST FREQUENTLY CITED BOOKS OF THE BIBLE APPEAR

This table indicates how many statements cite the books of the Bible most frequently cited in these statements taken together.

Number of statements citing this book		Listing of frequency by canonical order	
Matt.	11	Gen.	5
Rom.	11	Ps.	7
Isa.	11	Isa.	11
Luke	11	Jer.	7
John	10	Ezek.	6
Eph.	9	Matt.	11
2 Cor.	8	Mark	6
Ps.	7	Luke	11
1 Cor.	7	John	10
Jer.	7	Acts	5
Col.	7	Rom.	11
Heb.	7	1 Cor.	7
Rev.	7	2 Cor.	8
Ezek.	6	Gal.	5
Mark	6	Eph.	9
Gen.	5	Col.	7
Acts	5	Heb.	7
Gal.	5	Rev.	7

TABLE VI: REFERENCES FOR MOST FREQUENTLY CITED
BOOKS OF THE BIBLE IN EACH STATEMENT

This table lists references for the books of the Bible most frequently cited in each statement, in descending order of frequency.

BAPTIST
Matt. 5:9; 25:21ff.; 28:19-20 [3]
Jas. 4; 4:1-2, 2 [3]
Eph. 2:12, 14ff. [2]

CATHOLIC
Matt. 4:17; 5:3-10, 39-42, 44-48; 6:14-15; 8:5-13; 10:34; 12:18-21, 34; 18:21-22; 21:12-17; 28:16-20 [12]
Luke 6:27-28, 29-31, 37; 11:4; 12:32; 14:31; 17:3-4, 20-21; 22:35-38, 51; 23:34; 24:44-53 [12]
John 3:13-25; 4:19-26, 46-53; 14:27; 15:12; 20:19, 19-29, 20, 26 [9]
Isa. 2:4; 7:1-9; 30:1-4; 32:15-20; 42:2-3 [5]
Jer. 6:14; 8:10-12; 37:10 [3]
Eph. 1:10; 2:13-22; 6:10-17 [3]

EPISCOPAL
Matt. 5; 5:9; 6:44, 44, 44; 7:24-30, 28; 15:12-28; 22:15-22, 21, 21, 21; 27:54 [13]
Luke 6:17-49, 27; 7:1-10; 20:20-26; 23:47 [5]
Rom. 12; 12:18; 13:6, 6, 9-10 [5]
Mark 12:13-17; 15:39; 25:14-30 [3]

EVANGELICAL
Matt. 5:9, 38-39, 43-44, 48; 22:37-39; 28:18-20 [6]
Isa. 2:4; 11:6, 9 [3]
Luke 10:25-27, 29-37; 19:13 [3]
Prov. 18:17; 24:11-12 [2]
Rev. 21:1, 4 [2]

HPC
Heb. 1:1-3; 2; 2:9; 4:15; 6:6; 7:27; 9:11, 12, 14, 22; 10:18; 11:1; 13:12-13 [13]
Gen. 1-2; 3; 4; 6; 6:5-13; 9; 11; 12:1-3 [8]
Isa. 2; 2:4b; 9; 10; 11; 29:14; 44:24–45:7; 52-53 [8]

63

1 Cor. 1:18, 25; 1:18–3:3; 3:18–4:3; 4:12-13; 11:5; 12:29; 14:3 [8]
Prov. 8; 8-9; 19:11; 20:17, 22; 21:6-7; 22:8 [7]
Matt. 4:1-11, 36; 5:9, 9, 11; 10:16, 18 [7]

LUTHERAN

Rom. 1:28-32; 2:15; 4; 5:1, 10; 8:18-25; 12:1-2, 19; 13:2-3, 4, 4, 7, 8; 16:16 [14]
Gen. 1:3; 3:9, 21; 4:9, 14-15 [5]
Matt. 5:9, 44; 24:6; 26:52; 28:19-20 [5]
Luke 2:10-14; 3:14; 6:20-23; 7:22; 10:8-9 [5]
Pss. 10:17-18; 68:5; 72:1-14; 82:1-3 [4]
Isa. 1:17; 2:2-4; 11:6-9, 9 [4]
John 14:27, 27; 17:5; 20:21 [4]

METHODIST

John 3:16; 14:27; 20:19, 20, 26 [5]
Isa. 32:16-18; 40–66; 48:18; 54:10 [4]
Matt. 5; 5:9; Matthew [3]
Col. 1:19-20, 20; 2:15 [3]
Ezek. 37:26; Ezekiel [2]
Rom. 5:1-2; 8:36-39 [2]
Eph. 2:14-19; 6:11-12 [2]

ORTHODOX

Gen. 1; 1; 1–2; 1:1, 1, 1-2, 2, 4a, 4, 10, 12, 18, 25, 26ff., 26ff., 26-28, 26-28, 26-30, 27, 27, 28, 28, 28, 28, 31; 2:5, 7, 8, 8, 15, 18, 20, 21-22; 3:8, 12-13, 15, 18, 18; 8:21-22; 30:33, 33; 49:10 [42]
Rom. 1:19-20, 21; 2:14-15; 3:10-20, 23-24; 5:1, 5; 6:4, 22; 8:2, 6, 17, 18-24, 18-25, 19-22, 19-25, 21, 22, 22; 11:36, 36; 12; 12:4, 5; 14:17, 19; 15:13; 16:1, 20 [29]
Isa. 1:17-23; 2:4, 4, 4; 6:1-7, 11; 9; 9:7; 11; 11:5ff.; 21:6-8; 26:12; 30:15ff.; 32:16-17, 17; 42:5, 59; 48:18; 52:7; 54:9-10; 55:12; 59:8; 60:17; 66:12; deutero-Isaiah; trito-Isaiah [26]
Pss. 8:6ff.; 24:1, 1; 29:10-11; 33:6; 45:4, 6-7a; 72:1, 2-4, 3, 3, 6, 7, 7, 7, 8, 15-17, 16; 85:10; 93:1; 96:1, 10; 97:1-2 [23]
Matt. 4:1ff.; 5:9, 14-16, 35-37, 48; 10:34; 11:28-30; 13:8; 18; 22; 23:8; 24:45-51; 25; 25:14-30, 35-37; 28:10 [16]

PRESBYTERIAN
Pss. 34:14; 37:11; 85:8, 10, 10 [5]
Isa. 2:4; 9:5-6; 53:5; 54:10-17; Isaiah [5]
Jer. 6:13, 14, 14, 14 [4]
Matt. 10:34; 22:37-39; 25:31-46 [3]
Luke 2:14; 13:29; 19:41 [3]
Col. 1:19-22, 19-22, 20 [3]

REFORMED
Eph. 1:10, 10, 20ff.; 2:1ff., 13-22; 3:10; 6:10-18, 12, 12, 12 [10]
Col 1:15-17; 16; 2:13-15, 13-15, 15, 15; 4:8 [7]
Rom. 1:25; 5:1-11; 8:31, 38f., 13:1 [5]
Isa. 31:1, 1; 32; 32 [4]
Matt. 5:39, 39-45; 26:52, 67 [4]
1 Cor. 2:8, 8; 15:24ff., 24 [4]
Pss. 34:14; 37:3, 3 [3]
Jer. 23:6, 6; 33:16 [3]
Rev. 13; 13:4; Revelation [3]

UCC
Jer. 6:13-14, 14; 7:1-10; 8:11; 22:15-16; 31:29-30, 34 [7]
Matt. 5:9, 9, 13-14, 13-14, 19; 11:19; 15:1-20 [7]
Eph. 1:14; 2; 2:14, 14, 14; 5:16; 6:15 [7]
Isa. 11:6-8; 39:8; 41:8; 52:7; Isaiah [5]
Ezek. 13:10, 16; 18:2; 34:25-29; 37:26 [5]
Heb. 1:1, 13, 16; 11:13, 16 [5]

TABLE VII: REFERENCES FOR MOST FREQUENTLY CITED
CHAPTERS OF SCRIPTURE IN EACH STATEMENT

This table lists the references for the chapters of the Bible most frequently cited in each peace statement. The books are listed in descending order of frequency.

BAPTIST
Jas. 4; 4:1-2, 2
Eph. 2:12, 14ff.

CATHOLIC
John 20:19, 19-29, 20, 26
Matt. 5:3-10, 39-42, 44-48
Luke 6:27-28, 29-31, 37

EPISCOPAL
Matt. 22:15-22, 21, 21, 21
Matt. 6:44, 44, 44
Rom. 13:6, 6, 9-10

EVANGELICAL
Matt. 5:9, 38-39, 43-44, 48
Luke 10:25-27, 29-37

HPC
Heb. 9:11, 12, 14, 22
Matt. 5:9, 9, 11
1 Cor. 1:18, 25; 1:18–3:3
1 Pet. 2:9, 13ff., 23-24

LUTHERAN
Rom. 13:2-3, 4, 4, 7, 8
Mic. 4:1-3, 4, 6-8

METHODIST
John 20:19, 20, 26
Isa. 32:16-18, 40-66
Matt. 5; 5:9
Col. 1:19-20, 20

ORTHODOX
Gen. 1; 1; 1-2; 1:1, 1, 1-2, 2, 4a, 4, 10, 12, 18, 25, 26ff., 26ff., 26-28, 26-28,
26-30, 27, 27, 28, 28, 28, 28, 31
Rom. 8:2, 6, 17, 18-24, 18-25, 19-22, 19-25, 21, 22, 22
Gen. 2:5, 7, 8, 8, 15, 18, 20, 21-22
Ps. 72:1, 3, 3, 7, 7, 7, 8, 16

PRESBYTERIAN
Jer. 6:13, 14, 14, 14
Ps. 85:8, 10, 10
Col. 1:19-22, 19-22, 20

REFORMED
Eph. 6:10-18, 12, 12, 12
Eph. 1:10, 10, 20ff.
Col. 2:13-15, 13-15, 15, 15

UCC
Matt. 5:9, 9, 13-14, 13-14, 19
Eph. 2; 2:14, 14, 14
Heb. 1:1, 13, 16

TABLE VIII: REFERENCES FOR MOST FREQUENTLY CITED CHAPTERS OF SCRIPTURE IN THE STATEMENTS TAKEN TOGETHER

This table lists Scripture references for chapters of the Bible most frequently cited in all the statements taken together. The books are listed in descending order of frequency. The chapters are listed in numerical order. I have included in parentheses references from deutero-Isaiah because they are so prominent in the church peace statements.

MATTHEW

   5; 5:3-10, 9, 9, 9, 9, 9, 9, 9, 9, 9, 11, 13-14, 13-14, 14-16, 19, 35-37, 38-39,
        39, 39-42, 39-45, 43-44, 44, 44-48, 48, 48 [25]

   6:44, 44, 44 [3]

   7:24-30, 28 [2]

   10:16, 18, 34, 34, 34 [5]

   22:15-22, 21, 21, 21 [4]

   25; 25:14-30, 21ff., 31-46, 35-37 [5]

   28:10, 16-20, 18-20, 19-20, 19-20, 19-20 [6]

ISAIAH

   2; 2:2-4, 4, 4, 4, 4, 4, 4, 4, 4b [10]

   9; 9; 9:5-6, 7 [4]

   11; 11; 11:5, 6, 6-8, 6-9, 9, 9 [8]

   31:1, 1 [2]

   32; 32 [2]

   (40–66; 41:8; 42:2-3, 5, 59; 44:24–45:7; 48:18, 18; 52:7, 7; 52:53; 53:5; 54:9-
        10, 10, 10-17; 55:12; 59:8; 60:17; 66:12; deutero-Isaiah; trito-Isaiah)

GENESIS

   1; 1; 1:1, 1, 1-2, 1-2, 1-2, 2, 3, 4a, 4, 10, 12, 18, 25, 26ff., 26ff., 26-28, 26-28,
        26-29, 26-30, 27, 27, 28, 28, 28, 28, 31; [28]

   2:1-4a, 5, 7, 8, 8, 15, 18, 20, 21-22 [9]

   3; 3:8, 9, 12-13, 15, 18, 18, 21 [8]

ROMANS

   1:19-20, 21, 28-32 [3]

   5; 5:1, 1, 1-2, 1-22, 5-10, 10 [7]

68

8:2, 6, 17, 18-24, 18-25, 18-25, 19-22, 19-25, 21, 22, 22, 35f., 36-39, 36-39
   [14]
12; 12; 12:1-2, 1-2, 4, 5, 18, 19, 19 [9]
13; 13:1, 2-3, 3f., 4, 4, 6, 6, 7, 8 [10]
14:17, 19, 19, 19 [4]

JOHN
14; 14:2, 16, 27, 27, 27, 27, 27, 27, 27, 27, 27 [12]
15:12, 13 [2]
16:33 [1]
20:19, 19, 19-29, 20, 20, 21, 26, 26 [8]

PSALMS
37:3, 3 [2]
72:1, 1-14, 2-4, 3, 3, 6, 7, 7, 8, 15-17, 16, 23 [12]
85:8, 10, 10, 10, 10-11, 10-11 [6]

LUKE
2:10-14, 14, 14, 46-47 [4]
6:17-49, 20-23, 27, 27, 27-28, 29-31, 33, 37 [8]
19:13, 41, 41-44, 42 [4]

3. Peace and God's Action against Chaos in the Old Testament

BEN C. OLLENBURGER

Introduction

The confession that peace is the apostolic vocation of Christians, in conformity with the New Testament's witness, has to confront the Old Testament. The dimensions of this requirement are historical, exegetical, and theological. Historically, the claim of the peace churches that peace *is* the apostolic vocation of Christians had to confront the counterclaim that the Old Testament severely qualifies or undermines their confession. As a result, this confrontation took the form, early on, of a serious disagreement about the relative weight to be given the Old and New Testaments. The disagreement was serious, because those who opposed the confession of the peace churches (an anachronistic term, if applied to the sixteenth century) argued that the Old Testament provides justification in principle for Christian participation in war. In response, those confessing peace as the apostolic vocation of Christians, on the basis of the New Testament, argued for a severe limitation of the Old Testament's bearing on the matter. Exegetically, the peace churches' confession has to establish the New Testament basis, not only for the confession itself, but also for just this limitation of the Old Testament. But even if the exegetical requirement is met, a theological requirement remains. This concerns not only the continuity of the Old and New Testaments but also and primarily the identity of God. To put it sharply, if the peace churches understand the identity of God as revealed in Jesus Christ, and thus as witnessed in the New Testament, to be radically discontinuous with the God to whom the Old Testament bears witness, then their confession cannot be sustained. It cannot be sustained, in that event, because the New Testament is consistent and unequivocal that the one whom Jesus calls Father is none other than Israel's God.[1] And in this the creeds are explicit and correct: God the creator of heaven and earth is the Father of whom Jesus our Redeemer is the Son. Whatever language we may need to devise, appropriate to our own time, in order to express this creedal conviction, the conviction itself cannot be sacrificed — not because it is creedal or episcopal or ecumenical, but because it is strictly conformed to the apostolic witness.

This essay was written with these historical, exegetical, and theological requirements in mind, but it does not and cannot intend to fulfill them. With them in mind, I can aim only to suggest the kind of resource or obstacle the Old Testament may be to the peace church confession that peace is the apostolic vocation of the Christian churches. In the following section I will define the scope of this essay, and in the second and third sections I will examine Old Testament texts that fit within that scope. Finally, I will propose some conclusions concerning the issue under discussion.

Peace, God's Action, and Order

A discussion of the Old Testament that deals with the question of peace must begin with the topic of war. It must do so because the Old Testament's statements about peace are at the same time statements about war. This fact, unsurprising as it may be on the face of it, is related to the specific situation that gives rise to statements about peace in the Old Testament: God's establishment, restoration, or preservation of peace against powers that threaten or destroy it. It would sidetrack our discussion to conduct it as an inquiry into what the Old Testament means by

---

1. Michael Goldberg shows this to be a problem confronting Christian confession generally, quite apart from the specific issue under discussion here. See his "God, Action, and Narrative: *Which* Narrative? *Which* Action? *Which* God?" *Journal of Religion* 68 (1988), 39-56. Reprinted in *Why Narrative? Readings in Narrative Theology*, ed. Stanley Hauerwas and L. Gregory Jones (Grand Rapids: Eerdmans, 1989), 348-65.

"peace," using the English term to guide the inquiry, or into what the Old Testament means by *shalom*. Each would be too narrow, or in other cases too broad, for this discussion. For that reason, I will mean by "peace" the outcome intended by God, as indicated by the texts, in situations where God intervenes or where God's purposes are effected in some other way. Since I have already narrowed the scope of this inquiry to Old Testament statements about God's action against powers that threaten or destroy peace, and have defined peace in terms of the outcome God intends in this action, it is already clear that peace is closely related to order.[2] This is not only a function of the constraints I have placed on this study; more importantly and in the first place, it is a conclusion from the texts themselves. It stands to reason that this correlation among peace, order, and the outcome intended in God's own actions would be clearest in texts that speak of creation. In this case, reason is confirmed by the texts. However, our theme is not limited to creation texts.

Creation and God's Action in History

Some of the Old Testament's earliest texts portray God's action on behalf of Israel against historical enemies. The song in Exodus 15 celebrates God's deliverance of Israel from Egypt at the sea. It opens in verse 3 with the claim that "Yahweh is a warrior,/Yahweh is his name."[3] In the battle that follows, Egypt's weapons are Pharaoh's chariots and army (v. 4), his sword and his "hand" (v. 9). The instruments of Yahweh the warrior are his right hand (v. 6) and the sea itself, which responds to

---

2. Jon D. Levenson offers an exceptionally fine treatment of the relation of creation (or order) to God's action against the powers that threaten it. See his *Creation and the Persistence of Evil: The Jewish Drama of Divine Omnipotence* (San Francisco: Harper and Row, 1988). Also instructive on the topic of this essay are Reiner Albertz, "Schalom und Versöhnung: Alttestamentliche Kriegs- und Friedenstraditionen," *Theologia Practica* 18 (1983), 16-28; and Walter Dietrich, "Ungesicherter Friede? Das Ringen um ein neues Sicherheitsdenken im Alten Testament," *Zeitschrift für Evangelische Ethik* 31 (1987), 134-61.

3. The translation follows a textual emendation suggested by Frank Moore Cross in *Canaanite Myth and Hebrew Epic: Essays in the History of the Religion of Israel* (Cambridge: Harvard University, 1973), 127, n. 53. Unless otherwise noted, translations are my own.

Yahweh's fury and breath by overwhelming the enemy (vv. 7-8, 10). The threatening power of the sea, elsewhere a symbol of chaos against which Yahweh's creative activity is directed (see below), is here the instrument of Yahweh's victory over Israel's enemy — who is at the same time Yahweh's enemy (v. 7). This victory is a demonstration of Yahweh's great majesty (v. 7), which is incomparable among the gods (v. 11).[4] The theme of Yahweh's majesty is again taken up, this time explicitly, in the song's conclusion, which affirms that Yahweh will reign forever (v. 18). Preceding this affirmation is a description of Yahweh's royal abode, which Yahweh has created (v. 17). Yahweh's abode, the throne and sanctuary on the mount of Yahweh's heritage (or patrimony), is the goal to which Yahweh leads Israel, whom Yahweh has also created, to the dismay of the nations (vv. 13-16). In Exodus 15, then, the redemption of Israel (v. 13) is set within the framework of Yahweh's rule, which includes Yahweh's action as creator. As creator, Yahweh commands the sea and its deeps, forms Israel, and establishes his own royal dwelling. These are the ways in which and the purposes for which, according to Exodus 15, Yahweh is a warrior.

In its literary context, between the Exodus and wilderness narratives, the song in Exodus 15 is accompanied by a prose account of the same event. While Exodus 14 precedes the song, it is most likely a later composite narrative that interprets Exodus 15. One feature of the song that seems to require interpretation is the absence of human agents in its portrayal of Israel's deliverance. All of the people mentioned — Pharoah and his army, the nations, Israel — are either the objects of Yahweh's action or the subjects of intransitive verbs; Yahweh alone is an actor. Exodus 14 interprets this absence of human activity by ascribing a particular responsibility to Israel. In 14:13-14, Yahweh instructs Israel, through Moses, to be fearless, to stand firm, and to witness Yahweh's action on their behalf: "Yahweh will fight for you, and you have but to keep silent" (v. 14; or, as the Koren version translates, "hold your peace"). The conclusion of the narrative reports that Israel did indeed witness the "great work" (literally, "hand") that Yahweh performed and that they feared Yahweh and "believed in Yahweh and in Moses his servant"

---

4. Verse 7 speaks of Yahweh's majesty *(g'wn)*, while v. 11 describes Yahweh as glorious *('dr)* and awesome *(nwr')*. The latter term appears in Pss. 89:7 [8]; 96:4; 99:3 in contexts of both kingship and creation. Where Hebrew versification differs from that of English versions, I will cite the English first with Hebrew in brackets.

(v. 31). In the conflict between the hand of the enemy (15:9) and the right hand of Yahweh (15:6, 12; 14:31), it was Yahweh's royal hand that prevailed. Israel's participation consisted of witnessing and believing.

The song of victory in Judges 5 presents a markedly different picture, with its enumeration of the clans who followed Deborah and Barak to the conflict with the kings of Canaan (vv. 13-19). However, in its description of the battle itself, the text mentions only two participants: the kings of Canaan (including Sisera) and the stars (vv. 19-20). To be precise, the stars fought from heaven against Sisera by flooding the Kishon River (vv. 20-21). The image of the stars producing rain is known from Ugaritic texts, especially in connection with the warrior goddess, 'Anat; one of them portrays her washing herself after battle in "dew that the heavens poured upon her, [showers] that the stars did pour upon her."[5] This text associates heaven and the stars, as does Judg. 5:20. In Num. 24:17, the star that comes from Jacob and the meteor (or scepter) that arises from Israel will crush Moab. In Egyptian and Mesopotamian literature as well the stars are weapons of divine warfare.[6] These references help clarify the otherwise surprising absence of Yahweh from the battle account in Judg. 5:19-21. This account describes the instruments of victory over Sisera and the Canaanite kings as divine weapons. The issue in this conflict was control of those instruments, which, as we have seen, are elsewhere at the command of the Canaanite goddess 'Anat. It is in the introduction to the song that the issue is clarified. Verses 4 and 5 portray Yahweh — "the one of Sinai" — marching from Seir in Edom, accompanied by earthquake and rain.[7]

5. A. Herdner, *Corpus des tablettes en cunéiformes alphabétiques* (hereafter *CTA*), 3.B.2.40-41. The translation is by J. C. L. Gibson in *Canaanite Myths and Legends* (Edinburgh: Clark, 1977), 48.

6. These last two examples are cited by Moshe Weinfeld, "Divine Intervention in War in Ancient Israel and in the Ancient Near East," *History, Historiography, and Interpretation: Studies in Biblical and Cuneiform Literatures,* ed. H. Tadmor and M. Weinfeld (Jerusalem: Magnes, 1984), 124-31.

7. On the geography of Yahweh's march in the south, see Theodore Hiebert, *God of My Victory: The Ancient Hymn in Habakkuk 3* (Harvard Semitic Monographs [hereafter HSM] 38; Atlanta: Scholars, 1986), 83-92. In his commentary, J. Alberto Soggin considers some further possible associations with Canaanite mythology in Judges 5 (*Judges: A Commentary* [The Old Testament Library (hereafter OTL); Philadelphia: Westminster, 1981], 79-101). Cf. J. Glenn Taylor, "The Song of Deborah and Two Canaanite Goddesses," *Journal for the Study of the Old Testament* 23 (1982), 99-108.

The instruments of Sisera's defeat in verses 19-22 are under Yahweh's command, not 'Anat's, and their effects — rain and flood — are the very effects of Yahweh's march from Seir in Edom. Just as in Exodus 15, Yahweh wins victory by commanding the forces of nature that spell chaos for Yahweh's enemies (Judg. 5:31). Yahweh acts, in other words, as the creator of these natural forces. That the victory belongs entirely to Yahweh is stressed in verse 8b: "Neither shield nor spear was to be seen among the forty contingents in Israel."[8] Israel's help was in Yahweh alone. In verse 23, Meroz and its inhabitants merit a curse for not seeking Yahweh's help against (or among) the warriors. Virtually everyone interprets this verse as if some otherwise unknown Israelite clan, Meroz, had failed to come to Yahweh's help because it had not answered the call to muster.[9] But the enumeration of Israelite clans — with comments on their participation or lack of it — occurs in verses 13-18, prior to the battle in verses 19-22. None of the clans who held back merit anything approaching a curse, and there is no reason to think Meroz would be an especially serious case. Furthermore, on analogy with texts such as Ps. 60:11-12 [13-14] and Isa. 20:6, 31:1-2, "Yahweh's help" should be understood as the help that Yahweh provides, rather than the help Yahweh needs someone like Meroz to provide. Meroz is contrasted not with the Israelite clans but with Jael (cf. vv. 6, 24-30), who is most blessed among women: She identified herself with Israel's cause, and Deborah's, and slew Sisera.[10]

The prose account of this episode in Judges 4 has a relation to Judges 5 similar to that of Exodus 14 to the hymn in Exodus 15.[11] Its

8. Robert Boling, *Judges* (Anchor Bible; Garden City: Doubleday, 1975), 110. In this context something like "contingents" seems more appropriate than "thousand" as a rendering of *'eleph*. Regarding this text's stress on the absence of weapons, see Patrick D. Miller, Jr., *The Divine Warrior in Early Israel* (HSM 5; Cambridge: Harvard University, 1973), 91-92.

9. For example, Baruch Halpern, *The Constitution of the Monarchy in Israel* (HSM 25; Chico: Scholars, 1981), 68-69. Halpern and others offer an interpretation of Judg. 5:13-18 different from the one I presuppose here (see Miller, *Divine Warrior*, 95-97).

10. See Millard Lind, *Yahweh Is a Warrior: The Theology of Warfare in Ancient Israel* (Scottdale: Herald, 1980), 71-73. Lind takes Meroz (perhaps a town) and Jael to be non-Israelites whose different responses to the conflict warranted, respectively, the curse and the blessing promised in Gen. 12:3.

11. Baruch Halpern, "Doctrine by Misadventure: Between the Israelite Source and the Biblical Historian," *The Poet and the Historian: Essays in Literary and Historical Biblical Criticism*, ed. Richard Elliott Friedman (HSM 26; Chico: Scholars, 1983), 46-49.

principal interest is in interpreting the story of Jael and Sisera (Judg. 5:24-30; 4:17-22) as fulfillment of Deborah's remark to Barak: "The road on which you are going will not gain you glory, for Yahweh will sell Sisera into the hand of a woman" (4:9). And unlike Exodus 14, Judges 4 places no particular stress on Israel's trust or belief. Its stress is on God's deliverance of Sisera into Israel's hands (v. 7), and specifically into the hand of Jael (cf. 5:26).

Neither Judges 4 nor Judges 5, nor any text of the Old Testament for that matter, is a pacifist tract. While killing is condemned in texts like Gen. 49:5-7, and pervasive violence is cited as a reason for the flood in Gen. 6:11, no Old Testament text suggests that participation in war is wrong in principle. Ancient poetic texts like Exodus 15 and Judges 5 make a different claim: Yahweh establishes order and thereby acts as the Lord of creation, and does so in battle against the forces of disorder. In Exodus 15, those forces are represented by Egypt's army, and in Judges 5 by the kings of Canaan. The decisive weapons against both are the forces of nature; by virtue of Yahweh's command, they are the forces of creation, and creation includes the peace that results (Exod. 15:17-18; Judg. 5:31b).

In both of these texts, Yahweh seems to have a home in the south, at Sinai (if that is Yahweh's mountain in Exod. 15:17)[12] and at Mount Seir (Judg. 5:4). The same is true in Deuteronomy 33, where Yahweh comes from Sinai, dawns from Seir, and shines forth from Mount Paran (v. 2). While this text includes no battle account, it does refer to the gathering of the tribes or their leaders under the Torah of Moses (vv. 4-5), and to God's victory over Israel's enemies (v. 27). Significantly, the formation of Israel and God's victory are explicitly connected with Yahweh's kingship: "Then [Yahweh] became (or was) king in Yeshurun." Most likely, this kingship was won over other, competing deities (v. 26).[13] Likewise, Habakkuk 3 locates Yahweh in the south, at Teman and Mount Paran, and in Midian (vv. 3, 7), this time with a highly mythological

---

12. In *Zion, the City of the Great King: A Theological Symbol of the Jerusalem Cult* (Journal for the Study of the Old Testament Supplement Series 41; Sheffield: Sheffield Academic, 1987), I rejected the identification of this mountain home of Yahweh with Sinai (190, n. 25). I still regard the question as open.

13. See Miller, *Divine Warrior*, 84-85. Deut. 33:26 describes Yahweh as the "rider of the heavens," which may echo the epithet of Baal "rider of the clouds." Prior to this description, v. 26 probably affirms that "there is none like El [God] of Yeshurun," though the text is difficult.

account of Yahweh's martial activity. The ancient deities Deber and Reshpeh are now part of Yahweh's retinue (v. 5), while the deities traditionally symbolizing chaos — Sea and River *(yam* and *nahar)* — are the objects of Yahweh's wrath (vv. 8, 15).[14] In Deuteronomy 33, Yahweh's victory over other gods is merely implicit. The same is true in Exodus 15, where ancient deities are made the instruments of Yahweh's victory, and in Judges 5, where the instruments of another deity are made the weapons of Yahweh. In Habakkuk 3, the gods themselves are defeated (or perhaps more precisely, the one deity, Sea/River [*yam/nahar*] is defeated). In each case, the victory confirms Yahweh's reign as Lord of creation and, as a consequence, wins Israel's security.

Creation and God's Defense of Zion

These themes are continued in other Old Testament poetic texts, but with a decisive change: a change in Yahweh's residence. We can see this in Psalm 68. This text, too, speaks of Yahweh's victory and of Yahweh's march in the south accompanied by earthquake and rain (vv. 7-10 [8-11]). And it appears to take the epithet of Baal, "rider of the clouds" or "rider of the heavens" (vv. 4 [5], 33 [34]), and to ascribe it to Yahweh.[15] In these respects, Psalm 68 follows the pattern we have seen in Exodus 15 and Judges 5. But the second half of Psalm 68, beginning with verse 24 [25], describes Yahweh's royal procession to Jerusalem, and specifically to the temple (vv. 24 [25], 29 [30], 35 [36]). According to the probable reading of verse 17 [18], Yahweh came from Sinai to the sanctuary,[16] which is the temple in Jerusalem (v. 29 [30]). In this way the psalm relates Yahweh's march in the south, a march of battle in which gods

---

14. Hiebert, *God of My Victory,* 92-94. On former deities become part of Yahweh's retinue, or emissaries and messengers, see Weinfeld, "Divine Intervention in War," 129-30.

15. It is common to emend Ps. 68:4 [5] and to translate it as "rider of the clouds," though I agree with John Day that something like "rider through the deserts" may be original; no emendation is required (Day, *God's Conflict with the Dragon and the Sea: Echoes of a Canaanite Myth in the Old Testament* [Cambridge: Cambridge University, 1985], 31-32).

16. Following the proposed emendation of *Biblia Hebraica Stuttgartensia* and others (cf. Hans-Joachim Kraus, *Psalms 60–150: A Commentary* [Minneapolis: Augsburg, 1989], 46).

and kings are dethroned, to Jerusalem as the site of Yahweh's dwelling as king.

It is especially in connection with Jerusalem/Zion that the theme of Yahweh's kingship is developed, and it is developed in relation to creation. Psalm 24 is instructive. It opens with the confession that the earth and everything in it, including its inhabitants, belongs to Yahweh. This is so because Yahweh "founded it upon the waters, and upon rivers he has created [established] it" (vv. 1-2).[17] Two points of this confession are significant. First is the explicit connection between Yahweh's creation and ownership of the earth. Having created it, Yahweh can legitimately claim to own it and rule it.[18] Second, the waters and rivers upon which Yahweh created the earth are symbols of chaos in the Old Testament, reflecting their personification in the twin Canaanite deities, Yamm (sea) and Nahar (river).[19] Both of these points are related to the liturgy in verses 7-10, which celebrates Yahweh's entrance into the temple. Here Yahweh is declared to be "the king of glory,/Yahweh powerful and mighty,/Yahweh mighty in battle . . . ,/Yahweh of hosts" (vv. 8, 10). The psalm is a celebration in the Jerusalem temple of Yahweh's kingship. We should understand that this kingship is exercised in battle against the powers that threaten creation; Yahweh exercises kingship, in other words, as creator.[20] This is the guarantee of the promise in verses 3-5: one with clean hands and a pure heart—one

---

17. The Old Testament frequently uses the verb *kwn*, especially in its polel stem, to describe God's acts of creation (Jörg Jeremias, *Das Königtum Gottes in den Psalmen: Israels Begegnung mit dem kanaanäischen Mythos in den Jahwe-König-Psalmen* [Forschungen zur Religion und Literatur des Alten und Neuen Testaments (hereafter FRLANT) 141; Göttingen: Vandenhoeck und Ruprecht, 1987], 23). John Gray offers an extensive treatment of God's kingship in the Psalms in *The Biblical Doctrine of the Reign of God* (Edinburgh: Clark, 1979), 39-116.

18. Martin Metzger discusses this connection in "Eigentumsdeklaration und Schöpfungsaussage," *"Wenn nicht jetzt, wann dann?"* (Festschrift for H.-J. Kraus, ed. H.-G. Geyer, J. M. Schmidt, W. Schneider, and M. Weinrich; Neukirchen: Neukirchener, 1983]), 37-51.

19. In the Ugaritic texts *CTA* 2.4.12-13 and 3.D.34-44, Yamm and Nahar are the opponents of Baal, whose victory over them will restore order to the world.

20. Day, *God's Conflict with the Dragon and the Sea*, 37-38; Tryggve N. D. Mettinger, *The Dethronement of Sabaoth: Studies in the Shem and Kabod Theologies* (Coniectanea Biblica, Old Testament Series 18; Lund: Gleerup, 1982), 70-71. I have explored the relation of Yahweh's kingship and creation in *Zion, the City of the Great King*, 23-80.

with integrity — has access to Yahweh's temple, and will receive blessing and vindication from Yahweh.

Several other psalms identify Yahweh as king and creator in celebrating Yahweh's victory over the chaos powers. Psalm 104 says that Yahweh set the earth on its foundations, and it will never be shaken (v. 5). The following verses (6-7) show how this took place:

The deep [*tehom*] covered it like a garment,
the waters stood above the mountains.
At your roar they fled,
at the sound of your thunder they ran away.[21]

The element of conflict remains implicit here, as in verse 26, where Leviathan — that chaos monster — is a playful sea creature. But it is against the deep (cf. Gen. 1:2) and the waters that Yahweh acts in creation, setting them in their place within boundaries that they cannot transgress (vv. 8-9).

However, in Psalm 89, Yahweh rules the raging (or arrogance) of the sea (*yam*) and stills its rising waves (v. 9 [10]). This action of creation is then described in terms of a conflict with the sea monster:

You beat Rahab like a corpse,
with your mighty arm you scattered your enemies.
Yours are the heavens, and yours also the earth;
the world and all that is in it, you founded them.

(vv. 10-11 [11-12])

Here, as in Psalm 24, Yahweh's ownership of the earth is grounded in creation, by which Yahweh establishes and maintains the world's order against the chaos powers that threaten it. This order reflects — or constitutes — the righteousness and justice that are the foundations of Yahweh's royal throne (v. 14 [15]). However, the emphasis in Psalm 89 is not on the ordering of the cosmos as in Psalm 104; rather, it is on the political extension of Yahweh's rule through a regent — David, Yahweh's

---

21. On the translation of v. 6, see Day, *God's Conflict with the Dragon and the Sea*, 29. The verb *g'r*, traditionally translated "rebuke" (as in RSV of v. 7), is closer to "roar," as shown most recently by James M. Kennedy, "The Root *G'R* in the Light of Semantic Analysis," *Journal of Biblical Literature* (hereafter *JBL*) 106 (1987), 47-64. See also Day, 29, n. 82.

servant (v. 20 [21]). David's opponents will suffer a fate similar to Rahab's (v. 23 [24]; cf. Psalm 2), and it will be David's hand—as an extension of Yahweh's—that rests on sea *(yam)* and river *(nahar)* (v. 25 [26]). So nearly is Yahweh's rule identified with David's in their joint maintenance of creation's order that Yahweh can call David "most high [*'elyon*] over the kings of the earth" (v. 27 [28]).

The political extension of creation, and thus of Yahweh's rule (but without mention of an earthly king) is celebrated as well in a series of enthronement psalms (93–99), so called because of their characteristic declaration: *yahweh malak,* "Yahweh rules as king."[22] In familiar language, Psalm 93 declares that Yahweh has created (established) the world (v. 1b); it follows this with reference to Yahweh's throne (v. 2), thus combining kingship and creation. Verse 3 introduces the element of conflict that we have already seen elsewhere, but this time the reference is to the continuing menace posed by those powers defeated in creation. The powers are again characterized as "rivers" or "floods" *(neharot),* the many waters, and the sea *(yam),*[23] but they are introduced only to declare that Yahweh—Yahweh on high (v. 4)—is mightier and more glorious than they are. In other words, Yahweh rules them. Psalm 97 carries this thought further, declaring Yahweh to be Lord of all the earth (v. 5b). While Ps. 89:27 [28] calls David most high *('elyon)* over all earthly kings, Ps. 97:9 declares Yahweh to be "most high [*'elyon*] over all the earth" and "highly exalted above all gods."[24] For that reason, Zion—the city of

---

22. For a discussion of translation and other issues related to the enthronement psalms, including Psalm 47, see Ollenburger, *Zion, the City of the Great King,* 23-52. Cf. Jeremias, *Das Königtum Gottes,* 15-29; Hermann Spieckermann, *Heilsgegenwart: Eine Theologie der Psalmen* (FRLANT 148; Göttingen: Vandenhoeck und Ruprecht, 1989), 180-86.

23. A. H. W. Curtis discusses these terms in "The 'Subjugation of the Waters' Motif in the Psalms; Imagery or Polemic?" *Journal of Semitic Studies* 23 (1978), 245-56.

24. This echoes Ps. 47:2[3], which says that Yahweh *is* "awesome 'Elyon [most high], the great king over all the earth." Verse 6[7] commands the gods to "sing praise to our God, sing praise to our king." These texts are concerned not only with Yahweh's exaltation but also, polemically, with Yahweh's identification as "the most high God," and thus with the issue of which god's order will govern the world. See Ollenburger, *Zion, the City of the Great King,* 44-45. Timo Veijola notes that the formulation in Ps. 89:27[28] has a parallel in Deut. 26:19, which says that Israel will be "most high [or exalted] over all nations" (*Verheißung in der Krise: Studien zur Literatur und Theologie der Exilszeit anhand des 89. Psalms* [Annales Academiae Scientiarum Fennicae 220; Helsinki: Suomalainen Tiedeakatemia, 1982], 52).

Yahweh's dwelling—rejoices (v. 8). And Psalm 99 opens with the declaration that Yahweh reigns, followed by "Yahweh in Zion is great,/and exalted is he over all gods."[25] The exaltation of Yahweh in Zion is symbolized by the ark, where Yahweh is enthroned on the cherubim.[26] In response, the peoples tremble and the earth quakes—not in response to Yahweh's march as a warrior, but in response to Yahweh's rule.[27] The justice and righteousness of that rule have been extended especially to Jacob (v. 4), and they have been exemplified in Israel's history (vv. 6-8). As victorious king over the chaos powers, and hence as creator, and as the Lord of history, Yahweh is exalted in Zion, "his footstool" (v. 5) and "his holy mountain" (v. 9; cf. Ps. 47:8 [9]).

God's rule on and from Mount Zion is especially prominent in three "Songs of Zion" (Psalms 46, 48, 76), each of which celebrates the refuge to be found in Zion because Yahweh defends it as king. Mount Zion is the site of Yahweh's royal dwelling (Pss. 46:1 [2], 5 [6]; 48:1-2 [2-3], 8 [9]; 76:1 [2]). In each of these psalms, Yahweh confronts an enemy. In Ps. 6:6 [7], that enemy is the raging nations; in 48:4 [5], it is the kings assembled for conquest; in 76:5 [6], it is soldiers. These are repelled by Yahweh and disarmed. When verses 3 [4] and 5 [6] of Psalm 76 say that Yahweh destroyed armaments and rendered soldiers harmless, and Ps. 46:9 [10] declares that Yahweh puts an end to war by shattering its instruments, we should understand these statements to be in essential continuity with the main themes of kingship and creation in the other psalms we have examined. These themes include Yahweh's displacement of other gods, to which Ps. 48:2 [3] alludes by calling Mount Zion "Zaphon" (otherwise, "north"), the mountain of Baal; it is Yahweh, not Baal, who reigns. Another such theme is Yahweh's conquest of and rule over the forces of chaos, whether these be sea and river, the many waters, Rahab and Leviathan (Ps. 74:14; Isa. 27:1), or the kings and nations through whom they threaten the peace. This rule, established in and by Yahweh's acts of creation, constitutes peace: the world ordered by Yahweh.

25. On the translation, see Ollenburger, *Zion, the City of the Great King,* 185, n. 159.

26. Mettinger, *The Dethronement of Sabaoth,* 19-37, provides the background and details of this imagery.

27. In *CTA* 4.7.29-32, the earth shakes when Baal utters his voice.

Creation and God's Defense of Israel

Psalm 104 describes creation as the effect of Yahweh's "roar" (v. 7). Similarly in Psalm 29, Yahweh's voice is the expression of divine power (vv. 3-9a), eliciting the cry "Glory!" in the temple (v. 9b; cf. Ps. 68:33 [34]). Following this is the declaration that Yahweh is enthroned as king over the flood (*mabbul*, v. 10). Yahweh's roar is an instrument of creation and its order. It is contrasted with the tumult of the chaos powers that threaten creation, such as the "waters" and "many waters" in Ps. 29:3. The same is true in Ps. 93:4, where the rivers and sea threaten by raising their voices; they threaten the ordered world of Yahweh's creation (93:1b). The stability of the world in Ps. 93:1 — "it will not totter" — is symbolized in Psalm 46 by Zion: "God is in her midst; she will not totter" (v. 5 [6]). In this psalm, Zion is threatened by chaos powers — not sea/river or flood or the deep or many waters, but nations and kingdoms. They rage, and *they* totter; Yahweh "gives voice, and the earth reels" (v. 6 [7]). In defending Zion, Yahweh defends creation against the powers that threaten it, a defense that sets the earth reeling and ends with the destruction of the instruments of chaos (v. 9 [10]).

The identification of nations with the powers of chaos is evident in Psalm 74. It attributes the destruction of Jerusalem to God's enemies, who "roared" in the midst of the very cultic center of Zion (v. 4).[28] God is thus urged to "redeem . . . Mount Zion, where you have dwelt" (v. 2b). The psalm complains that God's enemies appear to have triumphed, putting creation itself in peril. It is not God's voice that is heard but the voice of God's enemies; their din or tumult — their roaring — is constant (v. 23). The psalm bases its complaint on the confession that God *is* the creator and Lord of the earth: God shattered the sea, smashed the heads of the dragons on the waters, and crushed the heads of Leviathan (vv. 13-14).[29] It is to this creative activity, threatened by the roaring of God's enemies, that the psalm summons God; now the land is full of violence (v. 20).

It is especially the book of Isaiah that combines these various

---

28. Cf. Kraus, *Psalms 60–150*, 98-99. The verb here is *š'g*, not to be confused with *g'r*, also translated "roar."

29. See my essay "Isaiah's Creation Theology," *Ex Auditu* 3 (1987), 54-71, esp. 54-59.

themes within a political and military context. Central to Isaiah's theology is the notion that Yahweh dwells on Mount Zion as Yahweh of hosts (Isa. 8:18).[30] This is the God whom Isaiah encountered in chapter 6 as the king, Yahweh of hosts, enthroned in the temple on Zion (vv. 1, 5).[31] And it is from within this theological conception that Isaiah views his context and condemns the injustice practiced against the poor, the blindness and arrogance of the wicked, and the fear and faithlessness of Jerusalem's kings. All of this Isaiah takes to be an offense against Yahweh and examples of culpable pride: Yahweh alone is exalted, and Yahweh's exaltation entails the subordination of all (Isa. 2:6-22). Drawing on themes we have already seen in the Psalms, especially those associated with Zion and creation, Isaiah counsels that Jerusalem's best defense against the threat of military aggression is to exercise faith in Yahweh by giving rest to the weary and practicing quietness and trust (28:12; 30:15);[32] thereby, Isaiah returns us to Exodus 15 and its interpretation in Exodus 14 (see above).

These themes are explicit in Isa. 37:16, which is itself a conspectus of Isaiah's theology: "Yahweh of hosts, God of Israel, enthroned on the cherubim, you alone are God over all the kingdoms of the earth; you made the heavens and the earth." Creation is here the basis for the extension of Yahweh's rule over the nations, which are subject to Yahweh's purposes. On this basis in creation, Yahweh can say to the Assyrian king, Sennacherib:

Have you not heard? From long ago I have fashioned [made] it, from days of old I have formed it; now I have brought it to pass. . . . Because you have raged against me, and your roaring has come to my ears, I

---

30. It is unnecessary here to decide which, if any, texts in Isaiah 1–39 are from the eighth-century context in which the book places them. The options in contemporary scholarship range from ascribing virtually all of them to the eighth century (John H. Hayes and Stuart A. Irving, *Isaiah, the Eighth Century Prophet: His Times and His Preaching* [Nashville: Abingdon, 1987]) to ascribing virtually none of them to that time (Otto Kaiser, *Isaiah 1–12* [2nd ed., OTL; Philadelphia: Westminster, 1983]). In speaking of Isaiah, I mean the prophet portrayed in the book.

31. On the epithet "Yahweh of hosts," see Ollenburger, *Zion, the City of the Great King*, 37-38, and the literature cited there. Cf. C. L. Seow, *Myth, Drama, and the Politics of David's Dance* (HSM 44; Atlanta: Scholars, 1989). In what follows I draw extensively from my essay "Isaiah's Creation Theology."

32. J. J. M. Roberts, "Yahweh's Foundation in Zion (Isa 28:16)," *JBL* 106 (1987), 27-45.

will put my hook in your nose, my bit in your lips, and will turn you back on the way by which you came. (37:26, 29)[33]

The reference to creation grounds this text's claims about Yahweh's rule, which are specifically claims about the subject of this rule: the God enthroned on the cherubim on Zion, Yahweh of hosts. It is on this basis that Yahweh promises: "I will protect this city to save it, for my sake and for the sake of David my servant" (v. 35). And this promise is to guide King Hezekiah in his response to Sennacherib's aggression (36:1–37:35).

In Isa. 17:12-14, Isaiah uses the language of creation to express confidence that the nations cannot finally succeed in destroying Zion.

Ah, the tumult of many peoples! They rage like the raging of the seas. And the roaring of the peoples; they roar [*š'b*] like the roaring of mighty waters. [The nations roar like the roaring of many waters.] But [Yahweh] roars [*g'r*] at it, and it flees away, pursued like chaff on the mountain before the wind, or tumbleweeds before the storm. At evening there is terror; before morning it is no more. Such is the fate of those who rob us, the lot of those who plunder us.[34]

Isaiah here describes the security of Zion in terms that Psalm 104 uses to describe creation — the founding *(ysd)* of the earth — with the waters fleeing at the roar and thunder of Yahweh's voice (v. 7). The same confidence is expressed in Isa. 8:9-10, without the language of creation. This text concludes with the confession that "God is with us" — or "Immanuel" (cf. 7:14). It immediately follows a judgment against Judah (8:5-8) for refusing Yahweh's promise by acting in fear of the Syrian-Israelite coalition rather than in faith (cf. 7:9b). They have "refused the gently flowing waters of Shiloah" (8:6); instead, they will be flooded by river *(nahar)* and its mighty, many waters — in other words, Assyria (8:7), which will flood the land of "God is with us [Immanuel]."

33. On the translation, see Ollenburger, "Isaiah's Creation Theology," 56; and Hans Wildberger, *Jesaja: Das Buch, der Prophet und seine Botschaft* (Biblischer Kommentar: Altes Testament 10/3: *Jesaja 28–39*, Neukirchen-Vluyn: Neukirchener Verlag, 1982), 1418-19.

34. Verse 13a may be an explanatory gloss on v. 12b, or it may preserve an alternative reading; in either case, it would explain "mighty waters" in terms of the more common "many waters." Day discusses the mythological associations in Isa. 17:12-14 and especially its connection with Psalm 46 in *God's Conflict with the Dragon and the Sea*, 101-4.

In their references to "God is with us," to the waters of Shiloah and of the river *(nahar)*, and to Yahweh's chaos-defeating roar, Isa. 8:9-10 and 17:12-14 draw on the imagery and the theology of Psalms 46 and 76.[35] Behind the gently flowing waters of Shiloah stands Ps. 46:4 [5] and the river whose streams gladden the city of God; behind the promise of Immanuel stands Ps. 46:11 [12] and its declaration: "Yahweh of hosts is with us." And behind the promise of Isaiah stand Ps. 46:6 [7]: "Yahweh gives voice, and the earth reels," and Ps. 76:6 [7]: "At your roar, O God of Jacob, rider and horse lie stunned." This is the basis of the faith that Isaiah commends to Judah and to its kings. "Yahweh founded Zion, and in it the poor of his people find refuge" (Isa. 14:32). That promise is the guarantee of Zion's security, defended against every chaotic threat, whether in the form of international aggression, domestic injustice, or royal reliance on armaments and alliances. Trust in Yahweh is the only social or political strategy that Isaiah countenances in "the faithful city" (1:21), and it is the only realistic strategy for those who invoke the God who dwells on Zion and has founded it. As J. J. M. Roberts puts it, "The 'poor of his people' in Isa 14:32 corresponds to the 'one who trusts' in 28:16," in the face of imminent threat.[36]

The object of trust, in this case, is identical with the subject of creation. This can be illustrated, finally, from Psalm 65, which opens by confessing to Yahweh: "Praise is properly yours, O God, in Zion."[37] It continues by describing the God who "pacifies" the ends of the earth and the remotest peoples (v. 5 [6]),[38] who creates (establishes) the mountains by his strength, and who silences the roaring of the seas *and* the tumult of the peoples (vv. 6-7 [7-8]). The peace that is the result of creation extends to both the cosmic and the political realms, and it extends to nature as well (vv. 9-13 [10-14]).

Creation Theology and War

The creation theology that we have sketched from Exodus 15 to Isaiah is fundamentally a theology of Yahweh's universal reign (corresponding

35. Cf. Ollenburger, *Zion, the City of the Great King,* 121-24; Day, *God's Conflict with the Dragon and the Sea,* 101-4, 125-38.
36. "Yahweh's Foundation in Zion," 39.
37. On the text, see Kraus, *Psalms 60-150,* 27.
38. *Ibid.;* Ollenburger, "Isaiah's Creation Theology," 58.

to the first article of the creed).[39] In its conception, peace is the goal and result of God's action against the powers of chaos. There is no limit in principle on the forms that God's action can take, and there is no systematic correlation or disjunction between God's action and human military participation. There is, however, a strict disjunction in the order of necessity between trust in God and military means: The former is always and inherently necessary, the latter is not. This is explicit in Psalms 20, 33, 44, and 118, which relegate royal power and military armaments to strategic insignificance.[40] This disjunction, or asymmetry, can and does move in different directions. It moves in the direction of holy war, according to which trust in God is the necessary and singular condition of the military success — against improbable odds — that God promises and achieves to Israel's benefit.[41] It moves in the direction of God's separation from and opposition to Israel's wars, as in the classical prophets.[42] And it moves in the direction of war's transformation into liturgy, as in 2 Chronicles 20, where Israel prays, preaches, sings hymns, and witnesses the self-destruction of its enemies.[43] Finally, it moves into the future. Haggai and Zechariah expect that God will reconfigure the world in such a way that Yahweh's reign from Zion will again be evident; Isa. 65:17-25 expects that this will amount to a new creation. In these latter cases, God wages war to achieve peace, but Israel's military participation in that war would be irrelevant as well as foolish and arrogant. Ultimately, God's rule means that war will be forgotten, because the nations will find their peace in coming to Zion (Isa. 2:2-4); according to

39. I have argued that this belongs properly to the theme of creation, which should not be restricted to accounts of the world's origins, in "Isaiah's Creation Theology," esp. 59-63. There I also remark on the creed's first article in relation to the Old Testament's statements about creation.

40. Dietrich, "Ungesicherter Frieden?" 136-41; Ollenburger, *Zion, the City of the Great King*, 87-100. The same rhetoric appears among Israel's neighbors (*ibid.*, 136-44).

41. The Old Testament's holy war traditions depend on the traditions of creation and Zion, including the early poetic texts, rather than the other way around. See Ollenburger, *Zion, the City of the Great King*, 101-4; and my introductory essay, "Gerhard von Rad's Theory of Holy War," in Gerhard von Rad, *Holy War in Ancient Israel*, tr. and ed. Marva J. Dawn (Grand Rapids: Eerdmans, 1991), 24-30.

42. Albertz, "Schalom und Versöhnung," 22.

43. Lawson G. Stone argues that a similar, "spiritual" transformation of warfare occurs in the redaction of Joshua, in "Ethical and Apologetic Tendencies in the Redaction of the Book of Joshua," *Catholic Biblical Quarterly* 53 (1991), 25-36.

Isa. 45:14, 49:22-23, 60:4-14, 66:18-23; Zech. 14:16-19, they will come whether they want to or not.

This diversity means that it is impossible to find expressed within the Old Testament an answer in principle to the moral question of human (or Christian) participation in war. However, the consistency running through this diversity also means that the question of whether we should participate in any particular war is separable from a possible judgment that God is involved in it or wills it, or even that it is an identifiable expression of divine purpose. This is so even in the case of wars that could be defined by traditional criteria as justifiable.[44] Ahaz had just cause to fight a defensive war against Syria and Israel, but Isaiah told him that to do so would be unfaithful to Yahweh (Isaiah 7–8). Babylon's war of aggression against Judah was unjustifiable, either *ad bellum* or *in bello*, but Jeremiah said that God was behind it (Jeremiah 27). Cyrus lacked just cause for war against Babylon, but Isaiah said that Cyrus was Yahweh's anointed shepherd (Isa. 44:28–45:1). Each of these prophetic statements contradicted the judgment that its audience regarded as self-evident or reasonable, and each of them is based on God's sovereign rule over the nations.[45]

Such a conclusion does not easily conform to a contemporary insistence that God's behavior should be exemplary in all respects for our own. It also raises questions about the consistency of God's character.[46] Those questions inhere in Scripture itself and are raised starkly by

44. On the historical — if not inherent — tendency to justify wars by giving them the sanctity of holy wars, see Hans Süssmuth, "'Heiliger Krieg': Barriere des Friedens," *Saeculum* 22 (1971), 387-401. Robert M. Good's effort to show that just war notions were already alive in ancient Israel — primarily because Yahweh acts as judge — seems to me unsuccessful ("The Just War in Ancient Israel," *JBL* 104 [1985], 385-400).

45. Isaiah's statements about Cyrus in 44:28–45:1 depend on an argument from creation that begins in 40:12 (see Ollenburger, "Isaiah's Creation Theology," 63-68). Jeremiah's statements about Babylon in 27:6-7 rest on the claim in v. 5 that Yahweh is the creator of heaven and earth. Heinrich Gross discusses these texts and the general topic in "Weltherrschaft als Gottesherrschaft nach Genesis 11,1-9 und Daniel 7," *Gottesherrschaft-Weltherrschaft* (Festschrift for Rudolf Graber, ed. J. Auer, F. Mussner, and G. Schwaiger; Regensburg: Pustet, 1980), esp. 18.

46. Harry Huebner has raised these questions in "Christology: Discipleship and Ethics," *Jesus Christ and the Mission of the Church: Contemporary Anabaptist Perspectives,* ed. Erland Waltner (Newton: Faith and Life, 1990), 56-73, and in "Christian Pacifism and the Character of God," *The Church as Theological Community: Essays in*

the Nicene Creed: We believe in God, the Father, who as *pantokrator* is creator of heaven and earth, and in the Son, who is of the same essence but was crucified by a minor Roman official, suffered, and was buried. It is a matter of Christian conviction that these two articles do not and cannot stand in contradiction. It is also a matter of Christian conviction, hard-won and often contested, that the Old Testament bears witness to the God whom the creed identifies. In large measure, a judgment about the confession of the peace churches will rest on the way the creed's first two articles are related, and on the way the testaments are related.[47] But it will also rest on an interpretation of the Old Testament, whose statements about peace — and hence about war — confront the claims and confession of every Christian church. If it is difficult to justify pacifism on the basis of the Old Testament, it is no less difficult, on the same basis, to justify participation in the wars of our nations as a communal act of faithful trust in Israel's God and ours and in God's universal reign over the powers of chaos.

This essay has considered only a narrow range of Old Testament texts that speak of God's action against powers that threaten the peace. That range of texts, and the way this essay has treated them, is insufficient to answer the questions under discussion. I hope that it provides some help toward meeting the historical, exegetical, and theological requirements of that discussion.

Honour of David Schroeder, ed. Harry Huebner (Winnipeg: CMBC, 1990), 247-72. In neither article does Huebner mention the Old Testament, except to insist, in a concluding footnote, that "the story of Jesus" is "'an internal norm having priority'" over the Old Testament ("Christian Pacifism," 271-72, n. 47). Priority seems here to amount to annihilation. Compare Michael Goldberg's essay (n. 1, above), from an instructively different perspective.

47. I am not suggesting that the first article should be apportioned to the Old Testament and the second to the New. The New Testament bears on the manner in which God is "almighty," and the Old bears on the character of Christ's kingdom. Nor do I intend to ignore the third article, which confesses that the Holy Spirit did indeed speak through the prophets.

4. Yahweh: A Warrior God?

DIANNE BERGANT, C.S.A.

"For us as believers, the sacred scriptures provide the foundation for confronting war and peace today."[1] With this statement, the Catholic bishops, in their pastoral letter on war and peace entitled *The Challenge of Peace,* begin their discussion of the biblical foundations of the Church's position on the subject.[2] They admit at the outset that the Scriptures themselves contain no specific treatise on war and peace, but speak primarily of God's intervention in history. It is precisely the depiction of God's intervention as military action and the characterization of God as a warrior that many people find troubling and that this essay will address.

The sacred Scripture of ancient Israel frequently depicts its God as a God of peace. It seems almost inconceivable to the contemporary religious mind to juxtapose this image of harmony and serenity with one of discord and violence. Still, such a contradictory picture does emerge in the biblical tradition. Exod. 15:3 states: "Yahweh is a warrior;/Yahweh is his name."[3] According to the report found in this revered book, Israel

---

1. National Conference of Catholic Bishops (hereafter NCCB), *The Challenge of Peace: God's Promise and Our Response, A Pastoral Letter on War and Peace* (Washington: United States Catholic Conference, 1983), par. 27.

2. *Ibid.,* par. 27-55.

3. According to Raymund Schwager, S.J., "Approximately *one thousand passages* speak of Yahweh's blazing anger, of his punishments by death and destruction, and

had devised a plan to wrest Canaan, the Promised Land, from the people already living there, and this plan appears to have originated with the God whom Israel worshiped:[4]

> Therefore I have come down to rescue them from the hands of the Egyptians and lead them out of that land into a good and spacious land, a land flowing with milk and honey, the country of the Canaanites, Hittites, Amorites, Perizzites, Hivites and Jebusites. (Exod. 3:8, NAB)

How is this characterization of a bellicose God to be understood, especially at a time when women and men of faith are looking to the Scriptures for inspiration and direction in their own agonized search for peace in the world? How is one to interpret a tradition that not only seems to take war for granted as a part of life, but actually endows it with religious, even divine, legitimation? Is dismissal of such a religious heritage as irrelevant and even alarming the only recourse for socially sensitive believers, or might there be more than one way to understand biblical statements that not only sanction but actually encourage some kinds of war?

The issue of the legitimacy of war is further complicated when we admit that there are vastly different reasons for engaging in armed conflict. Unprovoked wars of aggression are significantly different from and cannot be compared with authentic struggles for liberation and freedom from oppression. Many believe that these latter conflicts can be justified. Still, methods of modern warfare, technologically sophisticated weapons with their great destructive capacity, and indiscriminate targeting of entire populations all throw into question the legitimacy of modern warfare. In an age when the very survival of the human race and the ecological future of the planet seem to be endangered, can a religious tradition that ostensibly justified and even advocated warfare speak to the contemporary problems of armed conflict?[5]

---

how like a consuming fire he passes judgment, takes revenge, and threatens annihilation." *Must There Be Scapegoats? Violence and Redemption in the Bible*, tr. Maria L. Assad (San Francisco: Harper and Row, 1987), 55.

4. The very name *Israel* comes from the Hebrew for "he fights" and "god."

5. According to Peter C. Craigie, the question of war in the biblical tradition raises three problems: the problem of a warlike God, the problem of the revelatory value of war literature, and the problem of such a tradition influencing contemporary ethics. *The Problem of War in the Old Testament* (Grand Rapids: Eerdmans, 1978), 11.

Preliminary Questions

Two fundamental questions must be addressed before attention can be directed to the biblical text itself. The first deals with the metaphorical character of theological language.[6] Very simply, theology is a human attempt to explain the ultimate mysteries of the world, the divine dimension of things, and the relationship that creation has with the creator. Our language, which originates in the empirical world of space and time, cannot adequately refer to the realm of the transcendent. We can only speak of God and the things of God by analogy. We live in a world of belief often explained in terms of philosophical abstractions and theological models and paradigms; our biblical ancestors lived in a "sacramental universe in which the things of this world, its joys and catastrophes, harvests and famines, births and deaths, are understood as connected to and permeated by divine power and love."[7] Our theology, which is frequently a hermeneutical construction, tends to be systematic and apologetic; their religious language attests to personal experiences of God, using whatever forms best communicate the revelatory character of that experience.

The religious language of the Bible is imaginative and paradoxical. Its metaphorical character opens one to possibilities of expression and insight that precise philosophical or descriptive discourse cannot provide. It generates impressions rather than propositions. It seeks to capture the power and emotion of the event of God and to draw the hearer (only secondarily the reader) into an experience that transcends both the past and the present and opens to the future. Such an understanding of religious language is necessary, not only for the sake of an interpretation that will provide new meanings (constructive theology), but also for the sake of an approach to history that will reveal old meanings (theological reconstruction).

The second preliminary issue is the matter of hermeneutical approach employed in biblical interpretation. Contemporary communication theory has helped us recognize the existence of three different

6. For an excellent treatment of the subject, see Sallie McFague, *Metaphorical Theology: Models of God in Religious Language* (Philadelphia: Fortress, 1982), 1-29. The use of "warrior" as a metaphor is discussed by the Catholic bishops of the United States in NCCB, *The Challenge of Peace*, par. 31.

7. McFague, *Metaphorical Theology*, 1-2.

worlds: the world out of which the text grew, the world created by the text, and the world of the reader. Each world is relatively independent of the others. However, the world of the text is indebted to the world out of which the text grew for its structure and for the fundamental meaning that structure expresses. This does not mean that the sense of the text is restricted to its original meaning and cannot generate a plurality of fresh legitimate meanings.

Interpretation is more than just the gathering of information about the text (historical criticism in a narrow sense). It can be defined as the meeting of the world of the reader with the world of the text in such a way that the meaning of the text takes hold of the reader. It is the explanation of the meaning of that text in a new context. This meaning may or may not be the original meaning of the text. However, when the text in question is revered as part of the sacred tradition of a believing community, a tradition somehow rooted in the self-identity of that community, some understanding of the historical continuity that the text has with that ongoing community seems essential for valid and historically coherent interpretation. The Bible is regarded as the inspired word of God and no believer will deny that it is revelatory. However, is its revelatory character limited to its original meaning? Is its revelatory importance limited to its normative content *(traditum),* or might it be found also in its formative process *(traditio)?*

It appears that throughout the process of tradition formation, the community exercised a great deal of creativity. This creativity was restricted, however, by the concept of self-identity that it inherited from the preceding generations. The biblical traditions that have come down to us illustrate this, and tradition criticism helps us to see that different generations grasped the essence of their self-identity and restated it in ways that were expressive of their own times. Interest in this process of transmission and reinterpretation has led to a new development in biblical study known as canonical criticism.[8] This interpretive approach is not so much interested in the historical dynamics that shaped the tradition (the concern of tradition criticism) as it is in the hermeneutical methods employed in this shaping. Advocates of this approach believe

---

8. Representative works by the chief proponents of this approach include Brevard S. Childs, *Introduction to the Old Testament as Scripture* (Philadelphia: Fortress, 1979) and James A. Sanders, *From Sacred Story to Sacred Text* (Philadelphia: Fortress, 1987).

that the methods that were operative in the formation of the Bible might well be used by contemporary believers as they seek to do in our day what our ancestors did in theirs, namely, to bring earlier traditions to life in new settings.

In order to accomplish this task, interpreters must analyze both the tradition as received and the sociopolitical situation of the community that expressed the tradition in new and more meaningful ways. From this they attempt to uncover the unrecorded interpretive method that lies in the text and between the lines of the text. This method may include approaches such as comparative midrash[9] or some manner of correlation[10] that can then be employed as the revelatory message is once again expressed in a new way for a contemporary community.

Interpretation

The biblical accounts can be examined on at least three different levels. First, there is the actual event or series of events that is the subject of the tradition (the factual circumstances of Israel's occupation of Canaan). Second, there is the explanation of the event(s) that the storyteller wished to pass on (Israel's occupation as realization of God's promise of land). Finally, there is the perspective of the editor(s), which influenced the way the events were ultimately remembered (the exilic version of the tradition, which sought to encourage a displaced and dispossessed people). Each point of view clearly reflects the specific concerns of a different historical period. Biblical interpreters go to great lengths to differentiate these levels of tradition development, lest the concerns of one period be mistaken for the concerns of another and the biblical message be misconstrued.

At issue here is the conception of God as a warrior.[11] Is this concept merely an unrefined image of God that Israel eventually outgrew, or was there really an experience of God in the midst of armed conflict? If the former is the case, does this fact undermine the revelatory value

---

9. Sanders, *From Sacred Story,* 66-67.

10. David Tracy, *Blessed Rage for Order* (Minneapolis: Winston-Seabury, 1975), 43-63.

11. Since military defense was one of the major responsibilities of the king, the images of warrior and king should be examined together. However, the limited scope of this paper prevents such an investigation.

of the early Israelite traditions? If the latter is true, can war nevertheless be judged unequivocally as immoral? Answers to these questions do not come easily. Only by a careful examination of the tradition can one hope to throw light on the complexity of the issue.

The context out of which ancient Israel spoke of God as a warrior and of the wars of Yahweh (see 1 Sam. 17:47; 18:17; 25:28) can be examined from historical, literary, and theological points of view.[12] These points of view raise several questions: (1) Do the accounts found in the text report actual events that have been embellished in transmission? (2) Are they merely literary inventions intended to portray deeper religious perceptions? (3) Are they culturally conditioned religious testimonies celebrating God's protection of Israel? (4) Do they perhaps contain elements of all three perspectives?

Historical Realities

Using both biblical material and findings from various branches of anthropology, interpreters have advanced theories about the manner of Israel's occupation of the land. The three most prominent explanations held today are: military conquest, peaceful infiltration, and social revolt.[13] The position taken relative to these three theories will significantly affect the way war stories are understood. However, regardless of which explanatory model is preferred, the portrait of the Israelite community that emerges from the narratives is fundamentally the same. This was a people who understood themselves as bound juridically, cultically, and militarily

12. The point of departure for investigation of this topic is Gerhard von Rad, *Der Heilige Krieg im alten Israel* (3rd ed., Göttingen: Vandenhoeck und Ruprecht, 1958). In his introduction to the English translation, *Holy War in Ancient Israel* (tr. and ed. Marva J. Dawn [Grand Rapids: Eerdmans, 1991], 24-30), Ben Ollenburger situates this book within the development of von Rad's own thinking on the topic and then summarizes the scholarly debates that preceded and influenced von Rad's work and that followed and critiqued it. This volume also includes an extensive and up-to-date bibliography documenting the scholarly debate on the topic. The current popular, uncritical use of the concept "holy war" contributes to animosity between nations of the East and the West; for this reason and because of the scholarly debate, the concept will not be used here.

13. For a concise summary of each model, see Norman K. Gottwald, *The Hebrew Bible: A Socio-Literary Introduction* (Philadelphia: Fortress, 1985), 261-76.

to each other and to their God in an overall societal agreement known as covenant. Israel enjoyed a kind of egalitarian tribal organization, with power distributed throughout the group. In this way it might be considered a kind of alternative community to the Canaanite city-state system, which it seemed intent on replacing, or at least resisting.

Like many traditional societies, Israel itself was most influenced by concepts of kinship and belonging. The early history of the people, as found in the Pentateuch and the historical narratives, attests to patterns of patrilineal descent that served to define both membership within the covenanted community and inheritance rights:

> When Abram prostrated himself, God continued to speak to him: "My covenant with you is this: you are to become the father of a host of nations. . . . I will maintain my covenant with you and your descendants after you throughout the ages as an everlasting pact, to be your God and the God of your descendants after you. I will give to you and to your descendants after you the land in which you are now staying, the whole land of Canaan, as a permanent possession; and I will be their God." (Gen. 17:3-4, 7-8, NAB)

The identity of the group as the special people of God played an important role in the establishment of social structures, in the customs and laws that secured these structures, and in the legitimation of these laws: "Therefore, if you hearken to my voice and keep my covenant, you shall be my special possession, dearer to me than all other people, though all the earth is mine" (Exod. 19:5). "They must not abide in your land, lest they make you sin against me by ensnaring you into worshiping their gods" (Exod. 23:33). Boundaries or limits were firmly fixed: "I will set your boundaries from the Red Sea to the sea of the Philistines, and from the desert to the River; all who dwell in this land I will hand over to you to be driven out of your way" (Exod. 23:31), and entrances and exits to the sociopolitical body were carefully guarded. Violation of these boundaries, whether geographic or social, was perceived as a threat to the sociopolitical integrity of the group. In addition, because the land was revered as a sacred possession of the sovereign deity (Israel only held the land as an inheritance [see Deut. 26:1]), and the people were considered a holy nation (Exod. 19:6), violation was also regarded as religious pollution.[14]

14. See Mary Douglas, *Purity and Danger: An Analysis of Concepts of Pollution and Taboo* (London: Routledge and Kegan Paul, 1966).

Finally, the relationship between violence and the sacred must be addressed.[15] First, social authorities believe that it is their responsibility to put order into undifferentiated reality lest this chaos reign unchecked. Such ordering has been considered a form of violence and, as a result, all social structures are regarded as violent modifications of the ever-present threat of even more violent chaos. The preventive measures intended to check unleashed violence usually fall into the social category of "the sacred." This happens because violence, which seems inescapable, must be legitimated. In the category of the sacred, the preventive measures themselves often assume a very violent character.[16] Secondly, since what is deemed sacred is culturally defined, the boundaries separating the ordered from the chaotic are socially constructed. At times these boundaries are marked and discernible to all. Frequently, they are not perceived by outsiders, who only see social behavior that may be quite violent but are unable to recognize what the insiders regard as sacred.

Literary Expression

The early traditions of Israel show that the central theme of its liturgical celebration was the victory of God over cosmic or historical enemies or both. Psalm 24:8 illustrates this:[17] "Who is this king of glory?/Yahweh, strong and mighty,/Yahweh, mighty in battle." The psalm begins with reference to God's cosmic victory in the primordial battle (v. 2). The account of this battle between the forces of two gods follows a mythical pattern that was common in the ancient Near Eastern world. One of the gods was the embodiment of order and the other was a comparable embodiment of chaos. Chaos was conquered and its forces were restrained. The victorious warrior god restored the cosmic order that had

15. Whether or not one agrees with René Girard's very radical statement that "violence and the sacred are inseparable," his insight lays bare the paradoxical nature of violence and serves as a helpful heuristic model for investigation of narratives that depict it. See René Girard, *Violence and the Sacred*, tr. Patrick Gregory (Baltimore: Johns Hopkins University, 1977), and Schwager, *Must There Be Scapegoats?*

16. Girard, *Violence and the Sacred*, 17-20.

17. For an extensive analysis of this psalm, see Frank Moore Cross, "The Divine Warrior," *Canaanite Myth and Hebrew Epic: Essays in the History and Religion of Israel* (Cambridge: Harvard University, 1973), 91-111. See also Pss. 74:12-17; 89:10-14.

been threatened,[18] entered triumphantly into the city, constructed and took up residence in the temple-palace, and thereby established peace. The procession into the temple, alluded to in this psalm (vv. 7-10), celebrated this exultant entrance.[19]

Although the psalm employs imagery reminiscent of the myth of creation and a ritual of enthronement, God is also described as "mighty in battle" (v. 8) and is called "Yahweh of hosts" (v. 10), references with military significance.[20] From this perspective, the entrance of Yahweh (vv. 7-10) might refer to the procession of the ark as it was carried into battle (see Num. 10:35-36). Thus the psalm praises the triumphant march of the primordial creator and warrior God who enters the cosmic temple and the Promised Land. In Israel's liturgical celebration, the oppressive powers of Egypt and the Canaanite states were portrayed as the concrete embodiment of cosmic chaos, the characteristics of the valiant warrior were attributed to Yahweh, and God and the people of God marched exultantly into the place where Yahweh would reign supreme.

Apart from the accounts of the myth of creation, the exodus-conquest tradition includes stories of both liberation from oppression and wars of aggression.[21] In both instances God is in the forefront leading the people and claiming the final victory. In the exodus tradition, the story of liberation from oppression, the victimized people cry out for release and God intervenes as a warrior in order to be their savior. From then on, Israel's valiant God is referred to as the one who "brought us out of Egypt with his strong hand and outstretched arm."[22] Throughout other Israelite traditions one

18. See Norman C. Habel, "'He Who Stretches Out the Heavens,'" *Catholic Biblical Quarterly* 34 (1972), 417-30.

19. Whether or not Israel observed an enthronement festival during which the drama described in this psalm would have been reenacted is not to the point of this study.

20. For a discussion of whether the Jerusalem cult, with this reenactment of cosmic victory, was a source of or a ritualization of the Yahweh war tradition, see Ben Ollenburger's introduction to von Rad, *Holy War in Ancient Israel*, 22-33.

21. According to T. R. Hobbs, *A Time for War: A Study of Warfare in the Old Testament* (Wilmington: Glazier, 1989), the battles fought during the time of tribal organization were defensive, while the wars of the monarchy were aggressive wars of expansion. For an entirely different interpretation of the theme, see Millard C. Lind, *Yahweh Is a Warrior: The Theology of Warfare in Ancient Israel* (Scottdale: Herald, 1980). His basic thesis is that "Yahweh as God of war fought for his people by miracle, not by sword or spear" (23).

22. Deut. 26:8; see also Deut. 4:34; 5:15; 7:19; 11:2; Ps. 136:11-12; Jer. 32:21.

reads again and again that God is actively involved in history, championing the cause of the exploited. The Scriptures look upon such divine interventions as wars of liberation. The ritual reenactment of the Passover continues to be a celebration of this deliverance. It is no wonder that liberation movements today turn to the exodus tradition for inspiration and affirmation.

The conquest narratives present an even greater dilemma for those concerned about war language, since they depict aggressive campaigns, and it is here that the image of God the warrior and the theme of Yahweh war are the most forceful. This is especially true in the first twelve chapters of the Book of Judges. Some recent scholarship claims that Israel's settlement of the Promised Land included more than military conquests:[23] Slaves in revolt against petty kings, mercenary troops, and oppressed serfs all joined forces with Israel. Other groups in Canaan allied themselves with Israel by treaty or were already related by ancestral ties. These disparate groups accepted the leadership of Joshua and began to worship Yahweh as supreme God and savior. If this was the case, then when the ancestors of Israel threw off the domination of these overlords, their struggle for self-determination and possession of the land in which they were already living was a struggle for liberation much as the exodus was for those people who came out of Egypt. This interpretation sheds an entirely different light on the meaning of the conquest. However, even those holding this view admit to the reality of some wars of aggression. Joshua 3–5 shows that the account of crossing the Jordan into the land was ritualized in preparation for the conquest of the land. Hence, the problem of God's presence and action during these campaigns of war remains.

The texts that speak of divine violence can be grouped into four categories:[24] (1) In a small number of narratives, God's rage seems to be unreasonable. For example, Uzzah, whose devotion prompted him to prevent the ark from falling, was repaid by being struck dead (2 Sam. 6:6-7). (2) In most of the accounts, divine wrath bursts forth as a reaction to Israel's unfaithfulness (e.g., Deut. 29:23-27). (3) In several passages, God does not directly punish the evildoers, but instead delivers them into the hands of their enemies.[25] Much of the poetic material belongs

23. Gottwald, *The Hebrew Bible*, 261-76.

24. The following is a summary of Schwager, *Must There Be Scapegoats?* 53-71.

25. For a study of God's authorization of self-assertion on the part of the powerless, see Walter Brueggemann, *Revelation and Violence: A Study in Contextualization* (Milwaukee: Marquette University, 1986).

to this category (see Ps. 44:11-12; Isa. 19:2). (4) In the fourth set of texts, God withdraws and the evildoers become the victims of their own sin (see Prov. 26:27).

In the second and third categories, where God directly or indirectly punishes, the violence seems to be acts of human recompense interpreted as divine action. The fourth set of texts raises the question of causality: Does an action contain within itself its own consequences? If it does, God may be responsible for putting in force the cause and effect relationship, but the individual is responsible for the consequences of actions freely chosen. "The passages concerning God's direct or indirect avenging activity and the statements about the perpetrators' self-punishment thus point to one and the same reality: violence is always committed by human beings."[26] This statement may be helpful as a contemporary interpretation of difficult texts, but it does not explain why Israel chose such frightening metaphors to represent God. Nor does it deal with the first set of texts where violence cannot be explained on the basis of human belligerence. There it is clearly God who is violent. Only some understanding of the violence of Israel's experience and the way the people interpreted and managed that violence can explain this.

Theological Interpretation

It has been said that violence is inevitable.[27] Individuals as well as societies, threatened by the undifferentiated chaos of reality, establish boundaries that distinguish the familiar and regulated from the unknown and unrestrained. Those boundaries that are needed for survival must be defended — if necessary, even by force. If violence is inherent in human beings, then disregard for the boundaries of others will most likely engender violent seizure of what belongs to those others.[28] Consequently, both defense and aggression occasion violence. In order to save people from being consumed by the inevitable violence of their own group, whether defensive or aggressive, that violence is frequently sacralized (e.g., "holy war," "just war," "the cause of right"). Israel, being

26. Schwager, *Must There Be Scapegoats?* 66.
27. Girard, *Violence and the Sacred*, 2-3.
28. Girard claims that mimesis is at the heart of most human desire and is the origin of envy, covetousness, and conquest (*ibid.*, 146-49).

no different from other nations in intertribal and international relations, was not spared the horror of armed conflict. This is said not to justify Israel's warlike tendencies but to explain why they might be given religious legitimation ("Yahweh wars").

There is a thin line between actually experiencing God's help in the events of history and later interpreting these events theologically. Was God actually encountered as a warrior, or did Israel merely sacralize its own violence by so characterizing God?[29] This is a difficult if not impossible question to answer. It may have been inconceivable for ancient Israel to distinguish between characterizing God's presence and legitimizing its wars. (It is different for contemporary Western believers, who do not belong to the same kind of sacramental world.) Furthermore, belief in God's protection in times of strife may be envisioned as God's offensive, even military, action on behalf of the nation. This kind of interpretation flows from a blending of historical fact, theological perception, and literary creativity. It does not explain away the fact of Israel's belligerence, but it focuses attention toward the faith that lies behind both the literary expressions and the theological themes. To believe that God is a warrior may well have been the only way for Israel to understand and explain the providential and protective presence of God in the midst of the horror of war.

Contemporary denunciation of Israel's legitimation of armed conflict should not prevent us from prizing the religious traditions that explained such incidents, for it is the theological meaning of the events that is revelatory for us and not the events themselves. Furthermore, as important as may be our comprehension of how Israel understood violence and interpreted the brutal events of its history, we need not be satisfied with Israel's understanding and interpretation. Biblical interpretation is more than mere imitation. It may be that we are like our religious ancestors in that violence is just beneath the surface of our own apparent composure and just beyond the boundaries that we have established for our ordered society. But since our worldview is radically different from theirs, we cannot merely imitate their actions or appropriate their religious explanations. If their traditions are to shape our religious consciousness, they must be critically examined and carefully reinterpreted.

---

29. Craigie maintains that, since Israel believed that God was present in every event of life, God was also present during war, and the designation "holy war" was a way that Israel explained this presence theologically (*The Problem of War*, 33-43).

The idea of a warrior god evokes images of superior strength and uncontested victory. It also suggests that such a deity should not be challenged in the future.[30] The patronage of a warrior god assures victory for the people and protection in the midst of all forms of danger. Furthermore, myth and history could not be as easily separated in the thinking of ancient Israel as might be the case today. Historical battles were believed to have cosmic repercussions, and the cosmogonic victory that established universal world order also set the parameters of specific national and social order.[31] Since God waged war in order to restrain chaos and establish peace and order, the deity should be revered as a champion of justice rather than feared as a warmonger.[32] War was not a major divine preoccupation; good order and peace that flowed from it appear to have taken precedence.

We may well disapprove of the conflicts and wars that Israel fought; we may also find offensive the theological themes and imagery that were so much a part of the justification and narrative description of those wars. But we must try to grasp what was being expressed by means of these themes and this imagery. At least three important tenets of faith are expressed therein: *First,* it is clear that Yahweh was perceived as the sovereign God and that there was no other. Therefore, in any battle, primordial or historical, Yahweh emerged as conqueror, established order, and ensured peace. *Second,* the people believed that Yahweh was personally present in their lives as patron God of the nation, willing to defend them against all other peoples regardless of the cost. Even in times of great crisis, Yahweh was always present, leading them to the victory, security, and prosperity that they needed in order to survive. *Third,* other tribes or nations that threatened Israel were regarded as opponents of Yahweh as well, and their transgression of Israel's sacred boundaries was considered pollution. Since these other peoples were viewed as enemies of God, they deserved to be punished as such, and their violation of the sacred space of Israel had to be rectified by some rite of purification (Yahweh war).

30. Not only was the primal event one of violence, the tradition alleges that the eschaton too will be ushered in amid chaos and upheaval (e.g., Isaiah 24–27).

31. See Patrick D. Miller, Jr., *The Divine Warrior in Early Israel* (Harvard Semitic Monographs 5; Cambridge: Harvard University, 1973), 170-75.

32. Recent anthropological insights may throw new light on those passages where God appears to be angry for no reason. There may in fact have been some violation of sacred boundaries unfamiliar to the contemporary reader. Indeed, Uzzah did dare to touch the sacred ark (2 Sam. 6:6-7).

It should be clear from this brief summary that allegiance to the sovereignty of Yahweh, confidence in the uniqueness of Israel's election by God, and the conviction that Israel's people were obliged to rid the land of any and all polluting influences all contributed to Israel's theological interpretation/legitimation of its wars.

Even if critical analysis can establish Israel's war ideology as historically bound and culturally conditioned, the present-day believer is still confronted with the sensitive matter of the warlike language that describes God. Although this war imagery cannot be dismissed easily, awareness of the metaphorical nature of religious language reminds us that to ask "Is God a warrior?" is not unlike asking "Is God a father? Or a mother? Is God personal? Is God just?" Contemporary interpretation suggests that the questions be rephrased rather than answered. Ask instead: "What is there in the designation 'just' that is like God? What is in 'personal' that is like God? What is there in being 'mother' or 'father' that is like God? Is there anything in the idea 'warrior' that can describe God?" An affirmative response can be given to the last question only if the image of a warrior God and the theme of Yahweh war are viewed as theological expressions, historically bound and culturally conditioned. The language and imagery that originated in ancient Israel and conveyed profound theological insights into the relationship of the people with their God do not carry the same meaning in other socially constructed communities.[33] If we are to be shaped by the biblical faith that has been handed down to us, we must either open the literary expressions to a variety of new theological explanations or recast the theological message in fresh literary metaphors.

Conclusion

The conclusions of this study can be drawn by answering some of the major questions raised at its outset: (1) Do the accounts found in the text report actual events that have been embellished in transmission? Specific

33. Several scholars argue that the imagery should be retained so that God's action in history and our dependence on this action are clearly stated (e.g., Patrick D. Miller, Jr., "God the Warrior: A Problem in Biblical Interpretation and Apologetics," *Interpretation* 19 [1965]: 39-46; Richard Nysse, "Yahweh Is a Warrior," *Word and World* 7 [1987]: 192-201).

details of the accounts may be embellishments, but war literature likely had some basis in actual fact. Careful historical-critical examination will help distinguish the event from the embellishment. (2) Are these accounts merely literary inventions intended to portray deeper religious perceptions? To say that this is only imagery begs the question, for even in those cases where the historicity of the narrative is questioned, Israel chose to use war imagery. Clearly such imagery said something about Israel's perception of Yahweh that could not be as well said in another way. (3) Are these accounts culturally conditioned religious testimonies celebrating God's protection over Israel? An affirmative response to this question is appropriate, since all religious testimonies are culturally conditioned. The question remains: Do they testify to actual fact or to later understanding? Whether they testify to fact or to interpretation, they testify to Israel's faith. (4) Do they perhaps contain elements of all three perspectives (historical, literary, and theological)? Quite simply, yes!

The challenge for contemporary believers is not the historical question. Israel's experience of violence is beyond question and its religious interpretation of it is found in the Scriptures. The real challenge for today is our interpretation of these religious testimonies. We might ask: If they are to be taken seriously, need they be taken verbatim? To this we might answer: If they are taken seriously, should they not be taken contextually? To believe that God is a warrior may well have been the only way for Israel to understand and explain the providential and protective presence of God in the midst of the horror of war. We may find that the image of a warrior God and the theme of Yahweh war are no longer apt expressions of our theology.

5. Jesus and Peace

PAUL N. ANDERSON

It is a great irony of history that the cross, symbol of the ultimate triumph of peaceful means to peaceful ends, has been used as a standard in battle. Through the centuries soldiers espousing Christianity have fought bravely in war, claiming Jesus' cause or begging his help, but perhaps not following his example or furthering his kingdom. It is also ironic that differing views of Jesus' teachings on peace and their implications for his followers have been a cause of division within the church. Even in his own time people were confused about the nature of Jesus' mission. Some perceived him as the leader of a nationalistic revolt, intending to overthrow the Romans by any means. Others saw him as a prophet in the tradition of Moses and Elijah, and they interpreted his works as miraculous signs, prefiguring the exaltation of Israel. Using recent biblical scholarship, this essay seeks to clarify Jesus' teachings on peace and their implications for those who desire to follow his way.

For more than two centuries scholars have tried to discover what the "real Jesus" said and did, compared to ways his followers represented his life and teachings. This quest for the historical Jesus began with a question posed by the Hamburg scholar Hermann Samuel Reimarus (1694-1768): "What sort of purpose did Jesus himself see in his teaching and deeds?"[1] Reimarus's answer produced great upheaval. He claimed

1. Charles H. Talbert, ed., and Ralph S. Fraser, tr., *Reimarus: Fragments* (Lives

104

that Jesus must be viewed in the company of other first-century messianic figures who strove for the exaltation of Israel and the overthrow of the Romans. After Jesus' death, Reimarus claimed, Jesus' followers spiritualized his mission to prevent the death of the movement he began. Implicitly, it was during this reinterpretation that teachings on peace were added and attributed to Jesus. Though Reimarus did not address the peace question directly, the question persists: What was the character of Jesus' mission, and what did he teach about peace?[2]

Jesus and the First-Century Prophets

When one compares Jesus with other first-century prophetic figures in Palestine, one sees some interesting parallels, but even more significant differences. The ancient Jewish historian Josephus mentions five first-century prophets and messianic figures; Jesus stands in striking contrast to four of them. For instance, around 6 C.E., Judas the Galilean declared that paying taxes to Caesar was idolatrous and called for a tax revolt as an expression of loyalty to God.[3] Jesus, however, taught people to "give ... to the emperor the things that are the emperor's, and to God the things that are God's" (Matt. 22:21).[4] While other messiahs advocated armed re-

---

of Jesus Series, ed. Leander E. Keck; Philadelphia: Fortress, 1970), 64. See also John Riches's introduction to his *Jesus and the Transformation of Judaism* (New York: Seabury, 1982), 1-19.

2. See Albert Schweitzer's classic text, *The Quest of the Historical Jesus: A Critical Study of Its Progress from Reimarus to Wrede,* tr. W. Montgomery (New York: Macmillan, 1964), for an extensive treatment of this topic. Other texts of interest include James M. Robinson, *A New Quest of the Historical Jesus* (Studies in Biblical Theology 25; London: SCM, 1959); Marcus J. Borg, *Jesus, a New Vision: Spirit, Culture, and the Life of Discipleship* (San Francisco: Harper and Row, 1987); Hans Küng, *On Being a Christian,* tr. Edward Quinn (Garden City: Doubleday, 1964); E. P. Sanders, *Jesus and Judaism* (Philadelphia: Fortress, 1985); Edward Schillebeeckx, *Jesus: An Experiment in Christology,* tr. Hubert Hoskins (New York: Seabury, 1979); John Howard Yoder, *The Politics of Jesus* (Grand Rapids: Eerdmans, 1972).

3. One of the clearest and most succinct treatments of these first-century figures is David Hill's "Jesus and Josephus' 'Messianic Prophets,'" in *Text and Interpretation: Studies in the New Testament Presented to Matthew Black,* ed. Ernest Best and R. McL. Wilson (Cambridge: Cambridge University, 1979), 143-54.

4. All Scripture citations are from the New Revised Standard Version, unless otherwise noted.

sistance to occupying forces, bolstered by appeals to God and country, Jesus taught his disciples to turn the other cheek when slapped and to carry a Roman soldier's pack an extra mile (Matt. 5:38-42). This posture differed radically from what Josephus calls the "fourth philosophy" of Judaism, that of Judas's followers, and even more from the approach of the Zealots and the Sicarii ("dagger men") who came in Judas's wake.[5] According to these revolutionaries, the righteous had a religious obligation to rid the land of foreign occupiers and their aristocratic Jewish supporters. Jesus, on the other hand, did not model the liberation he proclaimed on Caleb and Joshua's conquest of Canaan or on King Cyrus's freeing of the Jews from exile in Babylon. Instead he came as the suffering servant. Like the Israel portrayed in Isaiah 40–55, his wounds would paradoxically become the source of healing and salvation.

Josephus also mentions three first-century false prophets, whose ministries differed significantly from that of Jesus. In 35 C.E., a Samaritan leader gathered hundreds of followers at the foot of Mount Gerizim, on which the Samaritans believed the sacred vessels of Moses were hidden. Their leader planned to ascend the mountain, uncover the vessels, and use them to attain liberation from the Romans. They hoped that these sacred vessels, like ancient Israel's ark of the covenant, would make them invincible and assure Roman defeat. Pilate caught wind of the uprising and put it down with such force that he was called to Rome to answer for the carnage. In contrast, Jesus taught that God's power is not confined to Mount Gerizim or to Jerusalem (John 4:21-25) but is present with all who worship in spirit and in truth. Furthermore, Jesus' kingship could not be characterized by military might; his power is the power of truth (John 18:36-37).

5. See the section of this chapter below on "Jesus' Third Way." The connection between Judas and the Sicarii is not entirely clear, as the Sicarii did not coalesce into a definite group until the 50s and 60s of the first century C.E. Richard A. Horsley and John S. Hanson, in *Bandits, Prophets, and Messiahs: Popular Movements in the Time of Jesus* (New Voices in Biblical Studies, ed. Adela Yarbro Collins and John J. Collins; San Francisco: Harper and Row, 1988), have convincingly reversed the tendency to group these three types (Fourth Philosophy, Sicarii, Zealots) together in a single movement. According to Horsley and Hanson, Judean peasants probably all resented Roman occupation, but they did not organize themselves into a Zealot movement proper until the Roman oppression of the mid-60s resulted in a series of fight-or-flight responses (190-243). In any case, Jesus' teaching clearly ran counter to much of the conventional religious nationalism of his time.

Unlike Theudas, who sought (ca. 45 C.E.) to reenact the miraculous entry into the promised land by leading a band of followers across the Jordan, Jesus commanded Peter to put away his sword (John 18:11). "My kingdom is not from this world," says the Johannine Jesus. "If my kingdom were from this world, my followers would be fighting. . . . But as it is, my kingdom is not from here" (John 18:36). The implication is not that Jesus' followers *may not* fight (a matter of permission), but that they *cannot* fight. A righteous cause cannot be furthered by violent means. Theudas told his followers that at his command the waters would part and that they would cross the river unscathed. In this reenactment of the exodus from Egypt and the conquest of Canaan, the Roman governor Fadus understood that the Romans were to play the role of the thwarted Egyptians and the conquered Canaanites. He sent troops to make a surprise attack, and then paraded Theudas's decapitated head around Jerusalem as a disincentive to further displays of nationalistic zeal.[6]

By contrast, the sea-crossing narratives in the Gospels portray Jesus' love for his disciples. They are not sensationalistic demonstrations but acts of saving concern for those in need. And after the feeding of the five thousand in John 6:1-15, the crowd wants to sweep Jesus away and make him their king, their new Moses, but Jesus flees their plans for his future and departs to the wilderness.[7] However Jesus understood his ministry, he did not cater to popular aspirations. He perceived his mission in spiritual more than political terms, and this is probably why he commanded the healed, exorcised, and confessing believers to tell no one

6. Horsley and Hanson, *Bandits, Prophets, and Messiahs,* 164-67. Luke, in Acts 5:36, dates Theudas's revolt about a decade earlier than Josephus. According to Luke, Gamaliel advised that the Sanhedrin allow the Jesus movement to fail on its own (as had the movements of Judas and Theudas), or to succeed if it was of God. Here Luke's source seems to be differentiating the Christian movement from other prophetic movements of the time.

7. The earliest manuscripts read *fugei* (fled, as a fugitive). Later manuscripts soften the verb to *anechoresen* (departed). Richard A. Horsley is correct in *Jesus and the Spiral of Violence: Popular Jewish Resistance in Roman Palestine* (San Francisco: Harper and Row, 1987) that the Zealots can no longer be used as a foil against which to display a pacifistic Jesus. But one must still consider seriously Jesus' teachings on peace, which stand in remarkable contrast to conventional ways of understanding redemption (in political and economic terms). Although Jesus was like contemporary leaders in seeking to build local community and solidarity, all four Gospels portray him as struggling against conventional notions of how that should be carried out.

about him.[8] His kingdom was not intended to be primarily political, though it clearly had political implications. Its origin and essential character were of a different kind.

Another figure offers a similar contrast to Jesus. A man whom Josephus and Luke call simply "the Egyptian" gathered a band of about four thousand followers on the Mount of Olives around 55 C.E. and proclaimed that at his command the walls of Jerusalem would fall and God would deliver the Romans into their hands. Felix sent soldiers and put a bloody end to this attempt to reenact Joshua's conquest of Jericho. The leader escaped, and the rumor that he would reappear is echoed in the Roman soldier's question to Paul: "Then you are not the Egyptian who recently stirred up a revolt and led the four thousand assassins out into the wilderness?" (Acts 21:38).[9]

In contrast, Jesus saw Jerusalem as suffering not primarily under the bondage of the Romans, but under the poor stewardship of its religious leaders. Like the irresponsible shepherds of Ezekiel 34, they had fed themselves and not the flock. Jesus therefore pronounced woes on the Pharisees, corrected the teachings of the scribes and Scripture lawyers, and in another kind of prophetic demonstration cleared the temple of its corrupting elements. He did not place blame for social problems on an external foe but sought to restore Judaism to its original vocation to be blessed and thereby become a source of blessing to the other nations of the earth (Gen. 12:1-3).

A fifth first-century prophet mentioned by Josephus is John the Baptist. John's paving the way for Jesus' ministry had two effects. First, Jesus built on the work of the Baptist in formulating his own prophetic ministry. Second, this association fed some popular misconceptions about Jesus' mission. John came preaching repentance from sin and was especially critical of the Pharisees and Sadducees (Matt. 3:7-10). He also spoke pointedly about Herod's way of life (Mark 6:14-18). Josephus describes Herod's killing of John as politically motivated. His account

---

8. It is probable that the "messianic secret," most prominent in the earliest traditions of both Mark and John, reflects struggles Jesus actually faced when dealing with the tensions between the popular aspirations of the Galilean peasantry and his own sense of mission. Even the Q tradition preserves the memory of these tensions in the temptation narratives (Matt. 4:1-11; Luke 4:1-13).

9. Hill, in "Jesus and Josephus' 'Messianic Prophets,'" writes of Theudas and the Egyptian: "These two individuals, at least, believed themselves to be involved in the imminent messianic release of the nation" (148).

reports that John was executed because he was articulate and persuasive with the masses, and Herod feared an uprising.[10] The populace must have believed that the Jewish leaders, and certainly Herod, were carrying out Roman policies among the Jews, and they must have thought Jesus' association with John indicated that he was following in the way of other contemporary nationalistic leaders.

But John was also different from the others. According to Josephus, more than other prophetic figures John followed the authentic tradition of the Hebrew prophets. John challenged those in authority to rectify their affairs and to promote justice and righteousness in the land. He called for renewed concern for the poor and powerless, and people saw him as a true prophet. John's ministry illumines Jesus' proclamation and prophetic mission. The challenge for Jesus must have been to build on John's ministry while avoiding being cast as a popular Messiah proclaiming revolt and political deliverance. The crowd's taunt, "What sign are you going to give us then, so that we may see it and believe you?" (John 6:30) echoes the devil's words in the temptation narratives (Matt. 4:1-11; Luke 4:1-13). But Jesus rejects the extrinsic use of signs and wonders to amass a following; his healing and saving work had intrinsic redemptive worth. Compassion was the motive of that work, and personal wholeness was its goal. While his intention may have paralleled that of his contemporaries, one of its distinguishing marks was his absolute commitment to peaceable means to peaceable goals.

Jesus' Teachings on Peace

Those who seek to follow Jesus must come to grips with his teachings on peace.[11] Unfortunately, Christians have often found it too easy to embrace some of Jesus' teachings without heeding the most central ones. Rationalizations abound: "Jesus' teachings weren't meant for the real world. They aren't practical." Or "The Beatitudes are for the millennium,

---

10. Flavius Josephus, *Antiquities of the Jews*, 18.116-19.
11. On this issue, see Martin Hengel, *Was Jesus a Revolutionist?*, tr. William Klassen (Facet Books Biblical Series 28, ed. John Reumann; Philadelphia: Fortress, 1971); and *Victory over Violence: Jesus and the Revolutionists*, tr. David E. Green (Philadelphia: Fortress, 1973). See also George R. Edwards, *Jesus and the Politics of Violence* (New York: Harper and Row, 1972).

after Christ returns. The kingdom ethic is intended for the future." Or again, "Nobody's perfect, and in an imperfect world harsh situations require harsh remedies."[12] These attempts to accommodate force and violence in an otherwise Christian ethic betray a profound misunderstanding of Jesus' teaching about the character of God's reign.

The kingdom of God is spiritual in its domain and compassionate in its character, and the Johannine insight into the implications of this orientation is profound. The reason Jesus' followers do not fight to further his kingdom is that that kingdom is heavenly in its origin and eternal in its scope (John 18:36). Jesus' reign is a reign of truth and cannot be furthered by human force or violent conquest. In fact, its advance is retarded and even set back by violent measures. Against a backdrop of religious nationalism, Jesus taught the radical notion that the God of love and peace expects God's children also to act in loving and peaceful ways. In other words, concern for righteousness is transferred from the domains of nation and law to the arena of human relationships. To love God is to love others as well, and this requires renouncing violence and adopting peaceable means to individual and corporate goals.[13]

12. Hengel's and Edward's concern is to counter the thesis of S. G. F. Brandon (*Jesus and the Zealots* [Manchester: Manchester University, 1967]) and others, who claim Jesus was an advocate of violent revolution. Hans Küng's assessment (in *On Being a Christian*) is pointed (187):

> We cannot make Jesus a guerrilla fighter, a rebel, a political agitator and revolutionary or turn his message of God's kingdom into a program of politico-social action, unless we distort and reinterpret all the Gospel accounts, make a completely one-sided choice of the sources, irresponsibly and arbitrarily work with isolated texts — whether Jesus' own sayings or community creations — and largely ignore Jesus' message as a whole: in a word, we would have to use a novelist's imagination instead of adopting a historical-critical method.

13. Jesus' teachings on peace may be explored further in Carol Frances Jegen, B.V.M., *Jesus the Peacemaker* (Kansas City: Sheed and Ward, 1986); John Lamoreau and Ralph Beebe, *Waging Peace: A Study in Biblical Pacifism* (2nd ed., Newberg: Barclay, 1981); Richard McSorley, *New Testament Basis of Peacemaking* (3rd ed., Scottdale: Herald, 1985); Vernard Eller, *War and Peace from Genesis to Revelation: King Jesus' Manual of Arms for the Armless* (Scottdale: Herald, 1981); Ronald Sider, *Christ and Violence* (Scottdale: Herald, 1979); James E. Will, *A Christology of Peace* (Louisville: Westminster, 1989); and Ulrich Mauser, *The Gospel of Peace: A Scriptural Message for Today's World* (Louisville: Westminster/John Knox, 1992).

As we consider Jesus' teachings, several directives become clear.[14] Jesus commands his followers (1) *to love unconditionally*. He reduced the law from ten commandments to two: consuming love of God and compassionate love of neighbor. This teaching is displayed centrally in all three Synoptic Gospels (Matt. 22:37-39; Mark 12:29-31; Luke 10:27), and John describes Jesus' "new commandment" as the appeal to love others as Jesus has loved his disciples. By the mark of sacrificial love will Jesus' followers be recognized (John 13:34-35). This love is authentic; it is not a means to an end or a bargaining chip in a transaction. Jesus' followers are to care for each other's needs as though caring for their own. They are to give freely, expecting nothing in return, for that is the character of unconditional love.

Jesus also calls his followers (2) *to love even their enemies.* The instruction to love one's enemies shows just how radical Jesus' teachings were and are. Doing good to those who do good first is common. Tax gatherers and Gentiles lived by that ethic (Matt. 5:46-47). But to respond to wrongdoing with good, to return good for evil, is uncommon. It requires divine enablement, first to understand the concept, and then to put it into action. This is not doormat passivity; it is active, proactive, even activistic. Oppression thrives on fight-or-flight intimidation, and to confront it with agapeic love instead of fear or challenge is to subvert its mode of domination. In teaching this approach Jesus shows us the way God works in the world. God's children, Jesus' said, must love their enemies and pray for those who persecute them (Matt. 5:44), for God makes the sun rise and the rain fall on good and evil alike (Matt. 5:45). Knowing this action is counter-conventional, Jesus taught that it was to be standard practice for all his followers. They are to love all God's children, because God does.

Jesus' counter-conventional way is further cast into sharp relief by

---

14. These seven directives are a digest of the early Christian memory of Jesus' teachings on peace. On the basis of the criterion of dissimilarity (it is unlikely that counter-conventional ideas would have been attributed to Jesus as the sort of thing that of course he would have said), and on the basis of thematic coherence (most of these basic themes are present in all four Gospel traditions), they deserve consideration as concerns close to the heart of Jesus' actual teachings on discipleship. They are also broadly represented in recent ecclesial statements on peace (see Howard John Loewen's chapter in this volume). To enhance our focus on the content of these teachings in this section, attention to literary and historical-critical issues will be minimal.

his instruction (3) *to renounce the right to revenge and to demonstrate a spirit of exceeding generosity.*

> You have heard it said, "An eye for an eye and a tooth for a tooth." But I tell you not to counter-strike an evildoer; but to him who strikes you on the right cheek, turn and face him, offering him the other as well. And to him who wishes to sue you for your tunic, let him have your cloak too. And for the one compelling you to walk with him a mile, accompany him for two. Give liberally to the one requesting it of you, and do not refuse the one wishing to borrow from you. (Matt. 5:38-42, my translation)

Jesus' audience must have been shocked to hear him countering popular justifications of violence even before they were voiced. "You can't expect us to let those Romans walk all over us, slap us around, take our possessions, and conscript us into forced labor, can you?" To these objections Jesus declares: "Blessed are you when people revile you and persecute you and utter all kinds of evil against you falsely on my account" (Matt. 5:11); "Give to everyone who begs from you, and do not refuse anyone who wants to borrow from you" (Matt. 5:42).

At work here is something more profound than a parental injunction to be nice. At the heart of Jesus' new ethic lies a radically different sense of the character of ultimate reality. Often in the world's thinking, reality is considered basically material, to be apprehended by the five senses. What we have must be defended, and what we want must be sought by whatever means necessary. James assessed it this way: "What is the source of wars and fights among you? Don't they spring from your hedonism, warring within your members? You lust after something you don't have; you murder and covet but do not obtain it" (Jas. 4:1-2, my translation).[15] But in God's government things are different. To follow Jesus is to invest in the world beyond the here and now. One's passion becomes to seek truth and to adhere to it. In the light of God's truth, hoards and self-interest lose their appeal. Things are transient and will fade away, but the way of God's kingdom abides forever.

Thus, Jesus invites his followers (4) *to seek first the kingdom of God and its righteousness,* promising that as one does so one's needs will be

---

15. Vernard Eller, *War and Peace from Genesis to Revelation,* 17ff., uses this passage from James as a central text from which to consider treatments of war and peace in the Old and New Testaments.

truly cared for (Matt. 6:33). Paradoxically, the needs of others are addressed as well. The kingdom of God is like a treasure hidden in a field, or like a pearl of great price, worth selling all one has in order to obtain it (Matt. 13:44-46). The value of the kingdom makes pale the valuables of this world. This is no mere exchange of outward loyalties but the forsaking of all attachment to anything but the reign of God. It also challenges directly all human claims to rule by divine mandate because there is only one source of authority and power, and no human institution or structure has the sole right to speak on God's behalf. Seeking God's kingdom first restores a dynamic theocracy, a divine rule, on a personal level. Jesus becomes Lord. When this decisive change is made, all things become new. Priorities are rearranged around human relationships and values. Pride and self-deprecation are replaced by genuine humility, by the ability to see ourselves as God sees us. The need to possess loses its grip in the presence of the one who did not count equality with God something to be grasped but poured himself out, even to the point of dying, for the healing of the world (Phil. 2:5-11).

An effect of this transformation is that we find our needs and the needs of others met in ways beyond our imagining. Much human anxiety orbits around this-worldly affairs: what to eat or wear, where to live, how to get by. But Jesus invites us to release what chokes the joy of living out of us (especially for those of us who live in the materialistic cultures of the developed nations). To seek God's government first is to release what has its tightest grip on us. Jesus promises that God will take care of our real needs, and sometimes this begins by changing our awareness of those needs. We may think that what we need most is food, shelter, and clothing, but our absolute dependence is on the Ground and Source of our being; our basic need is for God. We become drawn into the ultimate interpersonal relationship. When this happens, we paradoxically become especially sensitized to the material needs of others and become instrumental in their being met. All desire is ultimately a reflection of our deepest need, our need for God. When this need is addressed, the others tend to take care of themselves. We even become active partners with God in meeting the needs of others as well.

The way of the kingdom is also *to turn the values of the world upside down*. The first will be last and the last will be first (Mark 10:31). This changed valuation of worldly status is one of Jesus' central teachings, and also one of the most radical. It undercuts a key motive for using violence. Most violence is the result of trying either to acquire or to defend property, territory, or pride. Knowing that in the end the tables will be turned at the least gives one pause when considering defending one's position or possessions. Jesus commanded the rich man, "Sell what you own and give the money to the poor" (Mark 10:21). The man went away grieving *because* he was wealthy. His greatest asset was his greatest liability, and so it is with institutions as well as individuals.

Likewise, Jesus instructs his followers to seek the path of service rather than seeking to be served. "Whoever wants to be first must be last of all and servant of all" (Mark 9:35). Welcoming a child in Jesus' name, ministering to the poor and dispossessed, and assuming positions of lesser rather than greater status exemplify this posture. But this is not an easy idea to take in. Even in Jesus' day his followers struggled with it. In response to the request of the sons of Zebedee to become his vice-regents, Jesus declared pointedly,

> You know that those who are acknowledged as bearing rule over the Gentiles lord it over them, and that their great ones act in a tyrannical way. This is not how things stand as regards yourselves. On the contrary, if anyone among you should wish to rank high, he must be your servant; and if he wishes to come first, he must be everyone's slave. Indeed the Son of Man made his appearance not to be served but to serve, offering his very life as a ransom paid on behalf of a multitude of men. (Mark 10:42-45)[16]

This means that to become Jesus' follower one must be willing (6) *to embrace the cross.* Jesus' mission, set against the backdrop of conventional messianic expectations, anticipated a paradoxical rather than triumphal victory. In contrast to the dagger men following in the wake of Judas the Galilean, who believed that if they succeeded they would win the hearts of leaders and people alike and emerge as national heroes, Jesus taught his disciples that he would be rejected by the elders, the chief priests, and the scribes (Mark 8:31). And in diametrical opposition to the portrayal of the apocalyptic Son of Man in Enoch's Similitudes, descending from the clouds and defeating all God's enemies in holy warfare, Jesus declared that the Son of Man must suffer and die (Mark 8:31). The disciples' shocked response is telling. Peter took Jesus aside to rebuke him. Even his closest followers were confused about his mis-

---

16. This lucid translation is from Heinz W. Cassirer, *God's New Covenant: A New Testament Translation* (Grand Rapids: Eerdmans, 1989), 86.

sion, and it was not until the resurrection that they understood what he had meant (John 12:16). To follow Jesus is to embrace the cross. Says Jesus, "If any want to become my followers, let them deny themselves and take up their cross and follow me. For those who want to save their life will lose it, and those who lose their life for my sake, and for the sake of the gospel, will save it" (Mark 8:34-35).

To follow Jesus is to be willing to pay the ultimate price. Jesus never promised that following him would be easy, the path of least resistance, safe. He promised the opposite, and this is crucial to understanding the spiritual calling to the way of nonviolence. To be peaceable might not work. The nonviolent do get killed. Yet Jesus calls us not to pragmatic calculations but to radical faithfulness. Early Christians understood the cost of discipleship, and true discipleship is no cheaper today. It still involves a cross.

In the light of these teachings we see more clearly what Jesus means when he calls his followers (7) *to be peacemakers.* The Beatitudes say that people are truly blessed when they live by the way of the kingdom, not by the ways of the world: the poor (or poor in spirit) will possess the kingdom, the mourners will be comforted, the meek will inherit the earth, those who hunger and thirst for righteousness will be fully satisfied, the merciful will obtain mercy, the pure in heart will see God, and *the peacemakers will be called the children of God* (Matt. 5:3-9). Those who live in this way may be persecuted (v. 10) and may meet the fate of the prophets of old (vv. 11, 12). Jesus' followers in every age will be salt for a world grown tasteless and light in a world suffering an eclipse of vision.

Being a peacemaker involves at least two things: a commitment to peaceable responses to otherwise volatile situations and a commitment to working for peace proactively. On the pacifistic side, Jesus commands his followers to put away their swords (John 18:11). On the proactive side, Jesus calls us to be peace*makers,* not just nonhostile. This means forgiving others as we have been forgiven (Matt. 18:21-35). It means loving our neighbors as ourselves, and loving with the same quality of love as the one who gave his life for others. To follow Jesus is to be called to become a peacemaker,[17] and to do so is to take Jesus' "third way."

17. Independently, Glen Harold Stassen has come up with a similar outline based on central motifs from the Matthean Sermon on the Mount, the Lucan Sermon on the Plain, and Romans 12, 14–15. In his book, *Just Peacemaking: Transforming Initiatives for Justice and Peace* (Louisville: Westminster/John Knox, 1992), Stassen

Jesus' Third Way

One of the most provocative treatments of Jesus and peace in recent decades is Walter Wink's description of what he calls Jesus' "third way."[18] Conventional responses to evil, according to Wink, are fight or flight responses. Within such a structure, effective domination depends on insuring either response from the dominated. By keeping the upper hand with force, the dominator can deal expeditiously with attempts by the oppressed to resist. This causes the oppressed to assume a submissive posture, which itself becomes a symbol of the relationship. Eventually, tokens of domination can substitute for the actual use of force, and such symbols remind the subjects of their position. While Jesus' contemporaries inclined toward either violent resistance (fight) or cowering submission (flight), Jesus advocated a radical alternative to both in his teaching recorded in Matthew 5:38-42.

Wink writes in *Engaging the Powers* that this passage has been wrongly employed as "the basis for systematic training in cowardice" (175), when it actually outlines a radical strategy for nonviolent engagement. First, turning the other cheek must be understood in its cultural context. To have been struck on one's right cheek in that right-handed culture (the left hand was used only for unclean tasks), according to Wink, is to have been given a backhanded slap:

> We are dealing here with insult, not a fistfight. The intention is clearly not to injure but to humiliate, to put someone in his or her place. . . . A backhand slap was a way of admonishing inferiors. Masters backhanded slaves; husbands, wives; parents, children; men, women; Romans, Jews. *We have here a set of unequal relations, in each of which retaliation*

outlines these New Testament transforming initiatives for Jesus' followers: (1) Acknowledge your alienation and God's grace realistically; (2) Go, talk, welcome one another, and seek to be reconciled; (3) Do not resist revengefully, but take transforming initiatives; (4) Invest in delivering justice; (5) Love your enemies; affirm their valid interests; (6) Pray for your enemies, persevere in prayer; (7) Do not judge but repent and forgive; (8) Do peacemaking in a church or a group of disciples (53-88).

18. See Walter Wink, *Violence and Nonviolence in South Africa: Jesus' Third Way* (Philadelphia/Santa Cruz: New Society, 1987), and the third volume of his trilogy, *Engaging the Powers: Discernment and Resistance in a World of Domination* (Minneapolis: Fortress, 1992). Most of the following discussion is drawn from these sources.

would invite retribution. The only normal response would be cowering submission. . . .

Why then does [Jesus] counsel these already humiliated people to turn the other cheek? Because this action robs the oppressor of the power to humiliate. The person who turns the other cheek is saying, in effect, "Try again. Your first blow failed to achieve its intended effect. I deny you the power to humiliate me. I am a human being just like you. Your status does not alter that fact. You cannot demean me." (176)

Turning the other cheek is therefore far from cowering subservience. In the light of Wink's analysis, it must be understood as the refusal to allow the tokens of domination to be cashed in. The person who turns the other cheek stands with dignity in the face of intimidation and refuses the role of the humiliated. By being willing to accept the direst consequences the oppressor threatens, one faces him as a peer and in so doing declares one's liberation from the forces of dehumanization.

Second, to give one's undergarment to a creditor similarly subverts domination, this time in a juridical setting. Citing Exod. 22:25-27; Deut. 24:10-13, 17; and Amos 2:7-8, Wink points out that "only the poorest of the poor would have nothing but a garment to give as collateral for a loan. Jewish law strictly required its return every evening at sunset" (178). Jesus' instructions suggest a situation rife with indebtedness and usurious manipulation. According to Wink, heavy indebtedness was "the direct consequence of Roman imperial policy. Emperors had taxed the wealthy so stringently to fund their wars that the rich began seeking nonliquid investments to secure their wealth." In this system, exorbitant interest "created the economic leverage to pry Galilean peasants loose from their land" (178). Thus Jesus instructed people to respond to the merciless creditor's confiscation of their outer garment by relinquishing also their inner garment, thereby scandalizing the creditor with their nakedness. Nakedness was taboo in Israel, especially for the beholder, so this action turned the tables on the creditors. In doing so,

the poor man has transcended this attempt to humiliate him. He has risen above the shame. At the same time he has registered a stunning protest against the system that created his debt. He has said in effect, "You want my robe? Here, take everything! Now you've got all I have except my body. Is that what you'll take next? . . ."

The powers that be literally stand upon their dignity. Nothing depotentiates them faster than deft lampooning. By refusing to be awed by their power, the powerless are emboldened to seize the initiative, even where structural change is not immediately possible. . . . Jesus provides here a hint of how to take on the entire system by unmasking its essential cruelty and burlesquing its pretensions to justice. (179)

Third, Jesus' command to go the second mile must also be interpreted in the light of its original setting. It was common practice for Roman soldiers to press local subjects into forced labor, and Jesus' instruction here, as in the previous examples, shows how "the oppressed can recover the initiative and assert their human dignity in a situation that cannot for the time being be changed. The rules are Caesar's, but how one responds to the rules is God's, and Caesar has no power over that" (182).

Again, imagine the shock of those who expected the dominated to cower in grudging subservience, thus reinforcing structures of oppression. Wink believes the case can be made for the view that one mile was set as the legal limit for tolerable exploitation when it came to forcing a subject to carry a soldier's load. Perhaps this restraint functioned to justify an abusive practice for the dominated and the dominator alike. In answering objections to the oppressive system, one could always point to this supposedly merciful restraint. For a Jewish subject to carry a Roman soldier's load two miles, double the legal limit, and to do so cheerfully, must have put the soldier and his system off balance. Says Wink,

From a situation of servile impressment, the oppressed have suddenly seized the initiative. They have taken back the power of choice. The soldier is thrown off balance by being deprived of the predictability of the victim's response. He has never dealt with such a problem before. Now he has been forced into making a decision for which nothing in his previous experience has prepared him. If he has enjoyed feeling superior to the vanquished, he will not enjoy it today. (182)

Finally, Wink argues that these instructions must be read in light of Matt. 5:39a, which is often mistranslated, "Do not resist an evildoer." Wink judges that a more correct interpretation of the text does not negate resistance, but only violent resistance; what Jesus forbids is "to resist *violently*, to revolt or rebel, to engage in an insurrection" (185). One might also amplify the sentence to read, "But I tell you, do not counter-strike the evildoer; but if someone strikes you on the right cheek, turn and face him, offering also the other." The implication is that evil cannot be overcome by evil means. When one responds violently to violence, evil wins a double victory. First, its essential nature remains unexposed and thereby it prolongs its life. Second, it succeeds in seducing those with good intentions into its way. History is full of examples of revolutionaries who became what they had originally hated: oppressors. Jesus' strategy brings true reform and avoids this tragic end. Says Wink,

> His way aims at converting the opponent; failing that, it hopes for accommodation, where the opponent is willing to make some changes simply to get the protesters off his back. But if that fails too, nonviolence entails coercion: the opponent is forced to make a change rather than suffer the loss of power, even though he remains hostile. But Jesus' way does not employ *violent* coercion. (192)

The strength of Wink's interpretation of Jesus' teachings on nonviolence is that it clearly portrays the third way Jesus instructed his disciples to follow. Jesus advocated neither a fight nor a flight response to domination, but a nonviolent, redemptive engagement of the powers that be. While he did not aspire to be a political leader in the popular sense, his teaching was thoroughly political in its implications. It aimed at nothing short of creating a new earth in which God's just and loving will would be done as perfectly as in heaven.

But this is precisely where Wink's helpful work could be misinterpreted. All too easily these insights could lead one to believe that the main import of Jesus' teaching is instrumental. One could infer that Jesus simply gives us a more effective way to subvert oppressive groups like the Romans.[19] This approach misses the intrinsic ethos of his teaching. Matthew 5:42 concludes the classic paragraph on nonviolent engagement by calling us to adopt a spirit of exceeding generosity simply because this is the way of Jesus. Though his followers will experience dehumanizing treatment, Jesus calls them to resist dehumanizing the oppressor, as well as the needy: "Give to everyone who begs from you," says Jesus,

---

19. Wink himself would see this as a misinterpretation. He writes, "Jesus did not advocate nonviolence merely as a technique for outwitting the enemy, but as a just means of opposing the enemy in such a way as to hold open the possibility of the enemy's becoming just as well. Both sides must win. We are summoned to pray for our enemies' transformation, and to respond to ill-treatment with a love which is not only godly but also, I am convinced, can only be found in God" (*Violence and Nonviolence in South Africa*, 32-33).

"and do not refuse anyone who wants to borrow from you." Evil cannot overcome evil. Only good can expose, disarm, and overcome it.

Problems with Jesus' Teachings on Peace

Despite the clarity of Jesus' teachings on peace, they present some problems. One is the fact that some passages from the Gospels may seem to legitimate the use of force. These texts have led some Christians to object to any model of Christian discipleship that relinquishes their right to resort to violence under some circumstances.

One example is the story of Jesus' clearing of the temple and his overturning of the tables and seats of the money-changers and pigeon sellers (Mark 11:15-19; Matt. 21:12-13; Luke 19:45-46; John 2:13-22). Some Christians argue that this story justifies occasional use of violence. However, this reading is problematic for several reasons. First, a whip of cords (mentioned in John 2) was probably used for cattle and animals, as when a herder drove animals out of a pen. Nothing in the texts suggests that Jesus struck people. Second, overturning chairs and tables in the temple is entirely in keeping with the tradition of prophetic demonstration. The goal was not to bring change by doing damage but to expose the truth about a corrupt and dehumanizing system. Interpreting these actions as acts of prophetic judgment (rather than as acts of violence) is consistent with the way they are portrayed in the texts themselves. The Synoptic accounts refer to Isa. 56:7 and Jer. 7:11 to explain Jesus' action as prophetic, while John uses Ps. 69:9. Nothing in this prophetic demonstration legitimizes the use of violent force by Jesus' followers.

In several places in the Synoptic Gospels Jesus refers to the sword in ways that appear to sanction its use. For example, in Matt. 10:34, Jesus is quoted as saying, "I have not come to bring peace, but a sword."[20] To examine this statement in isolation may give a skewed notion of Jesus' intention. Even the verses that follow it, describing enmity between family members, may lead the reader to believe Jesus was advocating violence. Matthew 10:34-39 falls within the larger context of warnings about the hostile reception Jesus' disciples are about to experience as he sends them out on a healing, exorcising, and preaching mission to the lost sheep of

20. See also Ulrich Mauser's treatment of this motif in *The Gospel of Peace*, 36-64.

Israel. Luke represents the Q motif in parallel fashion: "Do you think that I have come to give peace on earth? No, I tell you, but rather division" (Luke 12:51). The point is that they should prepare for a cold reception, and that they should remain faithful in their mission regardless of the cost. The pivotal promise is: "Those who find their life will lose it, and those who lose their life for my sake will find it" (Matt. 10:39). This promise connotes the martyr, not the murderer.

Another problematic passage is Luke 22:36, in which Jesus is reported as saying, "And the one who has no sword must sell his cloak and buy one." After this his disciples come to him and say, "Lord, look, here are two swords," to which Jesus answers "It is enough" (v. 38). The meaning of the passage is obscure, and Luke's source and reason for adding it are matters of debate. Verses 35-38 appear to be a conflation of a commissioning narrative and Jesus' rebuke to the disciple who severed the ear of the high priest's servant. Again, the context is one in which Jesus warns of trials to come and the need to prepare for them. If Jesus were advocating use of the sword, why would he assert that two swords would suffice to protect them against Roman legions? Richard McSorley suggests that the exclamation *ikanon estin* is better rendered "Enough of that!" (as in "Stop it!"), rather than "It is enough" (as in "That will do fine, thank you").[21] This rendering is even more persuasive when one views it alongside Jesus' abrupt statement to the disciple who slices off the ear of the high priest's servant: "No more of this!" (Luke 22:51). Both commands seem to be saying essentially the same thing in a similar colloquial ways. Despite the obscurity of Luke's tradition here, corollary passages make Jesus' instruction clear. Those who think he advocated armed revolt have misunderstood. According to Matthew 26:52, Jesus said, "Put your sword back into its place; for all who take the sword will perish by the sword." The point is not to justify one's violent response to others' violent action, but to put a stop to the all-too-human readiness to fight force with force. John also understands the central implication here. According to John 18:11, Jesus told Peter, "Put your sword back into its sheath. Am I not to drink the cup that the Father has given me?" Although Jesus brings division between his followers and those who reject the gospel message, and

---

21. *New Testament Basis of Peacemaking*, 40-41. McSorley's overall counsel is sound: "The obscurity of the text should be settled by the total gospel context, which is opposed to all murderous violence" (41).

121

although he warns his followers to prepare for adversity, he nowhere instructs them to use violence. Instead, he consistently commands them to put their swords away.

A final passage that has been used to legitimize the use of violence is Jesus' statement "No one has greater love than this, to lay down one's life for one's friends" (John 15:13). This passage is a clear biblical teaching on the character of sacrificial love. It says nothing about taking the life of another person out of love for one's friends. Being willing to lay down one's life for a friend is commended; being willing to take another's life is not. The way of Jesus is always the way of *agape*, and it does not accommodate the use of violent force for any reason. Though these passages may seem at first to challenge an absolute nonviolence, none of them legitimates either individual or collective violence.

A second problem with Jesus' teachings on peace is that they are aimed primarily at people with no political clout and so are difficult to incorporate into an ethic for those who are in positions of power and responsibility. How is Jesus' ethic of peace relevant to those responsible for the vulnerable? To pay the price of martyrdom when one is faced with a defend-or-die situation is one thing. It is another thing to allow members of one's family or nation, or even people of other lands, to run the same risk. This course of action is especially problematic for those leaders entrusted with responsibility to care for the needs of their constituent group. When one becomes responsible for others, one's ethical orientation tends to shift from a principled approach to a utilitarian calculation. One must consider what is best for all concerned. And, as far as we know, Jesus did not draw out the implications of his teaching for those in such positions of responsibility. His teachings emphasized the agapeic responsibility of each person, or of the group of his followers. But Jesus did not leave his followers without direction. He promised the presence of his Spirit, to provide them with guidance and to lead them to truth (John 14–16). Often people resort to violence because of fear or frustration, because they cannot foresee the outcome of a perilous situation. To believe in a risen Lord, who teaches that good is not effected by evil means, is to be able to look beyond apparent dilemmas to redemptive possibilities. Even when dilemmas seem unsolvable, the dynamic Spirit of Christ offers more possibilities than do party platforms or church policies. This is the spiritual basis of Christian hope in a fallen world:

> I have said these things to you while I am still with you. But the Advocate, the Holy Spirit, whom the Father will send in my name,

will teach you everything, and remind you of all that I have said to you. Peace I leave with you; my peace I give to you. I do not give to you as the world gives. Do not let your hearts be troubled, and do not let them be afraid." (John 14:25-27)

In discharging their responsibility for the vulnerable, Christian leaders must remember that there are vulnerable people outside leaders' constituent groups.[22] To believe in the active reign of God is to see through the otherwise unchallenged doctrine of the sovereignty of nations to the power that transcends the state. No human reign is sovereign. And evils rationalized on the basis of national advantage or the immunity of the state must stir the conscience of Christians on whose behalf some of these actions are done. When leaders hear from their constituents that they value truth above group advantage, and when leaders act on the basis of conscience, this approximates the new order in which the will of God is done on earth as in heaven.[23]

A third problem with Jesus' teachings on peace is that they ultimately call us to act on the basis of principle rather than outcome. This may appear impractical or even unrealistic. Yet many appeals to use violent means to peaceable ends first sketch an obviously undesirable worst-case scenario. Our God-given love for family, friends, God, and country is used deceptively to construct dilemmas that seem to force us to relax principle to save those we love from harm. Sometimes life does require that we make tough choices. But often the powers that be use hypothetical dilemmas to weaken our principled consciences. If one asks, "What would I be willing to do to save loved ones from tragic violation?" one set of answers emerges. Conversely, if one asks, "How much evil would I be willing to commit in the name of good?" one comes up with another set of conclusions.[24] Harsh realities exist, but rarely is creative and peaceable mediation totally

---

22. Mark Twain's "War Prayer" depicts this reality with disturbing clarity. See also Paul Anderson, "On the Sovereignty of Nations . . . and the Kingdom of God," *Evangelical Friend,* March/April, 1991, 4.

23. See Robert Barclay's Proposition 14, in *Barclay's Apology in Modern English,* ed. Dean Freiday (Newberg: Barclay, 1991), 362-88.

24. See my treatment of L. A. King's excellent question, in "On Asking Better Questions . . . and Finding Better Answers," *Evangelical Friend,* March/April, 1992, 4. See also Wink, *Violence and Nonviolence in South Africa,* 66-68, where Jesus' third way is understood as gift rather than as law.

impossible. The deceptive posing of either/or dilemmas helps make violence acceptable.

On the other hand, people of clear Christian commitment have wondered how closely the Christian is bound to Jesus' teachings on peace, especially when faced with real atrocities, with real victims crying out for military intervention. We do live in a fallen world, and good answers are not easy to come by. The evil perpetrated by Adolf Hitler, Idi Amin, Saddam Hussein, and South African apartheid has caused some Christians to wonder whether love of neighbor might sometimes necessitate the use of violent force. Such renowned theologians as Paul Ramsey and Reinhold Niebuhr have advocated approaches to contemporary conflicts that include the option of force.[25]

But as Richard McSorley and others have pointed out, one cannot come up with a just war theory on the basis of Jesus' teachings.[26] This

25. See William R. Stevenson, Jr., *Christian Love and Just War: Moral Paradox and Political Life in St. Augustine and His Modern Interpreters* (Macon: Mercer University, 1987). Paul Ramsey, for example, interpreted Augustine's just war idea to be "love-transformed justice." "In other words," writes Stevenson, "the basis for justified warfare lay not in mere self-preservation, nor in natural justice alone, but in a meshing of Christian love and natural justice" (116). Reinhold Niebuhr, on the other hand, traced a long history of Christian justifications for the use of force and identified many cases of institutional domination that are sinful precisely because they pretend to be righteous while using violent force. He therefore adopted a posture of "Christian realism"; he believed that in a fallen world, where power must be answered with power, the Christian should be prepared to use coercion but not with the pretense of being righteous in doing so. There is no escape from guilt in history, according to Niebuhr, and the Christian politician must be willing to strive for the good with no guarantee that morally desirable options are available.

26. McSorley, *New Testament Basis of Peacemaking*, 81-102. Consider also the provocative essay, "Christians and War," by Alan Kreider and John H. Yoder (*Eerdmans' Handbook to the History of Christianity* [Grand Rapids: Eerdmans, 1977], 24-27), which identifies three classic Christian positions on war — holy war, just war, and pacifism — and states that only pacifism is based on the teachings and example of Jesus. Jesus' teachings and example do not provide warrants for using violent means to seek peaceful ends. Some Christians who have rejected pacifism (e.g., Reinhold Niebuhr and Dietrich Bonhoeffer) have recognized honestly that to do so involves acting on some other basis. Before attempting to assassinate Hitler, Bonhoeffer resigned his clerical status and was willing to forfeit his eternal destiny. He did not justify his action but cast himself on God's mercy. Niebuhr was convinced that Christians must sometimes use violence to oppose greater violence, but he believed that to do so was sin nonetheless. These approaches have more integrity than eisegetical attempts to sketch Jesus as the forerunner of the kind of revolutionary who speaks justice through the barrel of a gun.

theory was the work of Augustine and others, using political reasoning and scriptural allusions. McSorley contends that Christians' willingness to engage in warfare denies the core content of the gospel, especially in the context of nuclear weaponry. It is no accident that the church documents on peace analyzed by Howard J. Loewen earlier in this volume, which range across a spectrum of ecclesial traditions, were produced out of reflection on the massive destructive potential of nuclear weapons developed during the 1970s and 1980s. The sort of moral reasoning that led thoughtful Christians during the first part of this century to move from pacifism to a just war posture may now in the nuclear age be leading thoughtful Christians to move from a just war position toward pacifism.

Virtually all participants in armed conflict perceive their action as justified, either in defending themselves and others against tragic outcomes, or in retaliation for some wrong they have suffered. But a "justified" use of violence in one case often sets the stage for a series of justifications of violence. Conflicts "solved" by force in one generation fester to become the source of later conflicts and even longstanding animosities. Conversely, when mediated solutions are owned by both sides, peace is more stable and enduring. Living by the principle of agapeic concern for all involved may more effectively produce long-term peaceable outcomes than so-called realistic solutions that fall back on violence. Though nonviolence may not always work, history is full of failed attempts to establish lasting peace by using force.

The Way of Discipleship and the Paradox of the Cross

To follow Jesus is to embrace the cross. This is the scandal of discipleship, in New Testament times and now, and it challenges even the best human schemes for security. Truth is often paradoxical; it stands against the conventions of human wisdom, and without divine aid, without revelation, we cannot grasp it.

The paradox of the cross is central to an adequate understanding of Christian pacifism. This paradox is seen in the Hebrew Scriptures, is revealed in the incarnation, and applies to all followers of Christ. The suffering servant of Yahweh is a prototype of Jesus (the "eschatype"), according to New Testament accounts of his ministry. It is unclear whether Jesus himself made this connection, or whether his followers afterward made the association with this figure. In any case, the connection reflects an insightful interpretation of Israel's history: The suffering of one generation becomes the next generations' means of redemption.[27] In the servant psalms of Isaiah 40–55, several features stand out. First, the servant is called "Jacob" and "Israel" and is referred to in both the singular and the plural; the writer seems to shift back and forth between a particular individual and corporate Israel. Probably both forms should be understood as referring to corporate Israel.[28]

Second, while Cyrus, "the anointed," was stirred up from the east by Yahweh (Isa. 41:2), Abraham's descendants have been chosen and called from the farthest corners of the earth (vv. 8-9) by the Holy One of Israel. The servant will be anointed with Yahweh's spirit and will bring a just world order without breaking a bruised reed or snuffing out a smoldering wick (Isa. 42:1-7). He [they] will be a light to the Gentiles and the means of the world's salvation (Isa. 49:1-7). Yahweh can conscript Cyrus into service, though Cyrus does not know Yahweh (Isa. 45:1-5), but in Yahweh's work through the suffering servant there is a closer harmony between Yahweh's healing and saving ends and the means used.

Third, paradoxically, the exaltation of the servant will come through suffering. To appreciate the full significance of this promise, consider the humiliation and devastation Judah had experienced in the sixth century B.C.E. Judah had been spared from Sennacherib's siege more than a century earlier, during Hezekiah's reform, but they were not spared from Nebuchadnezzar's armies in 587. Their land was overrun, their wealth plundered, and the ablest of their number taken to Babylon as slaves. The phrase, "we accounted him [our nation] stricken, struck down by God, and afflicted" (Isa. 53:4b), reflects long pondering over the problem of theodicy: Why would a just and loving God allow this

---

27. Eller, *War and Peace from Genesis to Revelation*, 88-112, interprets the suffering servant of Yahweh as the central biblical type for the way God fights. He calls it "fighting in reverse" and sees its fulfillment in the "victory of Skull Hill." See also Wink's fourth chapter in *Violence and Nonviolence in South Africa*, 47-72, especially 68ff.

28. Although the reference on the surface seems to be to an individual (especially in Isa. 52:13–53:12), it was a common Hebrew practice to refer to a group by using a symbolic name (see, for example, Hos. 11:1-4, where "Ephraim" is used as an endearing name for the ten northern tribes). Nowhere in these servant songs is a name used that lacks a symbolic and corporate reference (e.g., Jacob, Israel), and all that is said of the servant is true of the experience of corporate Israel. Therefore, it seems most coherent to understand the initial referent of the servant of Yahweh to be corporate Israel, though Christians understand this type to be finally fulfilled in Christ.

devastation to happen to God's chosen people? "By oppression and judgment he was [our ancestors were] taken away. And who can speak of his [their] descendants [us]?" (v. 8a; my paraphrase). This lament must have reminded the sixth-century audience of their sense of abandonment in the aftermath of the Babylonian humiliation.

The Jews who now experienced relative comfort and hope, who had survived and even prospered some during the exile, must have felt deeply indebted to their predecessors because of the suffering they had endured.[29] As horrifying as their ordeals had been, through Yahweh's care the suffering of the past had become the source of present blessing. The audience of Isaiah 40–55 must have found comfort in the belief that God had brought them to a place of consolation, not just in spite of but by means of the suffering of earlier generations. They must have pictured the previous generation as a paschal lamb: "He was [our parents and friends were] wounded for our transgressions, crushed for our iniquities; upon him [them] was the punishment that made us whole, and by his [their] bruises we are healed" (v. 5). According to Isaiah 53, Israel, which had suffered terribly, had been faithful and had thus become the means of blessing. Later Jews perceived their return to Zion as the blessing brought about by the faithfulness in the midst of the suffering of those who had gone before. Through the struggles and faithfulness of one generation, future generations were being blessed.[30]

These insights drawn from the redemption accomplished through the vicarious sufferings of exilic Israel also apply to New Testament understandings of Jesus' mission. The Gospel of Mark with special clarity portrays Jesus as one who understood that his suffering and death would paradoxically bring about the redemption of others. As Judah had

---

29. One difference in nuance between the singular and plural references to the servant is that when the singular is used, the reference seems to be to Israel's past sufferings. The plural seems to be used in describing a more contemporary situation.

30. This discussion is speculative, but if it understands the origin of the suffering servant motif correctly, then new light is shed on the mission of Jesus and how Jesus' followers perceived that mission. This understanding also has implications for the present discussion on peacemaking in the Scriptures. If the suffering servant is a model for understanding how God wrests redemption from tragedy, we gain new insights for approaching difficult situations today. A violent response to a perceived threat ceases to be our first reaction or even our last resort, and previously unforeseen nonviolent possibilities emerge.

been devastated by Nebuchadnezzar's aggression, so Jesus' followers were shocked by his death. Not until the resurrection did their despair give way to recognition: They came to see his suffering as a fulfillment of Scripture and to interpret his death as the means by which he took their suffering on himself. Jesus' death was not an end but a beginning. Through it came victory over the ultimate foe, death itself. And by raising Jesus, God declared with finality that oppression and violence will not have the last word. The reign of God advances by spiritually binding "the strong man," the powers and systems of oppression and deception that beleaguer the vulnerable.

Jesus' followers are called to embody the same approach. The way of discipleship is always the way of the cross, and to follow Jesus is to embrace the cross. Jesus did not promise that peacemakers would be successful, or that they would be spared hardship. To pursue peace is often to increase one's vulnerability, not to diminish it. Jesus says to Peter, the crowd, and the rest of the disciples, "If any want to become my followers, let them deny themselves and take up their cross and follow me" (Mark 8:34). Some failed to understand Jesus' teaching on the cross, but some abandoned him precisely because they did understand. The Johannine tradition reports that Jesus' disciples were scandalized by his teaching, that some of them slid back and refused to travel with him any longer (John 6:51-66).[31] The Christian mission to embrace the cross and so become an agent of reconciliation in the world cannot be accomplished by evil means. As Albert Schweitzer wrote in 1906,

> He comes to us as One unknown, without a name, as of old, by the lake-side, He came to those men who knew Him not. He speaks to us the same word: "Follow thou me!" and sets us to the tasks which He has to fulfill in our time. He commands. And to those who obey Him, whether they be wise or simple, He will reveal Himself in the toils, the conflicts, the sufferings which they shall pass through in his fel-

---

31. Jesus' "bread" is his flesh given for the life of the world (John 6:51); this is a statement about the cross. He then invites his followers to eat his flesh and drink his blood, an invitation not simply to partake of the Eucharist, but an invitation (which uses graphic eucharistic imagery) to continue to embrace the cross of discipleship. See Paul N. Anderson, *The Christology of the Fourth Gospel: Its Unity and Disunity in the Light of John 6* (Wissenschaftliche Untersuchungen zum Neuen Testament 2; Tübingen: Mohr, 1994), for a fuller treatment of the Johannine tradition and its audience.

128

lowship and as an ineffable mystery, they shall learn in their own experience Who He is.[32]

Findings

Overwhelming evidence contradicts attempts to connect the historical Jesus with armed revolutionaries. Jesus' mission was different from that of other first-century prophets and messiahs in its absolute commitment to nonviolent means. All four Gospels portray Jesus as one who struggled against popular hopes that he would overthrow the Romans by force, who was committed to using peaceable means to attain peaceful goals. Jesus' program was not that of Cyrus, Judas Maccabeus, or the Zealots.

Jesus' teachings were pervasively pacifistic, and following him entails serious reflection on his central teachings. These include admonitions to love enemies and to seek first God's reign. In this reign love and truth are supreme. As Ulrich Mauser has written, "It is . . . no exaggeration to say that the entire activity of Jesus, in word and deed, is the making of peace; and that the life of his community is given direction by his blessing on the peacemakers."[33]

But Jesus' ethic is not lofty idealism. His teachings had significant political implications. They provided people living under domination an effective means of nonviolent engagement aimed at laying bare evil systems of oppression and seeking to transform them into a just social order. Jesus taught an alternative to both violent revolution and doormat passivity, a third way which has been misunderstood both by pacifists and by those who would use force. Jesus' way is an ever-adaptable strategy for confronting the powers that be with the truth, forcing them into a public dilemma that may lead to their embarrassment or to repentance. Redemptive results are not guaranteed, but this third way can be used in any situation with creativity, initiative, hope.

Jesus' teachings on peace are clear but problematic. He did not give his followers directions about how to respond when those in their care face violent danger. But living by a kingdom ethic involves considering outcomes for all people involved, not just the members of one's own group. Then violent approaches may give way to creative alterna-

---

32. Schweitzer closes *The Quest of the Historical Jesus* with these words (403).
33. Mauser, *The Gospel of Peace*, 65.

tives. While Christians sometimes abandon pacifism out of concern to stop violence, even the effective use of force often eventually becomes the source of more violence.

Following Jesus always involves the cross. A disciple must be more concerned with minding the truth than with avoiding suffering. The suffering servant of Isaiah taught sixth-century (B.C.E.) Jews that God works to bring healing and hope out of the suffering of one generation; Jesus' followers perceive and experience the suffering of Jesus in a similar way. This model suggests that God works most powerfully in the world through such suffering. In our fallen world, there is no tragedy, ill, or injury that does not bear within itself redemptive possibilities. Following Jesus may increase our suffering, but we may be assured that if we are crucified with him we will also be raised with him. This is history's final paradox and the basis of the Christian peacemaker's hope.

6. Peace in the New Testament

RICHARD L. JESKE

The New Testament does not treat "peace" formally as a singular topic, though the word appears there more than ninety times, in every New Testament writing except 1 John. No New Testament author defines the topic in terms of its Christian sense. Writers offer short treatises on faith (Hebrews 11), love (1 Corinthians 13), the law (Romans 7), and even shorter ones on judging (Matthew 7) and church order (1 Timothy 3), but they give no parallel treatment of peace.

Yet a reading of the New Testament yields the impression that peace is sometimes at issue even when the word itself does not appear. The concept is central to the gospel message articulated in the New Testament; the Christian movement understood its mission as extending to the rest of the world what it had received, namely, God's offer of peace.

All New Testament writers presuppose that the life and work of Jesus of Nazareth has resulted in a new condition of peace between God and people. God's offer of peace has its persistent place in the stories that bracket the ministry narratives: the birth stories and the resurrection appearance stories. These stories make the point that the peace inaugurated by Jesus' life and ministry comes from God and is God's gift and blessing. This gift necessarily has implications for Christian behavior in the world. God's gift is to be articulated and used; Jesus' followers proclaim peace, and they also practice it.

Should Christians' practice of peace be adjusted at times to the evil nature of the world around them? New Testament writers from Matthew to John of Patmos answer in the negative. Jesus' followers know that the world is hostile to them, but they know God calls them to practice peace. From the church's earliest beginnings, its style of existence distinguishes it from other movements and groups. Jesus sent out his disciples with a word of peace to proclaim, with a mission to seek the children of peace (Luke 10:6; cf. Matt. 10:13). "The gospel of peace" is a phrase expressing the continuity between Jesus' preaching (Eph. 2:17; Acts 10:36) and Christian preaching after Easter (Eph. 6:15). And a specific kind of activity marked those who became Jesus' spokespeople in the world; they held the office of "the ministry of reconciliation" (2 Cor. 5:18). Even in 1 John, where the word "peace" does not appear, the practice of love toward other members of the community is the measure of one's love of God.

While peace is not defined in the New Testament, its many appearances there indicate its vital importance in Christian proclamation and life. So much do early Christian writers presuppose the notion and practice of peace that it soon appears in the conventional epistolary address: "Grace to you and peace. . . ."

Methodological Considerations

The general comments above will be supported by a review of New Testament peace texts. But first, some methodological considerations. Those who collect, categorize, and interpret such data must bear in mind the pitfalls of a word-study approach to the topic. If we confine our examination to occurrences of the Greek word *eirene*, we will miss vast portions of relevant New Testament material dealing with Christian attitudes toward adversaries, enemies, nonviolent action, and the use of weapons. For example, "peace" does not occur in the Sermon on the Mount (Matthew 5–7), only the compound "peacemakers" (Matt. 5:9); yet this material has much to say about Christian responses to others, including those who might threaten and attack. Theological assessments of the New Testament witness on peace must therefore include more than selected lexicographical data.

This study cannot and should not avoid theological interpretation of the data. But we will exercise caution when speaking about a "biblical theology of peace," or "the New Testament witness on peace." A variety of theologies, a variety of witnesses exist within the biblical canon. But this does not preclude some agreement among these theologies, some common thread among the biblical writings on this topic. Generally speaking, the biblical writers regard war as evil, but in some biblical accounts the people of God willingly and even enthusiastically wage war (Judges 5; 1 Samuel 15). Generally speaking, peace is regarded as good, but not when it rests on injustice or a false sense of security (Jer. 6:14; 1 Thess. 5:3). Where peace is a divine gift, it can also be taken away (Jer. 16:5).

The word "peace" takes on additional nuances when it appears with other significant terms: peace and love, peace and righteousness, peace and honor, peace and mutual upbuilding. These combinations offer possibilities for more precise definitions of peace. For example, peace and honor are eschatological rewards in Rom. 2:10, while in Rom. 14:17 peace and mutual upbuilding are present pursuits in the Christian community.

Finally, the question of the New Testament as a canonical whole will also bear on our study. Not only the perspective of each New Testament writer but also the collective authoritative witness of the New Testament as a whole has made its impact on the church's theology. Not only the authentic words of Jesus, but also Jesus' message as transmitted through the memory of the church has had a bearing on the formation of the church's witness through the centuries. Any review of the data must take into consideration the New Testament canon as a whole.

The Data

The noun "peace" *(eirene)* occurs in the New Testament 92 times, in every New Testament writing except 1 John. Forty-two occurrences are in the Pauline corpus. In none of these texts is peace something attained only after this life is over. At least thirteen peace passages are texts of parenesis (pastoral encouragement and admonition) dealing directly with Christian behavior practicable in the present. Some texts speak of peace among people in terms of general social tranquillity (as *shalom*). A preponderance of passages speak of the peace that human beings have before God because of the work of Christ, a peace that may be extended to relationships among people. About fifteen passages assume no such distinction: The peace that God gives inaugurates peace among people. Several passages speak of peace as a gift and blessing from God, while one (Gal. 5:22) sees peace as a fruit of the Spirit (cf. Jas. 2:14-18).

All four occurrences of the verb "have peace" or "live in peace" *(eireneuo)* appear as parenesis, as exhortations to live in peace with one another (Mark 9:50; Rom. 12:18; 2 Cor. 13:11; 1 Thess. 5:13). Twice the adjective "peaceful" *(eirenikos)* is used, neither with reference to human beings (Heb. 12:11 and Jas. 3:17). Matthew 5:9 speaks of the peacemakers *(eirenopoioi)* as God's own children, and Col. 1:20 refers to Christ as the Son who made peace through the blood of his cross.[1]

1. Gerhard Delling, "Frieden IV. Neues Testament," *Theologische Realenzy-klopädie* (hereafter *TRE*) XI (Berlin/New York: de Gruyter, 1983), 613-18; William Klassen, "Peace: New Testament," *The Anchor Bible Dictionary* (hereafter *AB*) V, ed. David Noel Friedman (Garden City: Doubleday, 1992), 207-12; Victor Paul Furnish, "War and Peace in the New Testament," *Interpretation* 38 (1984), 363-73; Victor Hasler, *"eirene," Exegetical Dictionary of the New Testament,* I, ed. Horst Balz and Gerhard Schneider (Grand Rapids: Eerdmans, 1990), 394-97; C. L. Mitton, "Peace in the NT," *Interpreter's Dictionary of the Bible* III, ed. George Arthur Buttrick (New York: Abingdon, 1962), 706; Werner Foerster, *"eirene* in the New Testament," *Theological Dictionary of the New Testament* (hereafter *TDNT*) II, ed. Gerhard Kittel and Gerhard Friedrich, tr. Geoffrey W. Bromiley (Grand Rapids: Eerdmans, 1964), 411-20.

See also the following important studies: Egon Brandenburger, *Frieden im Neuen Testament: Grundlinien urchristlichen Friedenverständnisses* (Gütersloh: Mohn, 1973); Klaus Wengst, *Pax Romana and the Peace of Jesus Christ,* tr. John Bowden (Philadelphia: Fortress, 1987); Gunther Klein, "Die Friede Gottes und die Friede der Welt," *Zeitschrift für Theologie und Kirche* (hereafter *ZTK*) 83 (1986), 325-55; Richard McSorley, *The New Testament Basis of Peacemaking* (3rd ed., Scottdale: Herald, 1985); Cain H. Felder, "New Testament Foundations for Peacemaking in the Nuclear Age," *Journal of Religious Thought* 42/2 (1985-86), 56-61; Daniel C. Arichea, Jr., "Peace in the New Testament," *The Bible Translator* 38 (1987), 201-6; John Dominic Crossan, "Jesus and Pacifism," *No Famine in the Land: Studies in Honor of John L. McKenzie,* ed. James W. Flanagan and Anita Weisbrod Robinson (Claremont: Scholars, for the Institute for Antiquity and Christianity, 1975), 195-208; Donald Senior, "Jesus' Most Scandalous Teaching," *Biblical and Theological Reflections on "The Challenge of Peace,"* ed. John T. Pawlikowski and Donald Senior (Wilmington: Glazier, 1984), 55-69.

The Sociohistorical and Religious Context of the Data

Greco-Roman Traditions

Greco-Roman traditions progressively displayed discontent with the heroic conception of war.[2] The Greek war-god Ares, though a son of Zeus and Hera, failed to achieve the full dignity of an Olympian deity and remained generally unpopular.[3] The goddess Athena, though active in war but not in random fighting, promoted and rewarded heroes' reflection on war and restrained conduct in war. In Homer's writings (eighth century B.C.E.) the fortunes of war were connected with the rule of the gods. But in Hesiod's works (seventh century B.C.E.) war was not caused by the gods but by Eris, strife (headstrong, incorrigible discord rather than honorable competition) at work among human beings.[4] Though the counsel of immortals stood behind the wars of mortals, the gods were in fact displeased about wars, especially those that began with the breach of a sworn treaty. Thus the ancients saw the need for critical reflection on the legitimacy, causes, and conduct of war, and the goal of such reflection was preventing rather than glorifying war.

By the time of Aristophanes (ca. 450-385 B.C.E.) the notion that military success rested on the wisdom of the gods was being rejected in favor of the belief that war was caused by human shortsightedness and by unscrupulous people pursuing their own narrow interests.[5] At the end of the first century C.E., the orator Dio Chrysostom could say, "Zeus wills that men should be friends to each other and that none should be the enemy of another."[6] If war broke out, human guilt and injustice were

---

2. Otto Bauernfeind, *"polemos,"* TDNT VI, 503-7; Peter Gerlitz, "Krieg I: Religionsgeschichtlich," *TRE* XX, 12; Abraham J. Malherbe, "Antisthenes and Odysseus and Paul at War," *Harvard Theological Review* 76 (1983), 143-73. Walter Burkert, *Greek Religion,* tr. John Raffan (Cambridge: Harvard University, 1985), notes that preliminary and subsequent rituals make it appear that war is understood in antiquity as "one great sacrificial action" (267); William Klassen, "War in the New Testament," *AB* VI, 867-75, observes that "the Romans more than the Greeks politicized all religion and tended to sacralize war" (869).

3. In the *Iliad* it is Ares who brings the "shameless butchery of war" (5.992-95), and Zeus describes Ares as "the most hateful to me of all the Olympians" (5.890-91).

4. Hesiod, *Works and Days* 14.

5. See Aristophanes' play *The Peace.*

6. Dio Chrysostom, *Discourses* 1.40-41. Cynic philosophers also complained about the senselessness of war (e.g., Diogenes, *Epistulae* 40; Heraclitus, *Epistulae* 7).

present on both sides. General assessments of the political reality of war remained unchanged, and there was little philosophical revision of the notion that while war was evil it was unavoidable[7] and that the only hope for overcoming war would be the establishment of a world state.

The Roman Empire

The Roman Empire under Augustus was, in fact, an attempt to construct a single world state. It is often referred to in conjunction with the peace it did establish, the *Pax Augusti* or *Pax Romana*. After his defeat of Antony and Cleopatra at Actium in 31 B.C.E., Octavian returned in triumph to Rome and gradually began replacing the existing republican structures with the principate, a more monarchic form of government. He assumed the title *Imperator Caesar Divi filius* ("Emperor, son of the Divine Caesar"), and the senate conferred on him the additional title "Augustus," an ancient sacral title, establishing Caesar's place in divine law and the emperor's mission as a divine mission. These shifts made inevitable a resurgence of worship of the emperor. The divine ruler cult promoted the belief that a higher will had brought about the imperial situation, which would put an end to war. The strong hand of the divine emperor assured peace,[8] a "glorious age" that would bring unparalleled prosperity and release from guilt and dread.[9] In the imperial period "peace" was used primarily of a state or time in which war had ceased, rather than of relationships among people.

Of course, this peace was more a reality in Rome and its environs and less in the provinces and frontiers of the empire. The many frontier wars during Augustus's time were waged ostensibly to secure the borders rather than for expansion of the borders. Vassal kingdoms, including that of Herod the Great in Palestine, were developed on the eastern and southern frontiers. The peace that existed was a "festering peace," to use Tacitus's term, endured by the people of the frontiers as servitude rather

7. Cf. Plato, *Phaedo* 66C.

8. One side of a denarius from the early period of Augustus's reign depicts Pax, the goddess of peace, with olive branch and cornucopia, and the reverse side portrays Caesar in military clothing with a spear. See Wengst, *Pax Romana and the Peace of Jesus Christ*, 11-12.

9. Cf. Virgil, *Eclogues* 4.11-15.

than enjoyed as tranquillity.[10] This had been the case for the Jews in Palestine since 63 B.C.E., when Pompey conquered and occupied the region.

Palestinian Judaism during the Roman Empire

Palestinian Judaism during the Roman Empire was the immediate social and historical context for the emergence of Christianity, a context marked by popular resistance movements, some with apocalyptic agendas, whose organized protests often ended in violence.[11] The tension between the government (Herodian puppet rulers and Roman governors) and the Jewish populace frequently erupted into open hostility. Although the first-century Jewish historian Flavius Josephus (ca. 37–ca. 100 C.E.) calls a number of rebels — Judas the Galilean, Simon of Perea, and others — "bandits," the movements they led were clearly messianic.[12] Social banditry, targeting both Roman military personnel and wealthy Jews, was common in the countryside and popular among the peasantry. It established the framework for wider rebellion against Rome.[13] Groups such as the Sicarii operated in urban areas and practiced terrorism especially against Roman collaborators.[14] After 40 C.E. such movements multiplied. A series of self-proclaimed prophets and kings led insurrectionist uprisings that promised deliverance from foreign oppression and from all suffering. Josephus writes that these leaders were "cheats and deceivers claiming inspiration" who "schemed to bring about revolutionary changes by inducing the mob to act as if possessed, and by

---

10. Tacitus, *Histories* 4.17.2.

11. See Richard A. Horsley and John S. Hanson, *Bandits, Prophets, and Messiahs: Popular Movements in the Time of Jesus* (New Voices in Biblical Studies, ed. Adela Yarbro Collins and John J. Collins; San Francisco: Harper and Row, 1988); Horsley, *Jesus and the Spiral of Violence: Popular Jewish Resistance in Roman Palestine* (San Francisco: Harper and Row, 1987).

12. See Horsley and Hanson, *Bandits, Prophets, and Messiahs*, 34-47, 88-134. Horsley and Hanson find evidence for the existence of popular messianic movements "in every major district of Jewish Palestine" (36).

13. Horsley and Hanson distinguish between local social bandits, brigands whom they describe as the Robin Hoods of Palestine, and the popular messianic leaders whose followers attacked Roman strongholds and troops as well as Herodian fortresses (204).

14. Flavius Josephus, *Jewish War* 2.254-56.

leading them out into the wild country on the pretence that there God would show them signs of approaching freedom" (cf. Matt. 24:24-26).[15] The government suppressed all these messianic movements, crucifying or otherwise executing their instigators as political insurrectionists. Within this highly charged atmosphere John the Baptist and Jesus appeared. Both developed followings that proclaimed their leaders' messianic character, and both were executed as political agitators.

Tensions between the empire and its Jewish subjects increased. The Emperor Caligula (37-41 C.E.) enacted harsh measures against them, and Claudius (41-54 C.E.), his successor, expelled the Jews from Rome. Under Nero (54-68), Christians were blamed for the disastrous fire in the city, and many were executed.[16] Finally, in 66 C.E., full-scale revolt broke out in Jerusalem. Zealots and other militant Jewish partisans seized the city, plunging the territory into the conflict known as the Jewish-Roman war of 66-70.

After 70 C.E., Christians began to find their place in greater Roman society. Their movement was viewed less and less as a threat to social stability, and they could even hold positions of civic responsibility (see Rom. 16:23). Still, in some provinces local persecutions of Christians did occur, especially in Asia Minor under Domitian (81-96) and Trajan (98-117). As late as 165 C.E. the execution of Polycarp, bishop of Smyrna, was followed by a pogrom of Christians there.[17]

The Hebrew Scriptures

The literary-religious context for understanding the New Testament witness on peace necessarily includes the Hebrew Scriptures. Here the picture of God's rule in war contrasts markedly with the Greek understanding of their deities' attitude toward such conflicts. In the Hebrew Scriptures, not only does Yahweh cause wars, but Yahweh also determines their outcome. The Greeks could not have conceived of wars of Ares or Athena, but Num. 21:14 speaks of "the book of the wars of Yahweh." This

15. Josephus, *Jewish War* 2.259, tr. G. A. Williamson (Middlesex: Penguin, 1970), 139.

16. Tacitus, *Annals* 15:44; Suetonius, *Lives of the Caesars: Nero* 16.

17. W. H. C. Frend, *The Rise of Christianity* (Philadelphia: Fortress, 1984), 180-84. Frend also mentions the martyrdoms in Lyons in 177 and in North Africa in 180 (pp. 179-84). "Only near the end of the century did the clouds begin to lift" (184).

expression conveys the concept of Yahweh's sovereign rule over the people, established with Yahweh's victory over the chaotic forces in the primeval battle (Psalm 29). Psalm 2, an enthronement psalm of great interest to New Testament writers,[18] presents the strong rule of Yahweh who gives power to Yahweh's anointed to maintain peaceful order in the midst of hostile foreign powers. Yahweh is guarantor and provider of peace for Yahweh's people (Ps. 85:9-14). Peace in its fullness is well-being established by God, and when such well-being is lacking, God's people can turn in lament to God with the petition that God act to restore it.[19]

This strong image of the rule of Yahweh who is warrior and guarantor of peace has a positive theological implication: Yahweh's people are to find their security in Yahweh alone. In contrast to the peace and security found in Yahweh is a false peace, resting on Israel's illusory sense of self-sufficiency.[20] God establishes the only true peace, and Israel (or the world, for that matter) does not experience peace unless God gives it. This belief is expressed most forcefully in the worship form called the Aaronic Benediction (Num. 6:24-26, especially v. 26), and in the pilgrim psalms (e.g., Ps. 128:6). Yahweh may also war against Yahweh's own people (Amos 2:14-16); lack of peace among people is the cause of lack of peace between God and God's people.

A permanent peace, among peoples and with God, has a place in the prophetic vision, though beliefs differ about how it will be realized. Isa. 2:2-4 and Mic. 4:1-3 describe the permanent peace of "the latter days" that will come about by the voluntary subjection of the peoples before Yahweh ("swords into plowshares"), while Joel 3:9-21 tells of a permanent peace for Judah and Jerusalem coming through the rallying of Yahweh's people for the great eschatological battle ("plowshares into swords").[21] In both texts Yahweh intends to bring peace, for Yahweh's people (in Joel) or for the whole world (in Isaiah). The goal of God's rule over creation is peace, a peace including but not limited to the cessation of military hostility, a state of complete wholeness and well-

18. See Acts 4:25-26; 13:33; Heb. 1:5, 5:5.
19. See Lam. 3:17 and the various psalms of lament (e.g., Pss. 35, 44, 55).
20. See Jer. 6:14; 8:11; 14:13-14; Amos 6:1-14.
21. Hans Heinrich Schmid, "Friede II: Altes Testament," *TRE* XI, 609, suggests that both texts are to be understood from the vantage point of Yahweh's instruction about waging war in Deut. 20:10: Before waging war an offer of peace must be made, and only after terms of peace are rejected can war be waged, and then waged fiercely.

being for humanity. The eschatological peace that both prophets antic-
ipate lies not beyond history but within history, for Judah and Jerusalem
(in Joel's case) and for all nations (in Isaiah's). God intends peace, and
God's reign means that "nation shall not lift up sword against nation,
neither shall they learn war any more" (Isa. 2:4; Mic. 4:3).

Hellenistic Judaism

Hellenistic Judaism was marked by a variety of viewpoints and traditions.
For instance, the Septuagint (LXX) translators indicate their uneasiness
with the depiction of Yahweh as a warrior: In every case (Exod. 15:3;
Isa. 42:13; Judith 9:7, 16:3), the LXX changes the Hebrew text from "man
of war" to "one who destroys war." However, the Maccabean conflict
(168-165 B.C.E.) raised messianic hopes. The ensuing hundred years of
Hasmonean rule, followed by the Roman conquest of Palestine, also
helped create a climate in which apocalypticism thrived. Various writings
speak of the final war of the end time, which will eliminate the ungodly
powers and do away with sin (*Testament of Dan* 5:10-11; *1 Enoch* 91:12;
100:4), a time of incomparable tribulation (Dan. 12:1). The War Scroll
of the Qumran community speaks of the great and final battle between
the children of light and the children of darkness. These texts understand
peace only as following the decisive conflict of the eschatological future.[22] The phrase "God of peace" occurs once, in the *Testament of Dan*
5:2. There it refers to God's protection of a repentant Israel from its
enemies. These enemies will face God's vengeance in the end time.

A number of rabbinic texts speak of the coming Messiah as one
who brings peace, as peace himself, bestowing peace among his creatures,
in the world above, and between himself and humanity. Josephus, writing
at the time of the Jewish-Roman War, admonished Israel not to fight
against Rome, because to do so would be to align oneself against God,
who will avenge God's people if they are wronged.[23] For the Hellenistic
Jewish philosopher Philo of Alexandria (ca. 20 B.C.E.–50 C.E.), external

---

22. *1 Enoch* 71:15: "He [the Son of Man] shall proclaim peace to you in the
name of the world that is to become. For from here proceeds peace since the creation
of the world" (*The Old Testament Pseudepigrapha*, I, ed. James H. Charlesworth [Gar-
den City: Doubleday, 1983], 50).

23. Josephus, *Jewish War* 5.375-78.

physical conflict resulted from conflict within the soul.[24] One attains spiritual peace by contemplating and exercising wisdom and virtue, by acknowledging that we all have one God, to whom we must listen and whose will we must practice.[25] Only then will the wild beasts of the soul be tamed.[26] The object of Philo's allegorical method of biblical interpretation was to discover the hidden, spiritual meaning underlying the terminology of the biblical texts.

The Ministry of Jesus in the Memory of the Church

Jesus' mission and ministry had political consequences, because it had much to do with the way people live together and treat each other. The New Testament Gospels tell us much about the way of life that Jesus lived and promoted, particularly about his table fellowship with social outcasts. The company he kept with tax collectors and sinners[27] offended his contemporaries; the early church would not have invented this feature of his ministry. In associating with these people, Jesus was acting out a parable; with loving acceptance God was drawing near to sinners. They celebrated this communion by eating and drinking at table together.

The Synoptic Gospels

In the Synoptic Gospels, Jesus' ministry is remembered as a ministry of teaching, preaching, and healing (Matt. 4:23). In the texts dealing with healing, the traditional biblical understanding of peace as wholeness can be seen. Jesus' form of dismissal, "Go in peace," is often coupled with the statement, "Your faith has saved you" (Mark 5:34; Luke 7:50; 8:48), an indication that physical healing is a component of wholeness before

24. Philo, *On the Giants* 51.

25. Philo, *On Rewards and Punishments* 115-17.

26. Yet Philo gives a rationale for men of peace waging war: "To fight against those who attempt to break treaties and ever practise the violation of the vows they have sworn. [Thus] . . . they take the field to resist those who would subvert the stability of the soul" (*On the Confusion of Tongues,* tr. F. H. Colson and G. H. Whitaker, Loeb Classical Library, Philo IV [Cambridge: Harvard University, 1949], 43).

27. For further definition of these terms see Horsley, *Jesus and the Spiral of Violence,* 212-31.

God. "Go in peace" is a congratulatory description of that wholeness: Let what is now in force for you in this moment continue! This formula therefore signifies both present reality and future possibility; a relational wholeness before God exists now and can exist in the future. That is God's peace. Luke 7:47-50 includes God's forgiveness as an ingredient in this peace. Therefore, when Jesus' disciples are sent out in mission to proclaim the nearness of God's reign, they are told to announce God's peace to those who receive them (Luke 10:5; Matt. 10:13).

The subject of Jesus' preaching and teaching was "the good news of the kingdom of God." For Jesus the kingdom of God was not limited to the future or to heaven or to an institution (the church or the nation). In contrast to those who looked backward with longing to the kingdom of David or who hoped for its future return, Jesus proclaimed that God's kingdom had now drawn near. He said that God's reign is a present reality and summoned people to live in it now (Matt. 12:28). Furthermore, according to Jesus, God's reign cannot be taken by force or appropriated on human terms. God's kingdom is a gift (Luke 12:32), something to be received (Mark 10:15). Therefore Jesus did not share the goals of the Zealots or of members of other movements that sought to establish God's reign by violently overthrowing the Roman government or its vassals. For Jesus, the kingdom is God's gift.

Matthew 10 and Luke 10 record Jesus' instructions as he sends out his disciples. They are told to make two announcements: "The kingdom of God is at hand" (Matt. 10:7; Luke 10:9) and "Peace be to this house!" (Luke 10:5; cf. Matt. 10:13). While other messianic movements were assembling followers to prepare for pitched battle, Jesus' followers were sent to search for the children of peace (Luke 10:6). They were not to divide the world into politically partisan camps, or condemn those who rejected them (judgment will come in due time [Matt. 10:15; Luke 10:12]), or categorize people as children of light and children of darkness. They were to seek the children of peace, and if they found none in the place they were visiting, their own commitment to peace was to remain visibly operative (Matt. 10:13; Luke 10:6). We have reason to believe that Jesus used the phrase "child of peace" to refer to those who responded to his message and that he was the first to use the phrase; no use of it by others of his time has been discovered.[28] The contrast with other

---

28. This was first proposed by William Klassen, "'A Child of Peace' (Luke 10.6) in First Century Context," *New Testament Studies* 27 (1981), 488-506.

messianic movements is clearly drawn with the announcement that the long-awaited kingdom of God has drawn near. That is the message of Jesus, and therefore it was to be the message of those he sent out. Other messianic movements also confronted sin and its consequences in the world: sickness, suffering, and death. But unlike adherents of other messianic movements, Jesus' followers do not destroy but restore. They offer healing to the sick, relief to the suffering, acceptance to the rejected, hope to those who are impoverished, and life to the dying (Matt. 10:7-8; Luke 10:9; cf. Matt. 4:15-17). Jesus' ministry is first and foremost a ministry to the poor and oppressed, and only secondarily to the rich and powerful: It is exceptional when a rich person enters God's kingdom (Mark 10:23; Matt. 19:23; Luke 18:24). Because Jesus' movement contrasted with other messianic movements, including that of John the Baptist, John wonders whether Jesus is really the one who is to come and is told, "The blind receive their sight, the lame walk, the lepers are cleansed, the deaf hear, the dead are raised, and the poor have good news brought to them. And blessed is anyone who takes no offense at me" (Matt. 11:5-6; also Luke 7:22-23). Those who do not take offense receive God's blessing. They are the peacemakers and as such are the children of God (Matt. 5:9).

"Blessed are the peacemakers, for they will be called children of God." This beatitude, along with other beatitudes, stands at the beginning of the Sermon on the Mount (Matthew 5–7) and provides a theological basis for all that follows. The Sermon on the Mount is first of all a composition of the Evangelist Matthew, presented to his readers as a compendium of Jesus' teachings on a variety of topics: the law, almsgiving, prayer, fasting, judging, and other subjects. As a compendium, the Sermon on the Mount is a statement of Jesus' mission and on what it means to be a follower of Jesus, a disciple (or learner; cf. Matt. 5:1-2). The Beatitudes stand at the beginning of the Sermon on the Mount to indicate that all that follows, all the admonitions and directives in the rest of the sermon, have their point of origin in the blessing of God. Only those so blessed are able to consider seriously for their own life-practice the admonitions and directives that follow. Only the blessing of God enables that mature relationship, that wholeness before God and before others, that makes all things new and creates Christian discipleship. Those who receive God's blessing according to the Beatitudes (Matt. 5:3-11) are those to whom Jesus' ministry is directed throughout the Gospels: those who are poor, suffering, rejected, and oppressed (see also Luke 4:16-22). Those who have experienced the healing and acceptance that Jesus' fellowship offers are now sent to proclaim to others what they have experienced. They have received God's blessing and have peace before God, which enables them to be different and to make a difference in the world; they are the salt of the earth and the light of the world (Matt. 5:13-16). The admonitions and the directives of the Sermon on the Mount, when seen from the vantage point of the Beatitudes, are at the same time descriptions of Christian discipleship in the world.[29]

This is especially true of Matt. 5:9, "Blessed are the peacemakers, for they will be called children of God." Though the word "peace" does not appear in the Sermon on the Mount, the rest of the sermon contains many examples of peacemaking in the world. When peacemakers are called "blessed," this means that their efforts are grounded in God's own initiative; God has made peace with them. Their own practice of peacemaking will bear witness to their special relationship with God, to their being God's children. This connection between making peace and being God's children occurs again in the sermon: "Love your enemies and pray for those who persecute you, so that you may be children of your Father in heaven; for he makes his sun rise on the evil and on the good, and sends rain on the righteous and on the unrighteous" (5:44-45). The admonition to love one's enemies is based on the good news of God's mercy toward those who are evil and unjust. Peacemakers, then, know themselves to be blessed and loved by God and are therefore able to demonstrate love and concern for their enemies. Peacemaking is not a passive posture of nonresistance, not mere passive suffering to maintain tranquillity. It is not even limited to acts to reconcile people. It is actively engaged in the practice of love of enemies. Luke 6:27 expands on how to do this: "Love your enemies, do good to those who hate you, bless those who curse you, pray for those who abuse you."

Jesus was not the first to ask his followers to practice kindness toward their enemies. Passages in the Old Testament (Exod. 23:4-5), in intertestamental literature (e.g., *Testament of Gad* 6), and in rabbinic writings speak of loving the other, of taking no vengeance against the evildoer, and of forgiving.[30] But Jesus was the first to make loving one's enemies the essence of being a child of God (Matt. 5:45).

---

29. Recent studies on the Sermon on the Mount include Robert A. Guelich, *The Sermon on the Mount* (Waco: Word, 1982); Peter Stuhlmacher, "Jesu vollkommenes Gesetz der Freiheit: Zum Verständnis der Bergpredigt," *ZTK* 79 (1982), 283-322.

30. Cf. *Derech Eretz Rabba* 11.

Whom does the term "enemy" refer to in the Sermon on the Mount? Another beatitude says, "Blessed are you when people revile you and persecute you and utter all kinds of evil against you falsely on my account. Rejoice and be glad, . . . for in the same way they persecuted the prophets who were before you" (5:11-12). Enemies, in the Sermon on the Mount, are those who persecute others on ideological grounds, on religious grounds; specifically, they persecute Jesus' followers because of their witness to him. An enemy is not simply a person with whom one has an ongoing personal quarrel. Enemies are people who persecute others because of their commitment to Christ. These are the people Jesus' disciples are called to love. Jesus' disciples are called to practice the most difficult kind of love, love for the hardest people to love. Jesus' admonition to love one's enemies, then, cannot be seen as a privatistic ethic to be practiced only toward individuals whom we know personally. It is a programmatic discipline that distinguishes Jesus' followers from others in the world and characterizes them as God's own children (Matt. 5:43-48; see also 20:25-26; Mark 10:42-45).

The distinctiveness of Jesus' fellowship, in contrast to other kinds of fellowship, is the frame of reference for Jesus' statement "Do not think that I have come to bring peace on earth; I have not come to bring peace, but a sword" (Matt. 10:34; see also Luke 12:51). The context of this statement indicates that it applies to family relationships (Matt. 10:35-37; Luke 12:52-53; 14:26). Jesus' mission and teaching may indeed cause division in the family fellowship, especially if the family's values run counter to Jesus' message. In that case, the disciple must make a decision and count the cost. Jesus teaches that we are not to find security in earthly social structures. We are not to rely on family to retaliate when we are attacked, nor are we to make commitments to retaliate on behalf of our family members. Such familial commitments create entanglements that are opposed to Jesus' ethic of peace toward those who revile, abuse, and persecute. Those who wish to be followers of the crucified one need to review such commitments critically (Matt. 10:35-38; Luke 14:26-27).[31]

Three traditions suggest that Jesus had a more overtly revolutionary attitude. All four Gospels report that Jesus overturned the tables of

31. Matthew Black sees this imagery as evidence that Jesus did expect an apocalyptic upheaval following his death ("'Not Peace but a Sword': Matt. 10:34ff; Luke 12:51ff," in *Jesus and the Politics of His Day*, ed. Ernst Bammel and C. F. D. Moule [Cambridge: Cambridge University, 1984], 287-94).

the moneychangers and traders in the temple (Mark 11:15-17; Matt. 21:12-13; Luke 19:45-46; and John 2:13-22). If Jesus and his disciples had attempted a full-scale assault and occupation of the temple, the result would have been a riot and a reaction from the Roman guard stationed nearby. Many scholars believe that these accounts embellish a prophetic word of Jesus or a more contained prophetic act directed toward restoring the holiness of the temple.[32]

In Luke 22:38, when Jesus' disciples present him with two swords, his reply, "It is enough," indicates that armed conflict is not what he has in mind.[33] That is also the sense of Jesus' rebuke to the lone swordsman who injured the high priest's slave, an episode reported in all four Gospels (Mark 14:47; Matt. 26:51-54; Luke 22:50-51; in John 18:10-11 the swordsman is identified as Simon Peter).

Throughout the New Testament, Jesus' messiahship is described as a messiahship of peace. Peace is the theological meaning given to his mission and ministry. The early Christian church saw Jesus as the Prince of Peace promised in Isa. 9:6; both Matthew (4:15) and Luke (1:79) understand Jesus' coming as a fulfillment of Isa. 9:1-2. The text of Jesus' sermon in the synagogue at Nazareth (Isa. 61:1-2, as recorded in Luke 4:18-19) also lies behind Matthew's presentation of the Beatitudes (Matt. 5:1-2). Zechariah's Benedictus in Luke 1 ends with a specific understanding of the purpose of the Messiah's promised mission: "to guide our feet into the way of peace" (Luke 1:79).

In the very structure of Luke's Gospel Jesus' messiahship of peace is most clearly shown. At Jesus' birth the multitude of angels announces God's peace to the world: "Glory to God in the highest heaven, and on earth peace among those whom he favors!" (2:14). Luke's record of Jesus' ministry draws to a close with Jesus' entry into Jerusalem. Then the multitude of disciples, recalling "the deeds of power that they had seen," respond as if antiphonally to the angelic Gloria at his birth with the shout: "Blessed is the king who comes in the name of the Lord! Peace

---

32. See Furnish, "War and Peace in the New Testament," 369; Marcus J. Borg, *Conflict, Holiness and Politics in the Teaching of Jesus* (New York: Mellen, 1984), 171-76; idem, *Jesus, A New Vision: Spirit, Culture, and the Life of Discipleship* (San Francisco: Harper and Row, 1987), 174-76.

33. G. W. H. Lampe, "The Two Swords (Luke 22:35-38)," *Jesus and the Politics of His Day*, ed. Bammel and Moule, 335-51, understands Jesus' answer as a sarcastic response to the disciples who were ready to engage in combat (351).

in heaven, and glory in the highest heaven!" (19:38). From beginning to end, the story of Jesus is remembered and narrated as a ministry of peace.

The Acts of the Apostles

In the Book of Acts, the word "peace" designates the resolution of a private conflict (7:26) and a political one (12:20); it refers to the absence of fighting and war (as in Luke 11:21 and 14:32). In Acts 24:2, Tertullus describes the governor Felix as a guarantor of peace, in terminology reminiscent of the Augustan imperial design. Acts 9:31 speaks of the development of the church in Palestine in peace. Christians are sent on their way "in peace" (Acts 15:33; 16:36), a traditional Hebraic usage. This usage is also apparent in the Nunc Dimittis (Luke 2:29): Simeon can now depart this life "in peace" because he has seen the Messiah and his patient waiting has been vindicated before God and other people. Acts 10:36, alluding to Isa. 52:7, describes Jesus as bearer of a message of peace that God has sent to Israel. Acts 13:26 further identifies this good news as "the message of salvation." In Acts, then, "peace" thus carries the full range of meaning evident elsewhere in the New Testament, from cessation of hostility between human beings, to reconciliation between God and humanity, salvation itself. What God has initiated comes to fruition in the lives of people. The Messiah of peace brings peace to people, and they in turn practice peace among themselves.

The Gospel of John

When we turn to the Gospel of John we come to a later stage in the church's memory of Jesus' ministry, at the end of the first century. At the conclusion of the Gospel the risen Jesus leaves his disciples a legacy: "Peace be with you" (John 20:19). This is a reminder that Jesus refused the role of popular Messiah (6:15), defined in terms of power (6:30-32). The disciples had misunderstood his kingship of peace (12:16) because it did not fit their expectations. But the risen Lord returns to give them the legacy of peace and to send them as he has been sent (20:21).

Elsewhere in John's Gospel the word "peace" occurs only twice, and both times it stands in juxtaposition to "the world." Both references are in farewell discourses, a literary form unique to John's Gospel. With these words, John's Jesus prepares his disciples for the time to come:

147

"Peace I leave with you; my peace I give to you. I do not give to you as the world gives" (14:27). "I have said this to you, so that in me you may have peace. In the world you face persecution. But take courage; I have conquered the world!" (16:33).

In John's Gospel, the world is hostile to Jesus and his followers; hatred is the dominant feeling the world expresses toward Jesus and his disciples: "The world . . . hates me because I testify against it that its works are evil" (7:7). "If the world hates you, be aware that it hated me before it hated you. If you belonged to the world, the world would love you as its own. Because you do not belong to the world, but I have chosen you out of the world — therefore the world hates you" (15:18-19). The world (which for John includes the established religious institutions) is hostile to Jesus because it worships a god who approves it and gives legitimacy to its conduct and ideas. The world's religion is a means to the world's self-affirmation, and Jesus' prophetic words are anathema to it (5:38; 8:39-40; 9:28). With this disturbing question, Jesus exposes the vested interests of the very religious: "How can you believe when you accept glory from one another and do not seek the glory that comes from the one who alone is God?" (5:44).

The world believes its security lies within its own capabilities. It needs institutions that perpetuate this self-deceived self-confidence and a god whom it can shape to its own will (6:30-31). But Jesus tells his disciples that their lives are not to be determined by the world's standards. They are not to take up arms to defend their Lord, for they are not to replace with their own cup the cup the Father has given Jesus to drink (18:11). The peace that the world gives, which is based on mutual anxiety and multilateral threat, is not the peace that Jesus gives to his disciples. He asks them to practice a new peace in the world, as a sign of their identity as his disciples.

One should not speak of the peace Jesus gives to his disciples as a peace that is manifest only in the Christian fellowship. Nor is the peace that the world cannot give a mere hope for the future, not meant to be practiced by Christians in the present. The farewell discourses (13:31–17:26) immediately precede the Passion narrative in John's Gospel. Their function is to prepare Jesus' followers for the time to come, when he has departed and they will mediate his presence in the world (15:27; 17:20-21). Jesus' disciples are not to be coopted by the world, for its standards have been overcome (16:33). Jesus' peace exists in the world and for the world, that it might be saved (3:17). Jesus' own are those who live out the peace they have been given, witnessing in the world to Jesus (15:27;

17:20). Following the crucified one, then, means no longer being coopted by the world or conformed to its standards; Christian witness is not to be shaped by the world's anxieties.

As a result, Jesus' kingship contrasts with other kingships: "My kingdom is not from this world. If my kingdom were from this world, my followers would be fighting to keep me from being handed over.... But as it is, my kingdom is not from here" (18:36). To understand Jesus' kingship as otherworldly or future, not present in this world, is to misunderstand Jesus' statement. His kingship is not defined by the standards of this world. His kingship, and therefore his glory (that is, his cross [12:23-28; 17:1-5]), stand in judgment on the world and its standards. His followers are to witness to and practice his kingship of peace in this world. The cross of Christ judges not only the world's standards but also the church's rationalizations when it allows its witness in the world to be defined by the world.

Jesus' peace differs from the world's peace because it is given. The peace of the world is not given but extracted. Jesus' peace is a gift. That peace is given unconditionally, offered by Jesus and his followers, as a relief from pervasive anxiety and multilateral threat. The peace that Jesus and his followers live and give is more than the cessation of hostility (the world's temporary peace). It offers community rather than isolation (16:32), cooperation rather than competition (4:29-30), mutual caring rather than exploitation (15:17), productivity rather than destruction (15:5), enjoyment rather than endless striving (15:11), a new life that looks forward to God's future (16:7). The community of Jesus is a place of new relationships: The disciple whom Jesus loved takes his mother into his home (19:27). Jesus' own do not belong to the world, and that means that they face danger (15:18-19). But the farewell discourses include Jesus' statement, "Take courage; I have conquered the world!" (16:33).

The Pauline Letters

About half of the ninety-two occurrences of "peace" in the New Testament are in the Pauline letters. The concept of peace would seem, then, to have a central place in the theology of Paul. For Paul, God is the God of peace, and Paul's letters invariably begin with a salutation extending the peace of God to his readers.[34]

34. Rom. 1:7; 1 Cor. 1:3; 2 Cor. 1:2; Gal. 1:3; Phil. 1:2; 1 Thess. 1:1; Phlm. 3.

RICHARD L. JESKE

Romans 5:1-11 contains a compendium of Paul's theology, with its terms "peace," "grace," "faith," "hope," and "love" standing in close proximity. God has established peace with humanity through Christ, and all people have access through Christ to God's grace (5:1-2). We are justified by faith (5:1) and can rejoice in hope (5:2) because God's love has been poured into our hearts (5:5). Furthermore, God has established peace not merely with sinners or the godless, but with God's enemies: "While we were enemies, we were reconciled to God through the death of his Son" (5:10). In a parallel text, 2 Cor. 5:18-21, Paul defines Christian ministry as a ministry of reconciliation, identical with the ministry of justification (2 Cor. 3:9). Through this ministry those who had been enemies of God call other enemies into a new reconciled relationship with God, a relationship offered to them purely as a gift, as a sign of God's love (Rom. 5:8). According to Eph. 6:15, this ministry, this Christian proclamation, is the gospel of peace.

Paul's theology of the estrangement and hostility between humanity and God is enunciated in Rom. 1:18–3:20. Both Gentile and Jew, though they are well aware of God's existence, are estranged from God because they cannot thank God. As long as they believe God is at their disposal (1:22-23), their posture before God cannot be one of gratitude. They believe their position before God is secured by their achievement, by their thinking or by their doing. Judgment and demand they know, because of the law written on their hearts (2:15). But with the law as the standard, no human being can be justified (3:20); all have sinned (3:23) and face God's wrath which is against all wickedness (1:18). Therefore God's acceptance comes to them as a gift, "through the redemption that is in Christ Jesus" (3:24), and as recipients rather than achievers they are able to thank God. God has reconciled the hostility and estrangement, and peace between God and people can now exist. This is the good news that Paul is not ashamed of (1:16), the message of the peace and reconciliation that God has accomplished in Christ. It is only natural, then, for Paul to refer to God as "the God of peace" (Rom. 15:33; 16:20; Phil. 4:9; 2 Cor. 13:11; see also 2 Thess. 3:16; Heb. 13:20),[35] the God who fills

35. Gerhard Delling views "God of peace" as another of Paul's ways of describing God as a giver; as God gives hope, joy, love, so God also gives peace ("Die Bezeichnung 'Gott des Friedens' und ähnliche Wendungen in den Paulusbriefen," *Jesus und Paulus. Festschrift für Werner Georg Kümmel zum 70. Geburtstag,* ed. E. Earle Ellis and Erich Grässer [Göttingen: Vandenhoeck und Ruprecht, 1975], 76-84).

150

us "with all joy and peace in believing" (Rom. 15:13), whose way is the way of peace (Rom. 3:17).

In the society of the church Christians celebrate the gift of God's peace, the result of God's grace, mercy, and love in Christ. The two terms "peace" and "grace" are joined in every Pauline letter in a formula of greeting that indicates the early Christians' understanding that they are a community called by God to the ministry of reconciliation: "Grace to you and peace from God our Father and the Lord Jesus Christ" (Rom. 1:7; 1 Cor. 1:3; 2 Cor. 1:2; Gal. 1:3; Eph. 1:2; 6:23-24; Phil. 1:2; Col. 1:2; 1 Thess. 1:1; 2 Thess. 1:2; 1 Tim. 1:2; 2 Tim. 1:2; Titus 1:4; Phlm. 3; cf. 1 Pet. 1:2; 2 Pet. 1:2; Rev. 1:4; 2 John 3; 3 John 15; Jude 2; 1 Pet. 5:14). This greeting, which has its roots in the ancient *shalom* greeting and which soon became a standard salutation in Christian circles, reflects an understanding of the church as a community of people at peace with God and among themselves because of the saving work of Christ. As a literary and liturgical greeting, it is both a recognition of the style of existence initiated by the church's Lord and a wish that that style continue to mark the church's communal behavior.

The texts of Pauline parenesis, of pastoral encouragement and ethical admonition, include statements relating the concept of peace directly to communal behavior. In a discussion of judgmental attitudes within the Christian community, Paul states that Christian life under God's kingship is not for the purpose of quarreling over opinions, but rather is justice *(dikaiosune)* and peace and joy in the Holy Spirit (Rom. 14:17). Two verses later another combination helps define the meaning of peace in the church: "Let us then pursue what makes for peace and for mutual upbuilding" (14:19). "To set the mind on the flesh is death, but to set the mind on the Spirit is life and peace" (8:6), for peace is a fruit of the Spirit (Gal. 5:22). The Christians' proper style of existence is to be at peace with one another, to let the peace of Christ prevail in their community (Rom. 12:18; 2 Cor. 13:11; Col. 3:15; cf. Mark 9:50).

Several texts of Pauline parenesis deserve special comment. In 1 Cor. 7:14-15, Paul writes that the Christian marriage partner is not bound to maintain a marriage if his or her unbelieving spouse wants to terminate it. The reason given is that "it is to peace that God has called you" (1 Cor. 7:15). Jesus' prohibition against divorce (7:10) and God's intention that the marital bond be permanent are set over against God's concern for peace between people. The marriage law is not meant to result in enslavement, and God's call to peace in some cases supersedes the permanence of the marriage bond.

In 1 Cor. 14:26-33, Paul's instructions about prophetic speech in worship services suggest an orderly approach to preaching: The preachers are to take turns rather than all attempting to speak at once. Paul gives this advice because "God is a God not of disorder but of peace" (14:33). This means, first, that glossolalia is not to be heard in public worship unless someone can interpret it, transforming it into intelligible preaching. Second, prophets speak in turn, each having their rightful place, and their accountability to the community is preserved by the prophets who weigh the words each speaks (14:29). The peaceful ordering of communal worship preserves the integrity of each person as well as the integrity of the service, "so that all may learn and all be encouraged" (14:31).

Another text of Pauline parenesis important to a discussion of peace in the New Testament is Rom. 13:1-7. Its opening words, "Let every person be subject to the governing authorities; for there is no authority except from God," along with its reference to (local) governing authorities as servants or ministers of God, have led to its use as a prooftext justifying uncritical obedience to governmental authority and acquiescence in the face of official political injustice.[36]

Romans 13:1-7 fits within the greater context of chapters 12-15, the parenetic portion of this letter, in which Paul discusses the gospel's practical consequences for Christian living. The focus of 13:1-7 is individual Christian behavior in one's immediate society, and the respect due to local secular authorities, "that circle of bearers of power with whom the common man may come in contact."[37] Romans 13:1-7 is simply the practical application of the programmatic admonition of 12:1-2:

36. See, e.g., Martin Scharlemann, "Scriptural Concepts of the Church and the State," in *Church and State under God,* ed. Albert G. Huegli (St. Louis: Concordia, 1964), 15-58: "Rebellion, resistance, and disobedience run counter to God's intent for society; hence they are evil. 'Therefore,' says St. Paul, 'one must be subject...'" (43). Cf. also Johannes Friedrich, Wolfgang Pöhlmann, and Peter Stuhlmacher, "Zur historischen Situation und Intention von Röm 13,1-7," *ZTK* 73 (1976), 162: *"Mit dieser Feststellung widerrät Paulus mit Nachdruck dem Versuch eines politischen Widerstandes von Seiten der Gemeinde"* (emphasis original).

37. Ernst Käsemann (*Commentary on Romans* [Grand Rapids: Eerdmans, 1980]) rejects interpretations of this passage that use it to define a "metaphysic of the state." According to Käsemann, such interpretations have led "not only to conservative but also to reactionary views even to the point of political fanaticism. In opposition to this it must be stated emphatically that Paul is not advancing any theoretical considerations" (354).

I appeal to you therefore, brothers and sisters, by the mercies of God, to present your bodies as a living sacrifice, holy and acceptable to God, which is your spiritual worship. Do not be conformed to this world, but be transformed by the renewing of your minds, so that you may discern what is the will of God — what is good and acceptable and perfect.

This is Paul's appeal that Christian worship of God not be confined to sacred time and sacred space and sacred acts, but be practiced in the secular world, in the existing structures of everyday life. Paul's appeal recognizes that God has made it possible for Christians to carry out their spiritual worship within the orders of this world. The term "spiritual worship" *(logike latreia)* has its origins in the Stoic and popular philosophical criticisms of the formalities of ancient sacrificial systems, in which one's responsibility before deity was satisfied by cultic acts.[38] Paul uses this language to apply the concept of worship *(latreia)* to the daily life of the Christian believer. Within the structures of daily existence, Christians are to make evident what the will of God is, namely, the good, the acceptable, the perfect.

This programmatic exhortation finds practical application in the ensuing verses of chapter 12. What looks like irreconcilable diversity in the church is instead evidence of the vast richness of the one body of Christ and an affirmation of individuality in members' exercise of God's gifts in the body of Christ (12:3-13). Within the structures of this world there is hatred and persecution, but God's people are not to be conformed to such manifestations of temporality and the imperfections of this age.

---

38. Texts are cited in C. E. B. Cranfield, *The Epistle to the Romans* II (International Critical Commentary; Edinburgh: Clark, 1979), 601-5; Ulrich Wilckens, *Der Brief an die Römer* III (Evangelisch-Katholischer Kommentar zum Neuen Testament; Neukirchen: Benziger, 1982), 3, 4-6; James D. G. Dunn, *Romans 9-16* (Word Biblical Commentary 38B; Dallas: Word, 1988), 711-12. In Stoicism, for instance, use of the word *logike* would connect with the understanding of the *Logos* as that divine Reason that permeates all of nature, to be apprehended and lived out by human beings. If Paul's use of the word carries an anticultic edge (as suggested by Rudolf Bultmann, *Theology of the New Testament* I [New York: Scribner, 1951], 115-16; Ernst Käsemann, *Romans,* 329), it is no doubt due to Paul's experience with a narrow spiritualism that does not draw out the implications of formal worship for responsible action toward others (see 1 Cor. 6:1-6; 11:17-34). Obviously, however, Paul would not advocate a cessation of formal worship activities, though such activities constitute only one piece of the Christian's total worship of God.

Instead they are to show God's will by transforming the interaction, by giving a blessing for a curse.

> Bless those who persecute you; bless and do not curse them. Rejoice with those who rejoice, weep with those who weep. Live in harmony with one another; do not be haughty, but associate with the lowly; do not claim to be wiser than you are. Do not repay anyone evil for evil, but take thought for what is noble in the sight of all. If it is possible, so far as it depends on you, live peaceably with all. Beloved, never avenge yourselves, but leave room for the wrath of God; for it is written, "Vengeance is mine, I will repay, says the Lord." No, "if your enemies are hungry, feed them; if they are thirsty, give them something to drink; for by doing this you will heap burning coals on their head." Do not be overcome by evil, but overcome evil with good. (12:14-21)

Therefore, according to Paul, God will avenge as God wills and has created the proper structures for this vengeance (13:4).

The constant, then, is worship of God. The variable, the temporal, is the structure in which each person finds himself or herself called to that service of worship. The ceremonial law — dietary regulations, liturgical calendars, ritual food restrictions (13:8–14:23) — all these belong to the temporally conditioned structures of human existence, through which the constant, our worship of God, finds opportunity for expression. Absolutizing the structure and making it the constant diverts our worship to an object that is not God and is idolatrous.

For Paul the issue is not whether a social structure is valid but how the Christian worships God within it. Slavery and patriarchy do not prevent slaves and women from worshiping God. The priority for all Christians, even those who are enslaved and oppressed, is to remain true to God's calling (1 Cor. 7:17). Yet Paul insists that in Christ a new structure impinges critically on prevailing social structures and makes clear their temporality: "There is no longer Jew or Greek, there is no longer slave or free, there is no longer male and female; for all of you are one in Christ Jesus" (Gal. 3:28). Absolutizing temporal social structures is foreign to Paul's thinking. As he wrote to the Corinthians, "The present form of this world is passing away" (1 Cor. 7:31).

The same is true of governmental authorities. The authority of government is a derived authority. God's creating activity provides structures for people so that they can perform their service of worship. Absolutizing secular political authority diverts our worship to an object that is not God, and thus initiates idolatry. Therefore, in Rom. 13:1-7, Paul is emphatic about the status of government officeholders. They are God's servants (so described twice in v. 4, and again in v. 6, where the more festive and priestly term *leitourgos* appears). Their position is not greater than this; they are not God. Their position is not less than this, because they are servants for our benefit (v. 4), serving both God and people in the temporally conditioned structure through which we and they render our service of worship to God.[39] Those who have secular political power, specifically local authorities, do not bear the sword in vain (v. 4). That is, they are vested with authority to maintain the order that is necessary so that Christians may make evident the will of God and perform their service of worship.[40]

When he calls Christians to be subject to government authorities, Paul is not absolutizing the state or requiring blind submission to one government or to one form of government. If he were, he would not be able to deal realistically with the concept of conscience (v. 5).[41] When he tells his readers to be subject he is warning against a spiritualistic withdrawal from earthly matters and urging Christian involvement in this world's structures. For Paul this age (12:2) is still a reality for Christians, and denying its pressures endangers their witness and presence within it. This age is still here, and God's perfect future has not yet arrived. But Christians, while living in this age, are not to be conformed to it. Instead they are to be transformed so that their bodies, earthly and temporal, historically and culturally conditioned, may be presented as a living sacrifice to God. Worship of God in daily life is the constant for Paul; social structures are conditioned, contingent, transitory, and variable.

What happens when structures become obstacles to Christian worship

---

39. A century later Aelius Aristides uses the term *diakonoi* to refer to imperial officials and soldiers in the provinces. They are, of course, *diakonoi* of Caesar. *Orations, Eis romen* 26.89 (in the edition by Bruno Keil, II [Berlin: Weidman, 1898]).

40. It is important to remember that "bearing the sword" in Romans 13 refers to internal political conditions rather than external or international conflict. The issue of confrontation between one governmental authority and another is not raised here.

41. Some find in the reference to conscience in v. 5 the real Pauline accent in the text; Friedrich, Pöhlmann, and Stuhlmacher, *Zur historischen Situation*, 163-64, and Hans-Joachim Eckstein, *Der Begriff Syneidesis bei Paulus* (Tübingen: Mohr, 1983), 276-99, see the concept of conscience as that capacity to evaluate behavior that results from the insights and decisions of the renewed mind of Rom. 12:2.

of God? What happens when Christian conscience, seeking to respond to God's authority, conflicts with the demands of an apparently demonic governing authority? Paul would say that the Christian is not free to absolutize the structure and practice idolatry. Instead Christians are called to worship God, to make evident what the will of God is, what is good, acceptable, and perfect. Christians are called to break through the mythologies of the prevailing cultural religiosity, exposing the gods who are not gods (Gal. 4:8-10; Col. 2:8-23). If idolatry prevails, Christians are not to engage in it, and resistance and revolution may well be a new social structure within which they find themselves called to do their service of worship.[42]

Romans 13:1-7 is not an isolated piece of Pauline parenesis. Its immediate context calls Christians to live within the structures of human existence in a way that makes evident the will of God (see 12:9-21). They are to bless, not curse, those who persecute them. They are to repay no one evil for evil. They are not to avenge themselves but to leave vengeance to God. They are to feed the hungry enemy. They are to overcome evil with good. As far as it depends on them, if the possibility is there, they are to live in peace with everyone.

In Paul's letters, then, the peace that God has established in Christ has implications for how Christians live in the world. Paul's letters include sections of parenesis, in which he indicates how the good news of God's peace is expressed or applied in believers' daily life. Rom. 12:18 and 1 Cor. 7:12-17, for example, make clear that peace is the Christian's practical posture toward those outside the Christian community as well. Paul's students were taught this well, as 2 Tim. 2:22 testifies: Christians are to make peace their aim, along with justice, faith, and love.

The Letters after Paul

After Paul's death the church increasingly began to make its way as an institution in the world, one distinct from Judaism. The letters written

---

42. Friedrich, Pöhlmann, and Stuhlmacher are correct in identifying Paul's argument here, that secular government is the manifestation of God's eschatological rule, the "coordinates" by which God's rule is carried out (*Zur historischen Situation*, 162). However, God's eschatological rule should not be limited in any one instance to an existing temporal authority. It is incorrect to assume that the apostle's argument would automatically, in every case, preclude revolution as also a manifestation of the eschatological rule of God.

after Paul's time portray the peace God established in Christ as offered to the world through the church. Christ is now "the Lord of peace" (2 Thess. 3:16), and Christians are to pursue peace (1 Pet. 3:11; 2 Tim. 2:22), particularly when persecuted (1 Pet. 3:15-17). In the letter to the Hebrews the Old Testament prototype of Jesus' priesthood is that of King Melchizedek of Salem, whose name means "king of righteousness" and also "king of peace" (7:2-3). The letter's readers are admonished to "pursue peace with everyone" (12:14). The message of peace is the continuity between the earthly Jesus and the post-Easter church. Jesus preached the good news of peace "to you who were far off and to those who were near" (Eph. 2:17; cf. Acts 10:36), and now the church's proclamation is the same gospel of peace (Eph. 6:15).

Early Christian Hymns

A number of early Christian hymns preserved in the New Testament speak of Jesus' victory and lordship. They testify that he has conquered the worldly powers, established peace between God and people and among people, and is now exalted at God's right hand. These hymns have a remarkably consistent pattern of thought (Phil. 2:6-11; Col. 1:15-20; Eph. 2:14-16; Heb. 1:3; 1 Tim. 3:16; see also 1 Pet. 3:18-19, 22; John 1:1-18). In contrast to apocalyptic conceptions of the messianic confrontation with the forces of evil, these hymns portray Jesus as the preexistent Lord, whose battle with the evil powers is a cosmic battle, which he wins by entering the human scene and disarming the principalities and powers, making a public example of them and triumphing over them (Col. 2:15). Paul's use of such hymns indicates his awareness of their contribution to the development of christology in the church, though his editorial addition in Phil. 2:8 ("even death on a cross") reflects his uneasiness about their cosmic, otherworldly dimension. Like the Gospel writers, Paul wants to link closely Jesus' victory over the powers with the concrete historical event of the cross. The hymns celebrate Jesus' reign over all creation, with every knee bending and every tongue confessing, "Jesus Messiah is Lord" (Phil. 2:11).

In Eph. 2:14-16 this cosmic victory is translated into a program of relationships among people. This hymn refers to Jesus as our peace, the one who has broken down the dividing wall of hostility between Jew and Gentile and so provided a social framework in which Jew and Gentile can experience unity and have access in one Spirit to the Father (2:18). That social framework is the church, the body of Christ, which now continues Jesus' ministry of fostering reconciliation among people and of bringing hostilities to an end (2:16; see also Col. 1:20).[43]

The Revelation of John of Patmos

The last book in the New Testament canon is addressed to the churches in which Paul had conducted his mission work. It is the only writing in the Christian canon presented as an apocalypse.[44] In many respects, however, this writing constitutes a criticism of traditional apocalyptic thought rather than a repetition of it, especially in its vision that in God's future this world will be transformed rather than destroyed.

The author, John of Patmos, is aware of the pervasiveness of conflict and its effect on the churches to which he writes. Now in exile on the island of Patmos, he shares in their tribulation and persecution (1:9). He knows that some Christians in these churches are being imprisoned (2:10), and mentions by name one believer who has been martyred (2:13). He has firsthand experience of this war of persecution waged against the churches by the Roman state (11:7; 12:17; 13:7; see also 6:9), yet he is also aware that war is a constant ingredient in human life (9:7, 9; 6:1-8). He can depict the present struggle in terms of the primeval cosmic struggle and as an extension of it (12:7, 17), and he portrays its resolution in terms of the great final battle of the end time (16:14; 17:14; 19:19; 20:8).

Using this traditional imagery, John could call his readers to do battle with the evil powers arrayed against them, but he does not. Instead he calls them to reject violent action, even as they are victims of violence:

---

43. Joachim Gnilka, "Christus unser Friede — ein Friedens-Erlöserlied in Eph 2,14-17," *Die Zeit Jesu* (Festschrift for Heinrich Schlier, ed. Günther Bornkamm and Karl Rahner; Freiburg: Herder, 1970), 190-207; Peter Stuhlmacher, "'Er ist unser Friede' (Eph 2,14)," *Neues Testament und Kirche* (Festschrift for Rudolf Schnackenburg, ed. Joachim Gnilka; Freiburg: Herder, 1974]), 337-58.

44. Other apocalyptic material can be found in the New Testament, but only piecemeal (e.g., Mark 13 [and parallels in Matthew 24 and Luke 21]; 1 Thess. 4:13-17; 1 Cor. 15:20-28; 2 Thess. 2:3-14; 1 John 2:18; 2 Pet. 2:1-3:13; 1 Tim. 4:1; 2 Tim. 3:1-9). Jude is almost fully apocalyptic in content, but presents itself as a letter (see Richard L. Jeske, *Revelation for Today: Images of Hope* [Philadelphia: Fortress, 1983], 13.)

"If you are to be taken captive, into captivity you go; if you kill with the sword, with the sword you must be killed. Here is a call for the endurance and faith of the saints" (13:10; see also 14:12; 6:9-11). John calls these Christians to love even those whose actions are deplorable (2:4-6), for only when they love do they represent in the world the one who loves us and died for us (1:5). Their oppression will be overcome not by returning violence with violence but by the advent of the Lord in God's good time. The forces of evil will be vanquished not by Christian participation in the last battle but by their Lord alone, who overcomes the foe by the sword of his mouth, by his word (19:15, 21), a pacifist symbol. The armies that follow him wield no other weapon, nor do they take the spoils (19:21). In fact, the one weapon of victory, the sword of Christ's mouth, may be turned against the church when it capitulates to secular pressures (2:16).

Though the writer presents it as an apocalypse (1:1), the Book of Revelation in many respects is a criticism of traditional apocalyptic expectation. Its emphasis is not on the future but on the present and on the churches' witness to Christ in the present (19:10). The churches, threatened by hostile forces, are in the world as God's instruments for healing among the nations (3:14-22). Therefore Christians should neither run into the wilderness to await Armageddon, nor pass the hours in feverish expectation and paranoid speculation, nor indulge in religious flights into the spiritual stratosphere. God's new world, the holy city, comes down to earth; God dwells among people (21:2) and offers them wholeness and well-being (21:4), healing to the nations (22:2). Far from urging his readers to look past their historical existence to a transcendent future in heaven, John repeatedly calls for their critical involvement in the process of history. The conqueror is the believer who endures in the present struggle, following the example of the crucified Lord (2:7, 11, 17, 26, 28; 3:5, 12, 21). Endurance, not escape; steadfast witness, not rationalizing about the evil world; healing, not hostility, are the marks of Christian life, the marks of God's new world. As Paul had said earlier, if anyone is in Christ, there is a new world (2 Cor. 5:17).

Concluding Observations

According to Luke's Gospel, when some soldiers asked John the Baptist about their penitential obligations, he told them not to extort money from anyone by threats or false accusations, and to be satisfied with their wages (3:14). Jesus encountered a Roman centurion whose faith he extolled (Luke 7:1-10; Matt. 8:5-13), and at the foot of Jesus' cross a Roman centurion confessed that Jesus was the Son of God (Mark 15:39; Matt. 27:54; cf. Luke 23:47).

However, the New Testament offers no evidence that Christians performed military service. There may be many reasons for this, among them the possibility that the first Christian generation enjoyed Judaism's exemption from conscription.[45] Certainly soldiers were recruited into the Christian community (see Phil. 1:13; 4:22), and the New Testament does not report whether they continued in their occupation.[46] However, well into the late decades of the second century, various church fathers wrote that the profession of soldier was not an acceptable one for Christians. Though New Testament writers had opportunity to offer at least a neutral word about the profession (comparable to comments on slavery), their writings are silent on the subject. Even later New Testament texts, which urge Christians to show respect for government (1 Pet. 2:13-17; Titus 3:1), contain no admonitions about being good soldiers.[47] Nowhere does the New Testament encourage Christians to participate in war or even to look forward to doing so in the great final battle of the end time.

45. N. T. Wright, *The New Testament and the People of God* (Minneapolis: Fortress, 1992), makes the point that the land no longer functioned as an identity mark for the new people of God: "If the new community consisted of Jew, Greek, barbarian alike, there was no sense in which one piece of territory could possess more significance than another. At no point in this early period do we find Christians eager to define or defend a 'holy land'" (366).

46. See Klassen, "War in the New Testament," 873.

47. In Eph. 6:13-17 Christians are told to engage confidently in their struggle against the hostile powers of this world. A catalog of military dress is given, with the precise steps for a soldier's preparation for battle: belt, breastplate, shoes, shield, helmet, sword. All of these are neutralized under the heading, "the armor of God": the belt of truth, the breastplate of righteousness, shoes for proclaiming the gospel of peace, the shield of faith, the helmet of salvation, the sword of the Spirit (the word of God). The clear implication is that in the Christian's struggle against the powers of this world, God's armor (truth, righteousness, the gospel of peace, faith, salvation, the word of God) is all that is needed.

7. The Christian Church and the Roman Army in the First Three Centuries

DAVID G. HUNTER

The appearance of this volume reflects a new sensitivity to the problems of peace and warfare emerging in the Christian churches. The many documents on peace issued during the past decade dramatically illustrate this. As the churches respond individually to the challenge of peacemaking, the question raised by this book acquires a new urgency: Is there a Christian vision of peace that can serve as a genuine point of unity among the world's Christians? This chapter reflects on this question from the perspective of early Christian tradition.

The period of the primitive church — from the post-apostolic generation to the accession of Emperor Constantine — is a critical one in the formation of the Christian tradition. The features common to most Christian churches (the canon of New Testament Scripture, creedal formulations, hierarchical structures of government) took shape in this formative period. While churches differ in the theological weight given to tradition relative to Scripture, even the most biblically grounded churches will not fail to acknowledge that the New Testament canon itself is a product of early Christian tradition. The evidence of early Christian thought and practice on war and peace, therefore, may provide some guidance on the question of how the biblical tradition was appropriated and interpreted in the life of the church.

The attitude of the early Christians on the subject of war and peace is a question of unusual complexity. There are, of course, the usual historical difficulties that beset any study of antiquity, such as the paucity of sources and the problem of interpreting materials from a distant culture. In this instance, however, the difficulties are compounded by several other factors. First, there is the fact that Christianity in the first three centuries underwent profound change as it developed from a small and insignificant sect within Judaism to become a major religious force in the Roman Empire. This change in the nature of Christianity brought with it a fundamental reevaluation of the relationship between Christians and the surrounding political and social world, including the question of participation in the Roman state and its wars.

Second, nearly all scholars agree that there was some degree of diversity of opinion and practice among Christians throughout the period under consideration here.[1] In other words, it will often be difficult (and sometimes impossible) to isolate and define *one* Christian position on the issue of war and peace even within a single period. Critical historical scholarship today is extremely sensitive to the pluralistic character of the early Christian movement, and there is a widespread reluctance among scholars to assume that there was always a normative form of early Christian belief or practice.[2]

Third, it will be important to examine closely the reasons early Christian writers gave for objecting to war and military service, when in fact they did object. Recent scholarly work on the question of early Christians and the Roman army has stressed that pacifism or objections to violence may not have been a predominant concern, even for those Christians who did reject military service. Objections to idolatry and to religious practices in the Roman army, some have argued, were the primary reason for early Christian resistance to military service.[3] While

---

1. Modern discussion on this topic was inaugurated by Adolf von Harnack in his little classic, *Militia Christi: Die christliche Religion und der Soldatenstand in den ersten drei Jahrhunderten* (Tübingen: Mohr, 1905). An English translation with a critical introduction has appeared: *Militia Christi: The Christian Religion and the Military in the First Three Centuries*, tr. David McInnes Gracie (Philadelphia: Fortress, 1981).

2. Some important caveats in this regard have recently been issued by Frances Young in "The Early Church: Military Service, War and Peace," *Theology* 92 (1989), 491-503.

3. This position has been most fully developed in the studies of John Helgeland: "Christians and the Roman Army A.D. 173-337," *Church History* 43 (1974), 149-63, 200; and "Christians and the Roman Army from Marcus Aurelius to Constantine," in *Religion (Vorkonstantinisches Christentum: Verhältnis zu römischen Staat und*

such views may be overstated, it remains true that when early Christians gave explicit attention to the question of military service, and when they opposed it, they cited a variety of reasons.[4]

It will be important, therefore, to recognize the complexity of thought of each ancient Christian writer whom we discuss and to try to acknowledge the full range of their intentions. Keeping these various difficulties in mind, this essay will offer an overview of the positions of Christians during the first three centuries on the question of war and peace. In the interest of sensitivity to the evolving contexts of the discussion, I will proceed chronologically. The next section of this paper will explain and provide a rationale for the particular historical framework I have chosen.

Historical Framework

The period under consideration is the first three centuries of Christianity, roughly from the death of Jesus (ca. 30) to the reign of Emperor Constantine (died 337). During this time Christianity underwent a number of dramatic transformations: From a messianic movement within Judaism it became a predominantly Gentile religion that worshiped Christ as God (ca. 50-150); from a new and relatively obscure sect in the Greco-Roman world it became a firmly established and universal church (ca. 150-250); from a minority and still-persecuted body it became the dominant and, eventually, official religion of the Roman Empire (ca. 250-400).

Christian discussion of war, peace, and military service follows the course of the broader development of the church. These different stages in the church's own self-understanding provided new contexts in which the questions of war and peace were addressed. During the earliest phase, especially in the first century, Christians by and large did not expect the

---

heidnischer Religion), ed. Wolfgang Haase, *Aufsteig und Niedergang der römischen Welt: Geschichte und Kultur Roms im Spiegel der neueren Forschung* (hereafter *ANRW*) II.23.1, ed. Hildegard Temporini and Wolfgang Haase (Berlin/New York: de Gruyter, 1979), 724-834. See also John Helgeland, Robert J. Daly, and J. Patout Burns, *Christians and the Military: The Early Experience* (Philadelphia: Fortress, 1985).

4. For a critique of the views of Helgeland and an evaluation of the contemporary discussion, see my essay, "A Decade of Research on Early Christians and Military Service," *Religious Studies Review* 18/2 (1992), 87-94.

world to continue to exist in its current state. Adhering to Jewish apocalyptic notions, many early Christians expected that the return of Christ and the coming of God's kingdom would put an end to all worldly loyalties (cf. 1 Corinthians 7). The documents of the New Testament, therefore, offer only fragmentary and ambivalent guidance on the questions that confront later Christians.

In the second century, Christianity began to spread more widely in Roman society, and Christians had to confront the realities of Greco-Roman culture, including persecution by the Roman authorities. Christian writers known as "apologists" constructed sophisticated defenses of Christianity addressed to the educated elite of Roman society and to the authorities. But in spite of the apologists' efforts to argue for acceptance of Christianity by the Roman government, there is no explicit discussion of military service in any source prior to the end of the second century. The first phase to be discussed, therefore, will be the first two centuries, the period before the question of participation in the army clearly presented itself to Christians.

The second phase to be discussed is the late second and early third centuries. During this period we encounter the first explicit evidence of Christians wrestling with the question of participation in the Roman army, in the writings of Tertullian, Origen, and Hippolytus. As indicated above, this period also witnessed the widespread expansion of the church into the Roman world. During the third century the Christians emerged as a powerful force in the Roman Empire, one that could rival and eventually overcome other forms of Roman religion. In this period, when greater numbers of educated citizens were joining the Christian movement, the question of Christian responsibility to the Roman order presented itself more acutely.

Finally, the third phase to be discussed is the period around the accession of Emperor Constantine (later third and early fourth centuries). Constantine's conversion to Christianity is as well known as it is influential. From this point onward, Christians could no longer regard the Roman state as something alien to themselves. After Christianity became the official religion of the empire under Emperor Theodosius (ca. 391), the question of Christian participation in military service and war became unavoidable as the empire itself claimed the patronage of the Christian God.

It is critical, therefore, that the question of the attitude of the early Christians toward war and military service be treated with some sensitivity to these different phases of historical development. We must clarify

164

which early Christians we are discussing, that is, *when* they wrote, as well as *what* precisely they were (or were not) objecting to when they did (or did not) object to war and military service. We must also be willing to acknowledge that there may not have been *one* ethical position that had sole claim to be called Christian.

Phase One: The First Two Centuries

At the outset, two facts confront the student of the earliest Christian literature. One is the overwhelming emphasis on the peaceable (if not pacifist) nature of the Christian community. This attitude is first evident in the Gospel traditions of Jesus' Sermon on the Mount, which enjoin nonresistance and the love of enemies.[5] It is significant that these words are cited constantly by Christian writers in subsequent centuries. For example, the *Didache,* one of the earliest surviving Christian documents outside the New Testament, places Jesus' prescriptions about nonviolence at the very head of its moral instructions for Christians.[6] "Pray for your enemies," "Love those who hate you," "If someone strikes you on the right cheek, turn to him the other too"; these are some of the verses quoted by the *Didache.*

It is striking how often Christians in this period describe themselves as peacemakers. The theme is especially prominent in the writings of the second-century apologists. Justin Martyr, for example, writing in the middle of the second century, also cites the words of Jesus, while making the point that the peaceable nature of the Christian community offers an attractive witness to outsiders.[7] Justin also sees the spread of Christianity as a fulfillment of the biblical prophecies of Micah and Isaiah ("And they shall beat their swords into plowshares and their spears into pruning hooks").[8] "We who formerly killed one another," Justin writes,

5. Matt. 5:38-48; Luke 6:27-36.
6. *Didache* 1.3-4.
7. *First Apology* 16. The citations of the Sermon on the Mount both in the *Didache* and in the *Apology* of Justin indicate that early Christians regarded the teachings of Jesus as a normative guide for Christian ethics.
8. Justin, *First Apology* 39.2-3, citing Mic. 4:2-3 (Isa. 2:3-4); quoted from Louis J. Swift, *The Early Fathers on War and Military Service* (Message of the Fathers of the Church 19; Wilmington: Glazier, 1983), 35. This passage is also later cited by Irenaeus and Origen (see Knut Willem Ruyter, "Pacifism and Military Service in the Early Church," *Cross Currents* 32 [1982], 54).

"not only refuse to make war on our enemies but in order to avoid lying to our interrogators or deceiving them, we freely go to our deaths confessing Christ."

Similar sentiments are expressed by another apologist, Athenagoras of Athens, writing later in the second century.[9] Athenagoras repeatedly cites Christian nonresistance to evil as a distinctive mark of the church's ethic: "We have learned not only not to return blow for blow, nor to sue those who plunder and rob us, but to those who smite us on one cheek to offer the other also, and to those who take away our coat to give our overcoat as well."[10] Athenagoras then adds that Christians also refuse to attend public executions because "we see little difference between watching a man being put to death and killing him."[11]

It must be noted, however, that the same documents that stress the nonviolent character of the Christian community also assert strongly that Christians are loyal citizens and devoted to the well-being of the Roman Empire.[12] Both positions are arguments that serve the apologetic purpose of the authors. Christians in the second century were faced with Roman suspicions about their secret activities. There is also evidence that the Romans viewed Christians as a possible threat to the political stability of the empire. The Christian apologists responded by affirming both the peaceable nature of the community and the patriotic loyalty of Christians to the Roman state.

We must, therefore, be cautious about taking the statements of the apologists as absolute moral imperatives for all Christians. The apologetic stance of these writers led them to give ideal descriptions of the Christians and their activities; they were not necessarily offering absolute ethical prescriptions for all time. Nonetheless, it seems reasonable to assume that the view of Christians as a peaceable and nonviolent community was widespread enough to make the assertions of the apologists persuasive both to those inside and to those outside the Christian movement.

The second significant fact that confronts the student of early Chris-

9. Athenagoras's *Plea Regarding Christians* dates from 176-77.

10. *Plea* 1.4 (quoted from *Early Christian Fathers*, tr. and ed. Cyril C. Richardson [New York: Macmillan, 1970], 301). Like Justin and the *Didache*, Athenagoras alludes to the teachings of Jesus to illustrate Christian commitment to nonviolence. See also *Plea* 11.

11. *Plea* 35.5 (quoted from Richardson, *Early Christian Fathers*, 338).

12. Justin, *First Apology* 12; Athenagoras, *Plea* 37.

tianity and the military is that no Christian writer of the first two centuries actually deals directly with the question of the permissibility of warfare and military service for Christians. Furthermore this silence on the question corresponds to an absence of evidence that Christians actually participated in military service to any significant extent prior to the closing years of the second century.[13] In short, there is no firm evidence either of participation in the army or of discussion of military service before the end of the second century. How is one to interpret this silence?

Various explanations have been offered. Some scholars (usually those with a pacifist perspective) have suggested that a universal prohibition against military service must have been in effect.[14] In view of the clear New Testament injunctions against violence and retribution, the argument goes, most true Christians would have found it inconceivable to join the army. The Roman persecution of Christians, it is further suggested, would have strengthened this early Christian refusal to participate in military service.

While this argument has its attractiveness, it is not the only possible explanation or even the most likely explanation. More recent scholarship has emphasized that the question of military service simply may not have existed for Christians during the first two centuries, at least not in the form in which it was soon to present itself in the third and subsequent centuries. Membership in the army (with the exception of auxiliary troops) was not open to slaves or freedmen, and many early Christians would have belonged to these groups.[15] There was no involuntary conscription, so no Christian would have found himself forced to choose between enlisting and remaining a Christian.

Moreover, Christians had good reasons other than (or in addition to)

13. The earliest evidence of Christian soldiers dates from late second-century inscriptions. See H. Leclercq, "Militarisme," *Dictionnaire d'archéologie chrétienne et de liturgie* XI/1 (1933), 1108-81; Ruyter, "Pacifism and Military Service in the Early Church," 56-57.

14. Jean-Michel Hornus, *It Is Not Lawful for Me to Fight: Early Christian Attitudes toward War, Violence, and the State*, tr. Alan Kreider and Oliver Coburn (revised ed., Scottdale: Herald, 1980), 14-15; also Roland H. Bainton, "The Early Church and War," *Harvard Theological Review* (hereafter *HTR*) 39 (1946), 191. Both Hornus and Bainton, however, acknowledge that the issue did not really present itself to Christians until the late second century.

15. Louis J. Swift, "War and the Christian Conscience I: The Early Years," *ANRW* II.23.1 (1979), 842-43, is a balanced statement of the case; see also his *Early Fathers on War*, 26-27.

strict pacifism to avoid the Roman army. Foremost among these was the all-pervasive character of Roman army religion. In a series of publications on this theme, John Helgeland has demonstrated that membership in the Roman army entailed entry into a religious structure that shaped the entire life of the soldier: "It created a sacred cosmos in which the soldier lived from the day he entered until he died."[16] The military oath *(sacramentum)*, the cult of the legionary standards, the calendar of frequent military festivals timed to coincide with similar services at Rome, all combined to form a Roman army "religious world, a microcosm of Rome itself."[17]

The problem of idolatry and an aversion to Roman army religion, while not the sole reasons for the early Christian resistance to military service, must have been strong deterrents for any Christians who wished to join the army. On the whole, therefore, the lack of any real discussion of the issue suggests that few Christians in this period were confronted with the choice to enlist and that few converts had been made among those already in the army. While the second-century evidence suggests a strong bias toward nonviolence as a defining characteristic of the Christian community, this inclination did not result in any absolute prohibitions against military service. Furthermore, a reluctance to engage in military service may have been motivated as much by the dangers of Roman army religion as it was by a rejection of violence.

This general tendency for Christians to avoid military service is confirmed by a non-Christian source from this period. In the years between 177 and 180, a Roman philosopher named Celsus directed an attack on Christians in a work called *The True Doctrine*. Fragments of this work are preserved in the apology of Origen, the *Contra Celsum*, in which he attempted to answer the charges of Celsus. Among Celsus's criticisms of Christianity is the charge that Christians shirk their public responsibilities by refusing to take part in military service or public office. While Celsus was by no means a neutral observer of the Christian movement, his remarks must be given serious consideration, since he was the first pagan critic to have investigated Christianity thoroughly, and he knew a great deal about Christian beliefs and practices.[18]

---

16. Helgeland, Daly, and Burns, *Christians and the Military*, 48. See also Arthur Darby Nock, "The Roman Army and the Roman Religious Year," *HTR* 45 (1952), 187-252.

17. Helgeland, Daly, and Burns, *Christians and the Military*, 54.

18. On Celsus as a critic of Christianity, see Robert L. Wilken, *The Christians*

In the context of urging Christians not to abandon the worship of the traditional gods, Celsus had exhorted them, Origen says, to "help the emperor with all our power, and cooperate with him in what is right, and fight for him, and be fellow-soldiers if he presses for this, and fellow-generals with him."[19] Celsus went on to urge Christians to participate in public office "for the sake of the preservation of the laws and of piety."[20] It is clear that Celsus regarded Christian reluctance to worship the gods, abstention from military service, and reluctance to undertake public office as part of a general apolitical stance on the part of the Christian community toward the structures (both religious and political) of Roman society. In his view such a stance implied that the Christians were dangerously deficient in patriotism.

Origen's response to the criticisms of Celsus will be examined below. Here it is enough to note that Celsus's observation coheres with most of the available evidence from the second century. Christians were under no pressure to join the army and had little opportunity or reason to do so. Apparently few converts had yet been made among the soldiers, and there were good religious reasons — apart from the issue of violence — to avoid military service. While Christians in the first two centuries certainly seem to have regarded themselves as a peaceable people, there is no evidence to suggest that this led to any general proscription against military service. The issue simply had not arisen as such.

Phase Two: The Late Second and Early Third Centuries

A significant change is apparent in the later years of the second century and the opening years of the third century. Here we find for the first time several explicit discussions of Christian participation in the Roman army. In the most extended of these, that of the North African writer Tertullian, it is clear that there are some Christian soldiers who see no incompatibility between being Christians and being soldiers. The very

---

as the Romans Saw Them (New Haven: Yale University, 1984), 94-125; also R. Joseph Hoffman, *Celsus: On the True Doctrine: A Discourse against Christians* (New York: Oxford University, 1987).

19. Celsus in Origen, *Contra Celsum* 8.73, tr. Henry Chadwick (Cambridge: Cambridge University, 1953), 509.

20. *Contra Celsum* 8.75 (tr. Chadwick, 510).

fact that there is now some discussion on the subject indicates that some significant new developments have occurred.

The first change seems to have been a shift in the social composition of Christianity itself. By the early years of the third century, Christianity had spread widely in the Roman Empire and had begun to make deep inroads into the higher levels of Greco-Roman society. The very presence of learned exponents of Christianity, such as Tertullian and Cyprian in North Africa or Clement and Origen in Alexandria, suggests that Christianity was gaining adherents who had a new level of respectability and responsibility in society.[21]

At the same time, corresponding changes were occurring within the Roman army itself. From the time of Emperor Septimius Severus (193 C.E.), the power and prestige of the Roman military increased. Severus began a policy of tying military service more closely to local, rural communities. Soldiers also tended to take a greater role in civic offices. As the social historian Ramsay MacMullen has noted, "Many, for their full twenty-five years, did nothing but write; many attended magistrates as messengers, ushers, confidential agents, and accountants, measuring their promotion from chair to chair, from office to office."[22]

These parallel developments in the church and in the Roman army appear to have given encouragement to Christians to enlist. The prohibition against former slaves joining the army was also being relaxed at this time, and military service would have been viewed by many Christians as a path of upward mobility. Because avoiding bloodshed was a real possibility, the Roman army began to attract increasing numbers of soldiers, even from among the Christians.[23]

Christian documents of the early third century that begin to treat the question clearly reflect this situation. Tertullian, who later became a vociferous opponent of Christian military service, in his early *Apology*

21. On this theme, see W. H. C. Frend, *The Rise of Christianity* (Philadelphia: Fortress, 1984), especially 285-97 and 308-14; also Robert M. Grant, "The Christian Population of the Roman Empire," in his *Early Christianity and Society* (San Francisco: Harper and Row, 1977), 1-12.

22. *Soldier and Civilian in the Later Roman Empire* (Cambridge: Harvard University, 1963), 157.

23. For an interesting development of this point, see James Turner Johnson, *The Quest for Peace: Three Moral Traditions in Western Cultural History* (Princeton: Princeton University, 1987), 38-41; also Stephen Gero, "*Miles Gloriosus:* The Christian and Military Service according to Tertullian," *Church History* 39 (1970), 285-298.

for Christianity (ca. 197) notes that Christians serve in the army alongside non-Christians, though he adds that "according to our doctrine it is more permissible to be killed than to kill."[24] Tertullian is also the first writer to refer to the incident of the *legio XII Fulminata* (the so-called Thundering Legion), when the armies of the emperor Marcus Aurelius (ca. 173) were saved from a military defeat allegedly through the prayers of Christian soldiers.[25] In this early apology Tertullian seems indifferent, if not positively disposed, toward a Christian presence in the army.

In later works Tertullian appears much more intransigent on the issue. In his treatise *On Idolatry* he raises the twofold question: "Whether a member of the faithful can become a soldier and whether a soldier can be admitted to the Faith, even if he is a member of the rank and file who are not required to offer sacrifice or decide capital cases."[26] Tertullian's answer to this question is famous and uncompromising: "There can be no compatibility between an oath *(sacramentum)* made to God and one made to man, between the standard of Christ and that of the devil, between the camp of light and the camp of darkness. The soul cannot be beholden to two masters, God and Caesar."[27]

Tertullian is opposed both to baptized Christians joining the army and to enlisted soldiers being received into the church (unless they have abandoned the military profession). His primary concern seems to be the inherently idolatrous character of military service. It is not merely the officer, who actually conducts the pagan sacrifices or capital punishment, who is implicated in idolatry, Tertullian argues. Rather, the very presence of the Christian in the army camp is a sign of his participation in the cult of demons. The soldier's oath of allegiance to the emperor (the *sacramentum*), as Tertullian sees it, pledges an ultimate loyalty that stands in conflict with the Christian's baptismal commitment.

It is important to see, however, that Tertullian's rejection of military service is not based solely on the problem of idolatry or rival

---

24. *Apology* 37.4 (quoted from Swift, *Early Fathers on War*, 39).

25. *Apology* 5.6. The incident is recounted at length in Eusebius, *Church History* 5.5. While the event may have some basis in fact, the crediting of the victory to the intercession of Christians was probably a Christian apologetic invention. Contemporary pagan sources that mention the event do not speak of the Christian role. Cf. the discussion in Swift, "War and the Christian Conscience," 845; also Helgeland, Daly, and Burns, *Christians and the Military*, 31-34.

26. *On Idolatry* 19.1 (quoted from Swift, *Early Fathers on War*, 41).

27. *On Idolatry* 19.2 (quoted from Swift, *Early Fathers on War*, 41).

religious loyalties. He goes on in the passage just cited to speak specifically about the immorality of violence and bloodshed:

> Moses, to be sure, carried a rod; Aaron wore a military belt and John had a breast plate. If one wants to play around with the topic, Jesus, son of Nun [i.e., Joshua] led an army and the Jewish nation went to war. But how will a Christian do so? Indeed how will he serve in the army even during peacetime without the sword that Jesus Christ has taken away? Even if soldiers came to John and got advice on how they ought to act, even if the centurion became a believer, the Lord, by taking away Peter's sword, disarmed every soldier thereafter.[28]

Tertullian does not seem to distinguish clearly the strictly religious problem of idolatrous conduct from the more directly ethical question of the morality of killing. Both of these in his mind are incompatible with true Christianity; both idolatry and killing were forbidden by Jesus. Therefore, as Tertullian sees it, military service itself is forbidden to Christians because it violates their primary allegiance to the ethical and religious mandates of Christ.

It is worth noting that Tertullian's position was not the only one taken by Christians at this time. The very argument he presents in the treatise *On Idolatry* suggests that there were Christians who defended their presence in the army by appealing to examples from the Old and New Testaments (e.g., Moses, Aaron, Joshua, John the Baptist, and the Roman centurion who believed in Jesus). A later work by Tertullian, *On the Military Crown*, confirms the fact that many Christians in the army were untroubled either by the danger of idolatry or by the possibility of using violence.[29]

It is difficult to determine which position was dominant in the third century. Roughly contemporary with Tertullian is the church order known as the *Apostolic Tradition*, attributed to Hippolytus, a presbyter at Rome. Canon 16 of this document deals with a variety of professions (e.g., prostitution) and practices (e.g., concubinage) that are prohibited for Christians. Regarding military-service, the text notes that "a soldier under authority [i.e., in lower ranks] shall not kill a man. If he is ordered to, he shall not carry out the order; nor shall he take the oath. If he is

---

28. *On Idolatry* 19.2-3 (quoted from Swift, *Early Fathers on War*, 41-42).

29. The same situation seems to obtain in the work of Clement of Alexandria, who mentions in passing and without apparent concern the presence of Christians in the army (*Exhortation to the Greeks* 10.100.2).

unwilling, let him be rejected."[30] The document goes on to speak of higher ranks of soldiers: "He who has the power of the sword, or is a magistrate of a city who wears the purple, let him cease or be rejected."[31] Finally, the question of Christians enlisting in the army is raised: Catechumens or believers "who want to become soldiers should be rejected, because they have despised God."[32]

The *Apostolic Tradition* clearly forbids killing and thus should be regarded as a witness to the pacifist tendency in early Christian thought. It must be noted, however, that the text does not forbid a soldier to remain in the army, as long as he abstains from bloodshed. This concession is a tacit acknowledgement of the increasing numbers of Christians in the army. It also reveals the manner in which the Roman military gradually gained acceptance in Christian circles. But by absolutely forbidding enlistment, the text remains a powerful witness to the nonviolent tradition in early Christianity.

The antimilitarist strand in early Christian thought reaches a high point in the writings of Origen, a distinguished scholar who lived and taught at Alexandria and Caesarea in Palestine (died ca. 250). Rightly described as "the most articulate and eloquent pacifist in the early Christian Church,"[33] Origen discusses the Christian's participation in military service most explicitly in the *Contra Celsum*. As we have seen, Celsus complained that Christians failed to support the Roman Empire, refusing to participate in its wars or to undertake public service. Origen responds by distinguishing forms of service to the empire that are forbidden to Christians from forms that are permitted.

First, Origen strongly asserts that Christians are absolutely forbidden to participate in warfare or any kind of bloodshed. He bases this on the teaching of Jesus: "[Jesus] taught that it was never right for his disciples to go so far against a man, even if he should be very wicked; for he did not consider it compatible with his inspired legislation to allow the taking of

---

30. *Apostolic Tradition* 16.17. I have followed the translation of Geoffrey J. Cuming in *Hippolytus: A Text for Students* (Bramcote: Grove, 1976), 16. Dix and Chadwick translate the subject of the sentence as "a soldier in authority," i.e., an officer in the army. See *The Treatise on the Apostolic Tradition of St Hippolytus of Rome: Bishop and Martyr*, ed. Gregory Dix, reissued with corrections, preface, and bibliography by Henry Chadwick (London: SPCK, 1968), 26.

31. *Apostolic Tradition* 16.18 (tr. Cuming, 16).

32. *Apostolic Tradition* 16.19 (tr. Cuming, 16).

33. Swift, *Early Fathers on War*, 60.

human life in any form at all."[34] Christians, Origen continues, "have been taught not to defend themselves against their enemies; and because they have kept the laws which command gentleness and love to man, on this account they have received from God that which they could not have succeeded in doing if they had been given the right to make war."[35]

Origen here follows the primitive Christian tradition that we have seen in the writings of the apologists and in the *Didache:* a belief that the teachings of Jesus provide clear ethical precepts forbidding the use of violence or bloodshed. Later in the *Contra Celsum,* when responding directly to Celsus's exhortation that Christians should take up arms and fight for the empire, Origen states that Christians must abstain from killing, just as pagan priests must keep themselves undefiled from bloodshed in order to offer sacrifice in purity:

> If, then, this is reasonable, how much more reasonable is it that, while others fight, Christians also should be fighting as priests and worshippers of God, keeping their right hands pure and by their prayers to God striving for those who fight in a righteous cause and for the emperor who reigns righteously, in order that everything which is opposed and hostile to those who act rightly may be destroyed?[36]

This passage is of particular importance because in it Origen holds two positions that are in some tension. On the one hand, it is clear that the Christian is not allowed to participate directly in any sort of military activity that involves shedding blood. On the other hand, Origen freely admits that there is such a thing as a righteous emperor and such a thing as a righteous or just cause for war. Furthermore, Origen sees the Christian taking an active role in the battle for justice, but only in a nonviolent way. The Christian participates in the defense of political society by prayer, thereby going to the root of the problem.

Behind these assertions lies Origen's view that demons are the original cause of the evil of warfare. The positive role that Christians play for Roman society is to vanquish the forces of evil through prayer:

> Moreover, we who by our prayers destroy all daemons which stir up wars, violate oaths, and disturb the peace, are of more help to the

---

34. *Contra Celsum* 3.7 (tr. Chadwick, 132).
35. *Contra Celsum* 3.8 (tr. Chadwick, 133).
36. *Contra Celsum* 8.73 (tr. Chadwick, 509).

emperors than those who seem to be doing the fighting. We who offer prayers with righteousness . . . are cooperating in the tasks of the community.[37]

In these texts Origen sums up two distinct Christian traditions: He reaffirms the Christians' loyalty to the Roman state while at the same time reasserting the traditional Christian commitment to nonviolence.[38] By so doing, he bequeaths to posterity an ambiguous legacy. The pacifist tradition is stated with a precision and clarity unmatched in earlier writers. But, at the same time, some of Origen's statements point in the direction of what will later become the Christian just war theory.[39] While acknowledging a specifically Christian vocation to prayer and nonviolence, Origen admits that Christians have a genuine responsibility to pursue justice in the social order.

Phase Three: Late Third and Early Fourth Centuries

Origen's eloquent testimony to the pacifist character of the Christian community sums up the second phase in the church's reflection on the problem of war and military service. In the later decades of the third century and early years of the fourth century, a new period is entered. In the year 260 the emperor Gallienus, tired of fruitless attempts to suppress the Christian movement, issued an edict granting religious toleration to all sects in the Roman Empire.[40] For the next forty years the church experienced an unprecedented period of peace and was free to expand and develop unhindered by persecution. By the year 303, when the Great Persecution of the emperor Diocletian began, Christians were to be found at all levels of Roman society, including, it seems, among the troops closest to the emperor himself.[41]

---

37. *Contra Celsum* 8.73 (tr. Chadwick, 509).

38. On the former point, see Origen's citation of 1 Tim. 2:1-2 in *Contra Celsum* 8.73.

39. Helgeland, Daly, and Burns, *Christians and the Military*, 40; Gerard E. Caspary, *Politics and Exegesis: Origen and the Two Swords* (Berkeley: University of California, 1979).

40. Robert M. Grant, *Augustus to Constantine: The Rise and Triumph of Christianity in the Roman World* (San Francisco: Harper and Row, 1990), 171-72.

41. Lactantius, *On the Death of the Persecutors* 10.1-4, records that Diocletian's

Two distinct sets of evidence are available from this period immediately before the accession of Constantine. First, several accounts of
Christian soldier martyrs are extant and provide important information
about the actual practice of Christians between the years 260 and 303.
Second, the writings of Lactantius, an important Christian rhetorician
and apologist, offer a special insight into the pacifist tradition on the eve
of Constantine. Lactantius also provides evidence of the transformation
of this tradition under the Christian emperor.

The *acta* of the military martyrs present clear evidence that there were
Christian soldiers who found it possible to reconcile their faith with military
service; they also show that there were times when such accommodation
was impossible. The critical factor seems to have been the command to
sacrifice. For example, in *The Martyrdom of St. Marinus,* the story of a soldier
executed at Caesarea in Palestine around the year 260, we learn that
Marinus was a soldier who had been "honoured with many posts in the army
and was known for his wealth and his good family."[42] Only when Marinus
was eligible for a promotion that would have required him to administer
sacrifices did his Christian faith become an obstacle to military service.[43]

Later accounts of military martyrs from the reign of Diocletian
confirm this picture. Maximilian, a young recruit who was being forced
by his father to enlist (ca. 295), refused to accept the leaden military
seal.[44] It is not clear whether bloodshed or idolatry was the primary
problem; neither is mentioned explicitly. Maximilian's comment that the
military seal *(signaculum)* is incompatible with the seal *(signum)* of Christ[45]
echoes Tertullian and may suggest that religious loyalty was the main
issue. What is clear, however, is that not all Christians shared the reser-
vations of Maximilian. When the proconsul Dion pointed out to Maximilian that there were other Christian soldiers, even in the bodyguard

---

persecution began when certain soldiers made the sign of the cross during a sacrifice.
Diocletian, disturbed by the presence of Christians at these rites, demanded that all
soldiers be compelled to sacrifice. See also Eusebius, *Church History* 8.1.7.

42. *The Acts of the Christian Martyrs,* introduction, texts, and tr. Herbert Musurillo
(Oxford: Clarendon, 1972), 241. The text is from Eusebius, *Church History* 7.15.

43. Furthermore, the question of his suitability for higher office was raised
not by Marinus himself, but by a non-Christian rival who denounced him to his
superiors. According to the text, Marinus himself seems to have been willing to
accept the promotion (Musurillo, *Acts,* 241).

44. Musurillo, *Acts,* 244-49.

45. *Ibid.,* 246.

of the emperors, who served in the army without scruple, Maximilian simply acknowledged that "they know what is best for them. But I am a Christian and I cannot do wrong."[46]

Similarly, *The Acts of Marcellus* tells of a Roman centurion who was imprisoned for refusing to worship the gods during a joint birthday celebration for the emperors Maximian and Diocletian (ca. 298). Marcellus did say that "it is not fitting that a Christian, who fights for Christ his Lord, should fight for the armies of this world."[47] And yet Marcellus had advanced to the rank of centurion without any pangs of conscience. While some objection to bloodshed may be suggested in this text, the more dominant theme is Marcellus's objection to idolatry: "I am a soldier of Jesus Christ, the eternal king. From now I cease to serve your emperors and I despise the worship of your gods of wood and stone, for they are deaf and dumb images."[48] The supposition of the story is that Marcellus was in no danger until the issue of sacrifice had arisen.

Perhaps the clearest evidence that some committed Christians felt free to serve and fight as soldiers is the account of *The Martyrdom of Julius the Veteran*. Julius was a soldier who had served faithfully for twenty-seven years. How much of that time Julius was a Christian we do not know. What is known, however, is that it was only during the persecution of Diocletian, when soldiers were required to sacrifice, that the incompatibility between Christianity and the Roman army became apparent to Julius. When summoned before his superior, Julius stated:

> I cannot despise the divine commandments or appear unfaithful to my God. In all the twenty-seven years in which I made the mistake, so it appears, to serve foolishly in the army, I was never brought before a magistrate either as a criminal or a trouble-maker. I went on seven military campaigns, and never hid behind anyone nor was I the inferior of any man in battle. My chief never found me at fault. And now do you suppose that I, who was always found to be faithful in the past, should now be unfaithful to higher orders?[49]

Like the other *acta* of the martyrs, the story of Julius the veteran suggests that many Christians in the later years of the third century could serve

46. *Ibid.*, 247.
47. *Ibid.*, 253.
48. *Ibid.*, 251.
49. *Ibid.*, 261.

in the army and engage in warfare without fearing that this compromised their Christian faith. Only when confronted with the command to sacrifice to the gods, as a result of the policies of Diocletian, did the soldier martyrs take a clear stand against military service.

The final evidence in this period for the attitude of Christians toward the Roman army is the work of Lactantius. Lactantius's career spanned the closing decades of the third century and the opening years of the fourth. He was a native of North Africa who served as a teacher of Latin rhetoric in Bithynia at the invitation of Emperor Diocletian. In 303 Lactantius was forced to resign his position when Diocletian's persecution began. About 317 he was summoned to Gaul by the new emperor, Constantine, to serve as tutor to his son Crispus. Because of his experience and travel, Lactantius is a valuable witness to the diverse views of Christians in the period we are considering.

The primary source for Lactantius's views is his *Divine Institutes,* a long apology for Christianity written between the years 304 and 311. Throughout this work Lactantius speaks out strongly against any form of bloodshed, whether by capital punishment or in warfare. He appears to allow no room for exceptions:

> For when God forbids killing, he is not only ordering us to avoid armed robbery, which is contrary even to public law, but He is forbidding what men regard as ethical. Thus, it is not right for a just man to serve in the army since justice itself is his form of service. Nor is it right for a just man to charge someone with a capital crime. It does not matter whether you kill a man with the sword or with a word since it is killing itself that is prohibited. And so there must be no exception to this command of God. Killing a human being whom God willed to be inviolable is always wrong.[50]

Lactantius here echoes the pacifist views of Tertullian and Origen. The absolute prohibition against military service is based on an absolute prohibition against killing.

What is curious about Lactantius, however, is that he seems to have modified these views after the military successes of emperors who were sympathetic to Christians. In his work *On the Death of the Persecutors,* composed sometime between 316 and 321, Lactantius praises the victories of Licinius and Constantine over those emperors who persecuted Chris-

---

50. *Divine Institutes* 6.20.15-17 (quoted from Swift, *Early Fathers on War,* 62-63).

tians.[51] Lactantius is one of the ancient sources that records the famous story of Constantine's dream in which the emperor was instructed to put the sign of Christ on the soldiers' shields.[52] Furthermore, Lactantius can confidently regard Constantine as God's divinely appointed agent to restore justice and exact divine vengeance on the wicked.[53]

Lactantius seems to embody, at different stages in his life, both traditions that we have seen in the early church. In his earlier writings Lactantius followed the pacifist tradition represented by writers such as Tertullian and Origen; in later years, in response to the developments under Constantine, he appears willing to acknowledge a legitimate place for warfare, at least in the service of the Christian God. If, as Tertullian and other sources indicate, there were Christians serving in the army at least from the end of the second century, Lactantius's later position coheres with the stance of those Christians who found only idolatry, and not bloodshed, to be in conflict with the Christian conscience. Lactantius's volte-face anticipates the position that will become the majority view from this point onward.

Summary

I have suggested in this essay that Christian tradition in the first three centuries was divided on the question of warfare and military service. During the first two centuries there was a very strong emphasis on the peaceable nature of the Christian community. Although the question of Christian participation in the Roman army does not seem to have presented itself as such to most Christians, a strong current of opinion stressed that Christians did not resist evil with evil or violence with violence.

In the closing years of the second century and early years of the third, we find the first explicit evidence of a Christian discussion of the issue. Opinion was clearly divided, although the most vocal writers (Tertullian, Hippolytus, Origen) were clearly opposed to military service, especially when it involved killing. During the later years of the third century and early years of the fourth, there is increasing evidence of Christian participation in the Roman army. When Christianity was

---

51. See *On the Death of the Persecutors* 46.1-7 on the victory of Licinius over Maximinus.
52. *On the Death of the Persecutors* 44.5.6.
53. *Divine Institutes* 1.1.13-16 (quoted from Swift, *Early Fathers on War,* 67-68).

tolerated and pagan sacrifice was not enforced, many Christians seem to have justified their participation in the army. The only writer in this period to disapprove of military service, the apologist Lactantius, does not appear to have persisted in this opinion, especially after it became clear that an emperor might favor the Christian movement.

The Ecumenical Challenge

What does this survey of the ancient evidence have to say to the churches today in search of a common witness on war and peace? First, it can be argued that the pluralism of Christian witness among the churches today has a ground in the pluralism of the early church. From the very time when military service became a real option for Christians, there is evidence that Christians responded to it in a variety of ways. Recent scholarship, therefore, has challenged the views of an earlier generation that saw the early Christians as predominantly or exclusively pacifist.[54] The witness of the first three centuries does not provide the Christian today with a univocal mandate for pacifism.

Second, despite this pluralism in Christian practice, the evidence of the first three centuries suggests that there was a strong and consistent tradition that saw peacemaking as a primary mark of the church. This was a dominant theme in the writers of the first two centuries and in those writers of the third century who addressed the question of military service. Even later authors, such as Augustine of Hippo, who justify Christian participation in warfare in very limited respects, do not depart very far from the earlier pacifist strand in Christian thought.[55] Such a tradition is not to be taken lightly.

In other words, while it cannot be argued that pacifism was a moral

54. See my survey cited in note 4 above, in which I attempt to define the former "pacifist consensus" (characterized by the work of C. J. Cadoux, Roland Bainton, and Jean-Michel Hornus) and to chart the way in which this has given way to a "new consensus" that stresses pluralism.

55. This is the conclusion of a number of recent studies on Augustine. See R. A. Markus, "Saint Augustine's Views on the 'Just War,'" in W. J. Sheils, ed., The Church and War (Studies in Church History 20; Oxford: Blackwell, 1983), 1-13; F. H. Russell, "Love and Hate in Medieval Warfare: The Contribution of St. Augustine," Nottingham Medieval Studies 31 (1987), 108-24; D. A. Lenihan, "The Just War Theory in the Work of St. Augustine," Augustinian Studies 19 (1988), 37-70.

absolute in the early church, the witness of the first three centuries does provide the contemporary church with a model of how a degree of legitimate pluralism might be coupled with a common vision of peacemaking. Perhaps the task of the churches ought to be less that of determining what precise ethical position should be taken on the issue of participation in or abstention from warfare and more that of fostering the conditions that make peace possible in the world. A more positive agenda may prove to be a more reliable basis for Christian unity than a simple prohibition against violence.

Third, several of the ancient sources suggest that the issue of warfare and killing was inseparable from the broader issue of Christians' stance toward the world. Tertullian saw the question as one of Christians' ultimate allegiance to Christ, not to the Roman emperor. Origen looked at the matter from the perspective of a specifically Christian vocation to prayer and not to violence. Both writers challenge Christians to look beyond the (sometimes idolatrous) demands of particular nations and to recognize the common vocation of Christians and the final lordship of Christ. Such a challenge might serve as the basis of a common witness among the churches.

Finally, all Christian churches acknowledge the genuine need for continued growth in fidelity to the gospel of Christ. It may be the case that the Christian churches are only now beginning faithfully to hear Christ's call to peace. The prominent place given in recent church statements to pacifism as a legitimate Christian option is one illustration of how nonviolence may be a stance toward which the churches are growing.[56] In other words, the pluralism of ancient and modern Christianity on questions of war and peace does not preclude the possibility of a more unified witness in the future.

56. See, for example, National Conference of Catholic Bishops, *The Challenge of Peace: God's Promise and Our Response, A Pastoral Letter on War and Peace* (Washington: United States Catholic Conference, 1983), par. 111-21.

8. The Historic Peace Churches: From Sectarian Origins to Ecumenical Witness

DONALD F. DURNBAUGH AND
CHARLES W. BROCKWELL, JR.

During the sixteenth, seventeenth, and eighteenth centuries in European Christianity several ecclesial communities emerged that regard pacifism or nonresistance as a defining mark of the true church. Their pacifism is closely linked with their understanding of church-state relationships, which is in turn rooted in their scriptural hermeneutics. Seeking a return to the life and virtue of the primitive church, the evangelical radicals looked to the New Testament to guide their faith and practice. The old church to a greater extent and the Protestant state churches to a lesser extent held tradition as authoritative. This difference between the old church and the mainline Protestant state churches, on the one hand, and the progenitors of the historic peace churches, on the other hand, resulted in divergent definitions of the church and conflicting conclusions about how the church relates to the world. Thus these polarizations of this period center around different models of Christian community and witness.

Origins of the Historic Peace Churches

"The Anabaptists (now the Mennonites and the Hutterites), the Quakers, and the Brethren are popularly called the 'historic peace churches,' not because other churches are not concerned for peace but because these groups have refused to take part in war."[1] This generalization holds true for the formative periods of their beginnings: The Anabaptists emerged from the Radical Reformation of the sixteenth century, the Religious Society of Friends (Quakers) from radical Puritanism of the seventeenth century, and the Brethren from radical Pietism in the eighteenth century. Particularly in modern times, some members of these groups have entered the military, but the official positions of the churches have upheld the peace testimony.

The Unity of Brethren

Other communions have also held this witness. Prominent among them was the Unity of Brethren *(Unitas Fratrum),* also known as the Bohemian Brethren and Moravian Brethren (Czech Brethren). The Unity emerged from the radical wing of the Hussite movement in fifteenth-century Bohemia. The group formally separated in 1467 under the leadership of Brother Gregory of Rehor, nephew of the Hussite archbishop Jan Roky-cana. Some scholars suggest the influence of the earlier Waldensian movement in this formation. After 1467 they called themselves *Jednota Bratrska* (Fellowship of Brethren or *Unitas Fratrum*).

The intellectual leader of the Unity was Petr Chelcicky (ca. 1390– ca. 1460). In his classic work *The Net of Faith* and elsewhere, Chelcicky attacked the union of church and state, the class system, and Christians serving as soldiers. He taught simple living, adherence to the Sermon on the Mount, and strict church discipline. "His model Christian was the simple countryman — a farmer or village craftsman — who kept aloof from city life."[2]

By the end of the fifteenth century the Unity divided, as members of the nobility and bourgeoisie were attracted to the ranks. University-trained Lukas of Prague (died 1528) headed the victorious "Major Party"; he softened the earlier uncompromising asceticism and upheld faith without works. In 1495 at the second conference of Rychnov, Major

---

1. Roland H. Bainton, *Christian Attitudes toward War and Peace: A Historical Survey and Critical Re-Evaluation* (Nashville: Abingdon, 1960), 152.
2. Peter Brock, *Freedom from Violence: Sectarian Nonresistance from the Middle Ages to the Great War* (Toronto: University of Toronto, 1991), 23.

Party leaders decreed that the writings of both Gregory and Chelcicky should no longer be considered authoritative. Many members were added to the Czech Brethren, who made common cause with the Lutherans in 1542. Many of the Brethren migrated to Poland, where they united with the Calvinists in 1555.

Although the Unity flourished during this time, the Hapsburg rulers regarded them as heretics, and adherents faced increasing pressure during the Counter-Reformation. Finally, after the outbreak of the Thirty Years' War and the defeat of the Protestant cause at the Battle of the White Mountain in 1620, the Unity was totally suppressed. Their famous bishop, educator, and scholar, Johann Amos Comenius (1592-1670), and other leaders went into exile. Their church life as an organized body ceased.

For a century the hidden seed of the Unity was passed on secretly in a few persistent families, who occasionally gathered clandestinely in deep forests. In 1722 the remaining Brethren living in Moravia found refuge on Count Nicholaus Ludwig von Zinzendorf's Saxon estate, called *Herrnhut* (the watch of the Lord). In the wake of a Pietist revival in 1727, the Renewed Moravian Church was organized under the leadership of Zinzendorf (1700-60). It became known after 1732 for its remarkable efforts in foreign missions, first in the West Indies and North America, and later in other parts of the world.

The Moravians taught converts to follow peaceable pursuits. This was notably the case with their successful missions among native Americans. Tragically, belligerent American colonists did not acknowledge their nonresistant posture and conducted several bloody massacres of Moravian Indians in Pennsylvania and Ohio. Moravians for the most part held to their pacifist principles through the Revolutionary War but gave them up by the mid-nineteenth century.

Anabaptists / Mennonites

The Anabaptist movement of the sixteenth century crystallized almost simultaneously in several geographical areas — the Swiss cantons, southern Germany, central and northern Germany, the Netherlands, and elsewhere. Anticlericalism, peasant unrest, humanism, and apocalypticism merged to trigger radical religious activity. The reform ideas of Martin Luther, Ulrich Zwingli, Andreas Rudolff-Bodenstein von Karlstadt, and Thomas Münzer were in the air.

The Swiss Brethren movement in and near Zurich in the 1520s can stand as exemplary for other similar movements.[3] Younger associates of Ulrich Zwingli (ca. 1484-1531) in his reform of Zurich, including Konrad Grebel (ca. 1498-1526), Felix Mantz (1500-27), and Georg Blaurock (died 1529), became dissatisfied with the pace of reform and urged Zwingli to push ahead with changes in rite and practice with or without the approval of the city fathers. When Zwingli refused, they broke with him and proceeded to go their own way. The baptism of Blaurock by Grebel in January 1525 has been taken as the birthdate of the Anabaptist ("rebaptizer") movement.

Baptism of adult believers was seen as the hallmark of the movement, but it reflected more basic tenets. These new believers sought to follow Jesus Christ in all things as disciples, took the Scriptures as their authority, and came to believe that religious liberty was of paramount importance: The church should follow its Lord, unconstrained by the state. Church discipline, according to the rule of Christ (Matt. 18:15-20) was to become their pattern, resulting in an obedient and covenanted body looking to the primitive church as its model.

Anabaptist evangelists spread their views widely, and the authorities' attempts to punish their disobedience also resulted in the dissemination of their beliefs. In some areas entire towns (for example, Waldshut, under Balthasar Hubmaier [died 1528], the most articulate theologian to join Anabaptist ranks) accepted the new teachings. It soon became necessary to enunciate the core principles of Anabaptist belief because of challenges from the right (authorities and established churches) and the left (radical seekers who vested authority in their own revelations).

Early in 1527 a group of Anabaptist leaders gathered in Schleitheim, a town near the Swiss–South German border, and worked out the Brotherly Union, often referred to as the Schleitheim Confession of Faith. Michael Sattler (died 1527) was its principal author. The confession rests on a concept of the church as the community of those who imitate Christ. That community and all spiritual things exist in radical disjunction with the world. The confession's scriptural appeal is to the New Testament, especially to the Gospels. "Obedience, discipleship, and the imitation of Christ are the recurrent words in the Anabaptist confessions."[4]

---

3. We take this approach for the sake of brevity, aware that recent historiography of sixteenth-century Anabaptism has highlighted diversity within the movement rather than emphasizing common features.

4. Bainton, *Christian Attitudes*, 154.

The fourth and sixth Schleitheim articles are most relevant to our topic. Article four on separation provides the key: "Now there is nothing else in the world and all creation than good or evil, believing and unbelieving, darkness and light, the world and those who are [come] out of the world, God's temple and idols, Christ and Belial, and none will have part with the other." God calls us "to become separated from the evil one."

> From all this we should learn that everything which has not been united with our God in Christ is nothing but an abomination which we should shun. By this are meant all popish and repopish [mainline Protestant] works and idolatry. . . . Thereby shall also fall away from us the diabolical weapons of violence — such as sword, armor, and the like, and all of their use to protect friends or against enemies — by virtue of the word of Christ: "you shall not resist evil."[5]

The sixth and longest article deals with the sword, the state, and the state's use of violence: "The sword is an ordering of God outside the perfection of Christ." Citing Matt. 11:29 and John 8:1-11, the confession states that in "the perfection of Christ" the Christian should not "use the sword against the wicked for the protection and defense of the good, or for the sake of love."[6] Additional scriptural guidance is found in Luke 12:13-14; John 6:15; Mark 8:34 (Matt. 16:24; Luke 9:23); Mark 10:42-44 (Matt. 20:25-28); Rom. 8:29-30; and 1 Pet. 2:21.

The sword is of the flesh, Christians are of the Spirit. The citizenship of others is in this world, the citizenship of the Christian is in heaven. People of the world are armed with steel and iron, "but Christians are armed with the armor of God, with truth, righteousness, peace, faith, salvation, and with the Word of God. . . . Since the Christ is as is written of Him, so must His members also be the same, so that his body may remain whole and unified for its own advancement and upbuilding."[7] For these reasons, the Schleitheim confession's signers concluded that Christians should not become magistrates or become involved in government affairs. Government rested on coercion, and Christians could not use force.

---

5. John H. Yoder, tr. and ed., *The Legacy of Michael Sattler* (Classics of the Radical Reformation 1; Scottdale: Herald, 1973), 38.

6. *Ibid.*, 39.

7. *Ibid.*, 40-41.

While this programmatic rejection of violence was to become constitutive of the Anabaptist movement, there was one notable aberration. In 1534-35 revolutionary Anabaptists seized control of the town of Münster and defended it by force when it was besieged by Protestant and Catholic armies (who could agree on the dangers of Anabaptism). Violent leaders used terror to control residents and called true believers to flock to their banners to await the second coming of Christ. The Münster Anabaptists were bloodily suppressed. This isolated incident was used to discredit all Anabaptists as revolutionaries and terrorists.

In the wake of the Münster debacle, the Dutch former priest Menno Simons (1496-1561) provided a positive alternative for stricken Anabaptists in the Netherlands and northern Germany. His pastoral leadership and spirited written defense brought structure and support to the movement, which took his name in gratitude (and also to distance themselves from the Münsterites). Notable among Menno's writings was the *Foundation of Christian Doctrine* (1539).

Among Anabaptist refugees from the Tyrol and southern Germany who found asylum in Moravia, a communitarian group coalesced in 1528. They were called the Hutterian Brethren, after Jakob Hutter (died 1536), who gave them strategic leadership before he was captured and executed. Despite recurrent oppressive actions by the imperial authorities, local Moravian rulers provided a high degree of protection. This allowed the Hutterite movement to expand to a membership of about thirty thousand in one hundred colonies in the later sixteenth century, the group's golden age.

The forces of the Counter-Reformation dispersed this idyll, pushing the fleeing Hutterian Brethren into Hungary and Transylvania after 1622, and on to the Ukraine by the early nineteenth century. Many left the Ukraine in the 1870s because of the Czarist imposition of military conscription and found new places of refuge in the northwestern United States and the western provinces of Canada. Despite some difficulties during the world wars, the Hutterites continue to flourish in these locations.

The Religious Society of Friends

Radical Puritanism of the seventeenth century was the matrix of the movement that took the name Religious Society of Friends. They were mockingly called Quakers, a nickname for the society's adherents eventually used by both insiders and outsiders. The period of Cromwell's commonwealth and protectorate in England, following the overthrow of the monarchy, was a time of religious as well as political turmoil. Many religiously concerned people, called Seekers, dropped out of organized ecclesiastical activities to pursue their spiritual quest.

After 1652, under the guidance of George Fox (1624-91), James Nayler (1617-60), and others, a Society of Friends took shape from among these Seekers. The society grew rapidly, despite early lack of organization. Adherents traveled throughout the British Isles and abroad to give testimony to the faith that was in them. The movement persisted through the end of the century, through the restoration of the Stuart monarchy in 1660 and the reestablishment of the Church of England. Sharp repressive measures followed these developments, and fifteen thousand Quakers were jailed and nearly five hundred died as a result of imprisonment before the Act of Toleration was issued in 1689.

Although Friends became noted for their peace witness, the earliest period of their existence was not marked by complete pacifism. Some Friends served in Cromwell's Ironside Army, and Fox himself approved the use of force to oppose irreligion and the papacy. After 1660, however, the Quaker position against warfare and violence became clearer. Fox and other leaders distanced themselves from the violent attempt of the Fifth Monarchy Men to overthrow the government in 1661. They rejected war and fighting, which proceed "from the lusts of men" (Jas. 4:1-2). Fox elaborated his position in his writings. He stated his mission "to stand a witness against all violence and against all the works of darkness, and to turn people from the darkness to the light and from the occasion of the magistrate's sword. . . . With the carnal weapon I do not fight."[8]

Quakers would not personally participate in war because they regarded fighting as incompatible with the gospel. As Isaac Pennington put it, "Fighting is not suitable to a gospel spirit, but to the spirit of the world and the children thereof. The fighting in the gospel is turned inward against the lusts, and not outward against the creatures."[9] Quakers were not opposed to all participation in government and sought to influence policy regarding the use of the sword. They, like the Anabap-

8. Quoted in Margaret E. Hirst, *The Quakers in Peace and War* (London: Allen and Unwin, 1923), 57.
9. Quoted in Hirst, *The Quakers*, 124.

tists, made a distinction between the kingdom of Christ and the kingdom of the world. The sword was "carnal," meaning not only fleshly but irrational, "the entire lower nature of man."[10]

Roland Bainton highlighted three Quaker objections to war: First, war is not a method appropriate for achieving peace. Second, one's enemies may be convinced that their cause is just; killing them is not consistent with respect for their conscience. Third, we are not obligated to heed our leaders' call to arms when we know little of the reasons for the war or whose cause is right.[11]

The Church of the Brethren

Pietism was a reform and renewal movement within the Protestant churches in seventeenth-century German provinces. Some Pietists concluded that true reform along scriptural lines was impossible, given the tight state-church linkage. When their simple gatherings for Bible study, hymn-singing, and prayer were dispersed and declared illegal, they determined that their only recourse was to leave the church, to become separatists.

This was the background of the Brethren movement, which emerged in central Germany in 1708. Among radical Pietists who gathered in the county of Wittgenstein, a small number became convinced that complete obedience to the commandments of Christ entailed their (re)baptism and covenanting together as a society. In their view of the church they approximated the convictions of the earlier Mennonites, with whom they had many contacts and similarities. The chief difference was that these Pietists believed that baptism of adult believers should take place by a threefold immersion, after the practice of the early Christians.

Because they were reacting against the creedalism of the state church, Brethren did not write out a complete confession of faith. However, it is clear from the record and from their actions that they adhered to strict pacifism or nonresistance. Early Brethren converts refused to perform military service or even to carry the customary sidearms. Brethren tradition tells of Johannes Naas, a tall and well-built man who

10. Bainton, *Christian Attitudes,* 159.
11. *Ibid.,* 159-61.

was seized by recruiters to serve in the personal regiment of the ruler of Prussia. Despite torture, he refused to serve the prince, stating that he already had a commander to whom his loyalty was due, namely Jesus Christ.

By 1735 the Brethren had been transplanted to North America. Their nonresistance was put to the test in the French and Indian War (1756-63) and the American Revolution. They steadfastly maintained that their belief forbade violence. In 1775 they joined with Mennonites in an appeal to the Pennsylvania Assembly:

> The advice to those who did not find freedom of conscience to take up arms, that they ought to be helpful to those who are in need and distressed circumstances, we receive with cheerfulness toward all men of what station they may be — it being our principle to feed the hungry and give the thirsty drink; we have dedicated ourselves to serve all men in everything that can be helpful to the preservation of men's lives, but we find no freedom in giving or doing, or assisting in any thing by which men's lives are destroyed or hurt.[12]

This pattern of refusing military participation, joined with charitable outreach to those in need, continued through the nineteenth century. Even during the terrible years of the Civil War, the Brethren maintained their nonresistance, with the result that several members lost their lives. Those in the South were particularly hard-pressed because of the greater need for manpower in service of the Confederate cause.

Cooperation of the Historic Peace Churches

Although divided by historical origins and to some extent by doctrinal differences, the Mennonites, Quakers, and Brethren were drawn together by their common experiences in times of conflict. This happened primarily in North America, the place of their greatest proximity. Mennonites and Brethren supported the more activist Friends in their political leadership in colonial Pennsylvania. They also contributed generously to Quaker agencies set up to aid native Americans.

Because of their common conscientious objection to military service, the three bodies were consistently named together first in colonial

12. Quoted in Brock, *Freedom from Violence,* 201.

and later in state and federal legislation on conscription. As a result they often found it necessary to consult each other when they contacted legislators to petition for legislative relief. The degree of cooperation heightened in the twentieth century, as conscription became more sweeping and demanding. Whereas previously military involvement could be limited by paying commutation fees, in World Wars I and II, government demands were more comprehensive.

The experiences of conscientious objectors during World War I were as a rule unsatisfactory, in some cases intolerable, because of wartime hysteria and the Wilson administration's delay in defining acceptable noncombatant military pursuits. Peace church leaders determined to seek better arrangements, a resolution that acquired urgency in the 1930s as the rise of totalitarianism in Europe made the outbreak of war probable. At a meeting in Newton, Kansas, in the fall of 1935, peace church leaders made plans to work together to prevent war, and failing that, to secure the best possible service for conscientious objectors. They pursued this at the highest levels of United States government. A small continuation committee met periodically to coordinate joint efforts.

From this 1935 meeting comes the term "historic peace churches." Those gathered recognized the following commonalities: (1) Each group has been visibly active worldwide in relief for victims of war, in other kinds of service, and in fostering international communication. (2) Each group has assumed or affirmed the supranational quality of Christian fellowship. (3) Each group has historically taught that the Christian is called not to participate in war, even when required to do so by government.[13]

The result of these joint efforts, after the passage of the Selective Service Act, was the creation in 1940-41 of Civilian Public Service (CPS). This unique experiment in church-state relationships involved the Selective Service Administration's assignment of conscientious objectors to "work of national importance" in camps administered and financed by the historic peace churches. Beginning with conservation work in forests and farmland in large base camps, CPS workers eventually came to be

13. Douglas Gwyn, George Hunsinger, Eugene F. Roop, John Howard Yoder, *A Declaration on Peace: In God's People the World's Renewal Has Begun* (Scottdale: Herald, 1991), 107, n. 3; Donald F. Durnbaugh, ed., *On Earth Peace: Discussions on War/Peace Issues between Friends, Mennonites, Brethren, and European Churches, 1935-75* (Elgin: Brethren, 1978), 30-32.

involved in a broad range of projects serving the public interest: staffing mental hospitals and juvenile homes, becoming subjects of experiments in semi-starvation and infectious diseases, working with community development and hospitals in Puerto Rico, and more. A cooperative National Service Board for Religious Objectors was set up in Washington, D.C., to administer the extensive program, which cost the peace churches millions of dollars from 1941 through 1947, when the CPS project was phased out.

All three churches organized large-scale relief programs during and after World War II to bring food, medicine, and clothing to refugees, displaced persons, and other war-sufferers around the world. The agencies created to administer these programs — American Friends Service Committee (AFSC), Mennonite Central Committee (MCC), and the Brethren Service Committee (BSC) — typically worked together on location to raise funds and administer relief. Many staff people came directly from the CPS ranks. Their work brought public recognition to the peace witness of the churches, culminating in 1947 when AFSC was awarded the Nobel Peace Prize.

Since World War II the historic peace churches have created other agencies and movements to aid the cause of peace. Examples include the International Volunteer Service (IVS) program, which placed volunteers in Southeast Asia, the Eirene organization, which provided projects for European conscientious objectors, and the New Call to Peacemaking, which has stimulated peace witness in North America since 1976.

Ecumenical Discussions

In Amsterdam in 1948 a long process of ecumenical cooperation led to the formal organization of the World Council of Churches (WCC). One statement issued by the Amsterdam assembly addressed the issue of the morality of war; its title was "War Is Contrary to the Will of God." Drafters were unable to reach agreement on the question of Christian participation in war, and defined three positions. They confessed: "We must acknowledge our deep sense of perplexity in face of these conflicting opinions." Members called on theologians to address the unresolved issues.[14]

14. This document and other documents cited in this section have been published in Durnbaugh, *On Earth Peace.*

In 1949 representatives of the peace church agencies serving in postwar Europe were brought together by M. R. Zigler of the Church of the Brethren, to plan cooperative peace efforts in Europe. Zigler was particularly eager to address the challenge laid out in Amsterdam. A European continuation committee, modeled after the one developed in the U.S. in 1935, took up the task of drafting a peace church response. Their document, also titled *War Is Contrary to the Will of God*, was released in 1951 and sent to the WCC. It consisted of three individual statements from the peace churches, as well as one from the International Fellowship of Reconciliation. WCC staff members suggested that such a document would have more impact if it were a single unified statement representing all the peace churches.

A revision, "Peace Is the Will of God," was completed in time to be forwarded to the second WCC assembly in Evanston, Illinois, in the summer of 1954. There it encountered little direct response, but the following year Episcopal bishop Angus Dun and ethicist Reinhold Niebuhr published a rebuttal, called "God Wills Both Justice and Peace." To continue the conversation, the European continuation committee authorized a response, "God Establishes Both Peace and Justice." This was published, along with the earlier statements.

In 1955 peace church representatives met in a retreat center in Puidoux, Switzerland, to refine their joint positions and called in noted European theologians from the established churches as resources. The consultation developed into a full discussion of ecclesial and ethical issues dividing the peace churches and the European churches. Some called it a resumption of the dialogue broken off in the sixteenth century. This constructive exchange was deemed so valuable that participants urged that it be continued. Between 1955 and 1965, a series of "Puidoux" conferences ensued. Although they received little attention in North America, they had a significant impact on the European theological scene. Observers credit these conferences with stimulating interest in peace issues among European Christians and even with encouraging European governments to make provision for conscientious objectors to perform civilian service.

Also in 1955 the WCC's Study Department began a high-level study on the church and the nuclear threat. Two theologians involved were members of the International Fellowship of Reconciliation. Because the final statement of the study called for nuclear pacifism, the Central Committee of the WCC distanced itself from the report.

Peace church involvement continued in subsequent world assemblies of the WCC. The Third Assembly (New Delhi, 1961) called for a consultation between pacifists and nonpacifists; this took place after a long delay in the early summer of 1968. The Fourth Assembly (Uppsala, 1968) adopted a resolution inspired by the work of Martin Luther King, Jr.: It requested study of nonviolent methods of change. This resulted in a consultation at Cardiff, Wales, in 1972, with full peace church participation, and a document on "Violence, Nonviolence and the Struggle for Social Justice" (1973). Peace concerns were prominent in the Fifth Assembly (Nairobi, 1975), issuing in programs "to combat militarism."

The Sixth Assembly (Vancouver, 1983) spoke directly to the peace issue, adopting a document entitled "Confronting Threats to Peace and Survival" and endorsing an earlier statement (from Amsterdam, 1981) that called on the churches to "declare that the production and deployment as well as the use of nuclear weapons are a crime against humanity." Also at the Vancouver meeting a movement was begun to seek an international peace council to work for justice and peace, with primary initiative coming from East and West German Christians. This was taken up by the WCC under the heading "Justice, Peace, and the Integrity of Creation" (JPIC). Regional meetings, such as the "Peace with Justice" European Ecumenical Assembly in Basel in May 1989, culminated in a world convocation in Seoul, South Korea, in March 1990. The JPIC movement was made part of the WCC structure at the Seventh Assembly (Canberra, 1991). Historic peace church members took an active part in all of these initiatives and meetings.

Conclusion

Thus it is that the concern for peace that activated several smaller movements beginning with the Czech Brethren in the fifteenth century has now become a central cause for the combined Christian enterprise in the last decade of the twentieth century. Biblical scholar Otto Piper wrote in 1965 that the historic peace churches might be justified in continuing their separate existence "because they bring out an aspect of the Christian faith which no other denomination represents, the complete absence of which would result in a serious impoverishment of Protestantism."[15] As the peace concern has come to be seen as crucial

15. Otto Piper, *Protestantism in an Ecumenical Age* (Philadelphia: Fortress, 1965), 170.

for the ecumenical movement, these questions are raised: Are the historic peace churches remaining true to their traditional testimony of peace? As other Christians increasingly share their concern, is their continuing separate existence necessary? Are they pressing their peace witness in appropriate ways within the structures of ecumenical discussions? The current consultations on the apostolic faith and the churches' peace witness are an important arena for pursuing these issues.

9. Toward Acknowledging Together the Apostolic Character of the Church's Peace Witness

MARLIN E. MILLER

Most of the essays in this volume laid the foundation for the second consultation on "The Apostolic Character of the Church's Peace Witness." Some of the essays have been revised on the basis of the conversations during that consultation, which was held in October 1991 in Douglaston, New York. In contrast, this chapter has been written after the fact and without being tempered by the discipline of that broader lively dialogue. Nonetheless, it presupposes the other chapters of this volume and the consultation itself as summarized in the Summary Statement (which is included in the present volume). It also provides additional analysis of the issues that figured implicitly or explicitly in the consultation and proposes several steps that may be taken toward acknowledging together the apostolic character of the church's peace witness.

Recent Interest in the Church's Peace Witness

What is required for movement of the diverse church communions toward acknowledging together the apostolic character of the church's peace witness? As the essays in this volume by Howard Loewen (chapter 2: "An Analysis of the Use of Scripture in the Churches' Documents on Peace") and by Donald Durnbaugh and Charles Brockwell (chapter 8: "The Historic Peace Churches: From Sectarian Origins to Ecumenical

Witness") indicate, some churches have taken a renewed interest in war and peace issues since World War II and especially during the last two decades, in the face of potential mass destruction by nuclear weapons. For other church bodies, rejecting participation in violence and war has long been part of their teaching, practice, and identity. For still others, neither a long tradition of pacifism nor international tensions and the devastating capabilities of modern weaponry have made the church's peace witness a matter of major theological and ethical concern.

Because of this wide diversity among the churches, any impetus toward common recognition that peace witness belongs to the faithful church's calling in the world encounters resistance even at the initial point of raising the question of the church's peace witness. For some communions, the first step would therefore be the discovery, or perhaps the rediscovery, of compelling reasons to give the matter serious attention. Those who have participated in the consultations on the apostolic character of the church's peace witness hope that this volume may plant some seeds that will bear fruit in such a discovery or rediscovery.

For the communions that, whether for a few years or for many centuries, have believed that this subject warrants both theological discernment and concerted action, movement toward acknowledging together the apostolic character of the church's peace witness presents several challenges (see Summary Statement, I). Particularly in North America, the historic peace churches have been tempted to accept their vision of the church's peace witness as a denominational peculiarity rather than as a legacy of the common faith to be commended to all Christians. Lack of ecumenical conversation and mutual correction between historic peace churches and other communions until the latter half of this century have no doubt increased this temptation.

Other communions' interest in the church's peace witness during this century has most frequently been aroused by devastating wars and the threat of nuclear annihilation. These churches have often been tempted to limit peace witness to a particular social-ethical issue or to Christians' action in the public arena, rather than grasping it as a matter that also strikes close to the heart of the church's faithfulness and unity. Both renewed concern for the churches' active contribution to peace in a world of violence and injustice and the continuing commitment to a distinctive heritage should be encouraged. But neither will suffice to bring us to acknowledge together the apostolic character of the church's peace witness. If the question of the church's peace witness is one day to be answered in concert rather than in cacophony, all groups will need to give more attention to critical reexamination of scriptural foundations, to historical relations among the church communions, and to theological justifications that inform contemporary ways of putting the question.

From Historical Divisions toward a Common Peace Witness

Movement toward a common witness on peace calls into question not only the contemporary differences among the churches, but also the historical divisions that nurture and sustain these differences. Since the sixteenth century, the character of the church's peace witness has been a point not only of diversity but of explicit division among Christian communions. Latent differences over Christian participation in war and civil government, which had long existed and had sometimes surfaced within western Christendom, became matters of division and began to take on confessional status or its equivalent.

Among Anabaptist and Mennonite groups the principled rejection of violence and participation in war was given confessional status from their beginnings.[1] In response, both Lutheran and Reformed confessions explicitly affirmed Christian participation in civil government and in warfare, under certain conditions, and condemned the Anabaptists for their stance. For example, the Augsburg Confession (1530) states: "It is taught among us . . . that Christians may without sin occupy civil offices or serve as princes and judges, render decisions and pass sentence according to imperial and other existing laws, punish evildoers with the sword, engage in just wars, serve as soldiers. . . . Condemned here are the Anabaptists who teach that none of the things indicated above is Christian."[2] Similarly, the Thirty-Nine Articles of the Church of Eng-

---

1. See chapter 8 above. See also "The Schleitheim Confession (1527)" and "The Dordrecht Confession (1632)," in John Leith, ed., *Creeds of the Churches: A Reader in Christian Doctrine from the Bible to the Present* (3rd ed.; Atlanta: John Knox, 1982), 287-89, 303-5.

2. "The Augsburg Confession," Article XVI, in Leith, *Creeds of the Churches,* 72-73. See also the "Second Helvetic Confession," Article XXX, in Leith, 190-91, and "The Attitudes of the Reformed Churches Today to the Condemnations of the Anabaptists in the Reformed Confessional Documents," in *Mennonites and Reformed in Dialogue* (Studies from the World Alliance of Reformed Churches 7, ed. Hans

land affirm Christian participation in military service and war. Although this confession does not explicitly condemn other positions, Article XXXVII, on the power of civil magistrates, English Edition of 1571, asserts: "It is lawful for Christian men, at the commaundement of the Magistrate, to weare weapons, and serue in the warres."[3] In later centuries, the Society of Friends and the Church of the Brethren explicitly and consistently rejected participation in violence and war. Although they did not express their conviction in formal confessional statements, its authority in their communions was comparable to that of the confessionally defined positions of other communions.

With an acute awareness of these historical divisions, participants in the consultations on the apostolic character of the church's peace witness recommended that "further attention be given to . . . conversation and reconciliation between the churches whose historical teaching and practice on war and peace have been an occasion for strife, division, condemnation, and persecution" (Summary Statement, VII.2). Fortunately, some attention has been given to conversation and reconciliation among some of these churches in recent years, after centuries of recrimination and silence.[4]

Georg vom Berg, Henk Kossen, Larry Miller, and Lukas Vischer; Geneva: World Alliance of Reformed Churches, 1986).

3. In Leith, *Creeds of the Churches*, 280. Not only Christians commanded by magistrates, but also magistrates as Christians are confessionally authorized to wage war, according to "The Westminster Confession (1646)," Chapter XXIII, in Leith, 219-20. This confession also asserts that it "is lawful for Christians to accept and execute the office of a magistrate"; in fulfillment of their duties magistrates "may lawfully, now under the New Testament, wage war upon just and necessary occasion" (220).

4. Formal conversations between representatives of the Lutheran and Mennonite communions have taken place in both France and Germany. For the French conversations, see *Les Entretiens Luthero-Mennonites. Resultats du colloque de Strasbourg, 1981-1984, avec une préface de Pierre Widmer et une présentation de Marc Lienhard* (Montbéliard: Christ Seul, 1984). For the German dialogues, see "Die lutherisch-mennonitischen Gespräche in der Bundesrepublik Deutschland 1989-1992," *Texte aus der VELKD* 53 (1993).

Conversations between Reformed and Mennonite groups have taken place in the Netherlands through the sponsorship of the World Alliance of Reformed Churches and Mennonite World Conference. See *Mennonites and Reformed in Dialogue* (note 2 above) and *Dopers-Calvinistisch Gesprek in Nederland* (The Hague: Boekencentrum, 1982); *Mennonites and Reformed in Dialogue* contains a summary in English of the latter (pp. 61-71). See the select bibliography in this volume for information on how to obtain these documents. See also Ross T. Bender and Alan P. F. Sell, eds., *Baptism, Peace, and the State in the Reformed and Mennonite Traditions* (Waterloo: Wilfrid Laurier University, 1991).

A summary and brief analysis of the salient points in the recent dialogue between Lutherans and Mennonites in Germany may illustrate what has been accomplished by such conversations and why we should invest more in such efforts.[5] The Lutheran participants in the conversations acknowledged that in general the Augsburg Confession's condemnations of the Anabaptists were frequently based on insufficient information and were indiscriminately and incorrectly applied to more people and more groups than was appropriate. They noted that condemnation language would not be used today and that, in any case, identifying doctrinal differences and even false teachings should not become an occasion for inciting or justifying discrimination against people in either ecclesial or social arenas. Further, they believe persecuting the Anabaptists in the sixteenth and later centuries has left Lutherans with guilt that has encumbered their relations with Mennonites. For this they now ask forgiveness, in order to put these relations on a new spiritual level. Moreover, they commit themselves to additional conversations and encounters, which may help Lutheran and Mennonite Christians take more steps toward each other in the context of "reconciled diversity."

Both Mennonite and Lutheran conversation partners agreed that modern Mennonites do not characterize participation in civil government and in the police as un-Christian in the way that the sixteenth-century Anabaptists who wrote the Schleitheim articles did.[6] Today, both Mennonites and Lutherans are ready to accept responsibility for public affairs and cooperate in shaping them. Both also agree that the church is to be the messenger of the kingdom of God in the world and is to be clearly differentiated from the state and from the broader society. Simultaneously, the church needs to maintain a critical stance in relation to the state in order to carry out its prophetic witness and service in the world. Within these broad lines of agreement, Mennonites continue to consider use of armed force problematic, even when it is authorized by the state. They remain convinced that Christians who exercise political responsibility do not need to follow standards that differ from those used by other Christians.[7]

5. The conversations covered several themes; here only points directly related to the church's peace witness are summarized.

6. See chapter 8 above on Anabaptists and Mennonites.

7. In varying degrees and with differing emphases, other bilateral conversations have come to similar conclusions. See *Mennonites and Reformed in Dialogue*, 70-71; *Les Entretiens Luthero-Mennonites,* 45-46; *Baptism, Peace, and the State,* 235-37.

Both the measure of convergence and the degree of divergence became more accentuated when conversation turned to military service. Lutheran and Mennonite representatives share the belief that the church is the fellowship of those who have received the gift of reconciliation and that Christians are therefore liberated from the way of violence and called to be ministers of peace and reconciliation, using and advocating nonviolent means of resolving conflicts. They diverge on the specific implications of this belief for military and peace service. The Mennonites continue in principle to reject military service and to accept the call to live as a peace church, rendering peace service. While respecting individual decisions of conscience, they recommend that members refuse military service and enter an alternative peace service. The Lutherans consider it possible for Christians under certain conditions to participate in armed conflict in order to reestablish peace, to preserve justice, and to protect those who have no weapons. They base this conviction on Article XVI of the Augsburg Confession and on the Lutheran two-kingdom doctrine. Simultaneously, they agree that Christians may refuse military service for reasons of conscience.

In spite of continuing disagreement on military service and service in civil government, participants in the conversations discovered that they agreed in their basic understanding of the gospel. They concluded that the differences remaining do not have church-dividing significance.[8]

Though the conclusions of the Lutheran-Mennonite dialogue in Germany have not yet resulted in a final agreement between the two church bodies,[9] they illustrate how such conversation can lead communions that have been divided toward acknowledging together the church's peace witness. This experience demonstrates how much we need this conversation and discernment. For example, participants came to recognize that both communions now view the once-divisive issues in ways that differ from their sixteenth-century forebears' approaches. The present shape of convergence and divergence has shifted since the sixteenth century, when conversation broke off. Participants needed to reassess the ways each communion has viewed the other's teachings and practices

8. This general conclusion applied to the other issues examined, not only to questions related to participation in civil government, the police, and military service.

9. The report on the dialogue and the summary of convergence and divergence are being commended to the two church bodies for discussion and comment; the conclusions do not constitute a final statement of agreement between the two church groups.

with regard to Christian faithfulness and unity. Further, the way toward reconciliation has been opened by confessing past wrongs, by extending forgiveness, and by praying together.

Nevertheless, these bilateral conversations stopped short (perhaps appropriately) of raising several basic questions that are implicit in the historical controversies and still crucial for faithfulness and unity in the church's peace witness. Is a Christian pacifist stance, together with participation in war and violence under certain conditions, compatible with the apostolic faith? Are communions that accept both Christian pacifism and Christians' participation in war and violence under certain conditions acting in harmony with or contrary to the apostolic faith (see the Summary Statement, VI, questions 6 and 7)? These questions raise the issue of *commonly accepted and appropriate criteria* for discerning the apostolic character of the church's peace witness and its faithful expression in a world of violence and war. This issue remains pertinent for all church bodies, irrespective of the measure of convergence some communions may reach on matters that have historically been explicitly church-dividing.

The Christology of the Nicene Creed and the Church's Peace Witness

Through the initiative of the World Council of Churches, the Nicene Creed has been commended to the churches for study and recognition as a common expression of the apostolic faith and thus as a broadly ecumenical criterion for discerning what is in agreement with the apostolic faith. General questions about the sufficiency of the creed for expressing the Christian faith, about its relationship to Scripture, and about its relation to what should be included in a common expression of the apostolic faith today have figured prominently in Faith and Order discussions.[10]

More specific questions arise about using the Nicene Creed as a criterion for discerning apostolicity when we consider what steps we need to take toward acknowledging together the apostolic character of the church's peace witness. Apparently the church's earliest peace witness

10. See, for example, the Odessa (1981) and Rome (1983) reports in *Apostolic Faith Today: A Handbook for Study* (Faith and Order Paper 124, ed. Hans-Georg Link; Geneva: World Council of Churches, 1985), 245-56 and 257-66.

included a refusal to condone violence and war. Was there a major shift away from this position before the creed's formulation and widespread acceptance, a shift to church support for Christians' participation in warfare? If so, does the creed presuppose both theological and nontheological aspects of such a shift? Does the creed limit concern for apostolicity to specific points of doctrine while omitting reference to specific patterns of action and conduct (such as Christians' witness for peace) that may belong integrally to the apostolic faith? Finally, does the christology of the creed implicitly encourage or discourage the recognition that "the New Testament unambiguously calls the church to accept and proclaim the gospel of peace, to follow the way of Jesus in loving enemies and rejecting violence, to carry out a ministry of peacemaking and reconciliation, and to practice the justice of God's reign?" (Summary Statement, IV).

It is hardly controversial to say that the church's peace witness underwent a significant shift between the second and fifth centuries. The extent of the shift, how it should be assessed, what brought it about, and what consequences it should have for Christian theology and ethics remain matters of debate. This is particularly true of understandings of the church's relation to the state and society and of matters such as the specific nature of Christian peace witness and response to violence.[11]

Some churches and Christians regard the shift as a deviation from the apostolic faith or even a betrayal of it; others regard it as an appropriate or even natural development in harmony with the Holy Spirit's leading in the changed context in which the church was to carry out its vocation. Those who see the shift as a departure from the apostolic faith usually appeal to Scripture and to the tradition of the first two or three centuries as the primary and secondary criteria of apostolicity (though they may not use that terminology).[12] Those who regard the shift as an

---

11. See chapter 8 above on the Unity of Brethren, Anabaptists and Mennonites, and the Religious Society of Friends; compare the conclusions in chapter 7.

12. For the Quakers, the active presence of Christ's Spirit in the community of believers is considered decisive, along with Scripture and the practices of the apostles. See Dean Freiday, "Apostolicity and Orthochristianity," *Apostolic Faith in America* (Grand Rapids: Eerdmans, 1988), 43-52. In "The Authority of Tradition" (*The Priestly Kingdom: Social Ethics as Gospel* [Notre Dame: University of Notre Dame, 1984], 63-79), John Howard Yoder argues that the just war tradition as it developed in Christendom "is a fundamentally new political ethic, not organically evolved from the social stance of the early Christians, as that stance had been evolving up to and

acceptable development of the apostolic faith generally appeal to the relative weight of changed circumstances and the breadth of ecclesial consensus as additional criteria for the church's faithfulness and unity.

However this shift is understood, adopting a creedal statement from the late fourth century as the measure for common expression of the apostolic faith at least tends to render movement away from an earlier Christian stance less open to critical reassessment. At most, it excludes the possibility of regarding such changes as deviations from the apostolic faith. But it is precisely that possibility that needs to remain open to further examination if there is to be movement toward recognition of the apostolic character of the church's peace witness today sufficiently ecumenical to include the witness of the pre-Nicene church, the historic peace churches, and Christians of similar persuasion in other communions. The emphases of the creed and the ecclesial, social, and political contexts that influenced it and within which it functioned doubtless resolved particular controversies and provided a common reference for orthodox expression of apostolic beliefs. But the creed may also reflect questionable assumptions about the apostolicity of the church's peace message and the church's participation in the state, in military service, and in war.[13]

Perhaps the most serious questions raised about the Nicene Creed, with regard to theological criteria for the apostolic character of the church's peace witness, have to do with the creed's christological formulations. Are the terms of the creed in sufficient continuity with the New Testament's witness to the fully human as well as the fully divine Son of God? Do they ascribe fundamental importance to Jesus' life, teaching, and call to follow the way of the cross? Or do the categories of the creed

---

through Tertullian and Origen" (75). This ethic "rejects the privileged place of the enemy as the test of whether one loves one's neighbor. It rejects the norm of the cross and the life of Jesus Christ as the way of dealing with conflict" (75). In short, Yoder contends, "a change has taken place which must be described as a reversal" (76). He then draws out several implications of this assessment for current ecumenical discussion on the relation between Scripture, Tradition, and traditions (76-79).

13. See Thomas Finger, "The Way to Nicea: Some Reflections from a Mennonite Perspective," *Journal of Ecumenical Studies* 24 (1987), 212-31. Note also Dean Freiday's survey of several communions and Christian movements that have emphasized the importance of faithful practice and authentic experience and his proposal that practice and experience be included in reciprocal relationship with right beliefs as dimensions of apostolicity ("Apostolicity and Orthochristianity").

discourage or perhaps even preclude acknowledging the normative significance for the church's peace witness today of Jesus' love for the enemy, his rejection of violence, and his proclamation of God's reign? Modern biblical scholarship has rediscovered the historical, social, and political significance — that is, in traditional terms, the fully human dimensions — of Jesus' messiahship, teaching, and example. This rediscovery has often been interpreted as a corrective, and sometimes as an alternative, to traditional christology.[14]

The essays in this volume by Paul Anderson (chapter 5: "Jesus and Peace") and Richard Jeske (chapter 6: "War and Peace in the New Testament") draw heavily on the fruits of this rediscovery and on their potential significance for Christian life and the church's peace witness. Although Jeske and Anderson do not play the historical expressions of Jesus' messiahship off against traditional christological categories and emphases, the language and priorities of their portrayals differ significantly from the classical dogmatic concepts and concerns. If the directions of their interpretations are persuasive and stand up to further scrutiny and practice, then they will raise implicitly the question of the relationship between Scripture and the creed, specifically in relation to the theological basis for the church's peace witness. To be sure, the theological and biblical foundations for the church's peace witness are not limited to christological considerations. Nonetheless, these considerations are crucial. Movement toward recognizing together the apostolic character of the church's peace witness will thus require further conversation, clarification, and convergence on the basis for that witness in the churches' confession of Jesus Christ and in their christology.

14. Liberal Protestant scholarship has frequently portrayed the Christ of the creed and the Jesus of the Gospels as reflecting radically different christologies. This posing of stark alternatives has also been attractive to some Christian pacifists, both in the historic peace churches and in other communions, because it seems to give increased normative ethical significance to Jesus' example and teaching. Others have argued that an emphasis on Jesus' teaching and example is a needed corrective but is also compatible with orthodox christology (see Thomas Finger, "The Way to Nicea"; John H. Yoder, *The Politics of Jesus* [Grand Rapids: Eerdmans, 1972], 106-7). Even more strongly, A. James Reimer claims that "trinitarian orthodoxy," as reflected in the Nicene Creed, is not only compatible with a Christian peace ethic based on the Jesus of the Gospels, but essential to it ("Trinitarian Orthodoxy, Constantinianism, and Theology from a Radical Protestant Perspective," in *Faith to Creed*, ed. S. Mark Heim [Grand Rapids: Eerdmans, 1991], 129-61; see especially 156-61).

Interpretation of Scripture and the Church's Peace Witness

In addition to the diverging confessional traditions, differing appeals to Scripture have contributed to division among the churches on questions of peace and war. Authentic movement toward acknowledging together the apostolic character of the church's peace witness will thus also need to be measured by the criterion of Scripture. Indeed, the scriptural criterion for discerning apostolicity has been even more broadly acknowledged than the creedal standard in both the just war and the peace church traditions. Nevertheless, their respective interpretations of Scripture have all too frequently become captive to the traditional positions and have thus reinforced the divisions between church communions rather than encouraging movement toward a unity measured by Scripture as the primary common criterion of apostolicity.

For that reason, the consultation for which the essays in this volume were originally prepared gave primary attention to clarifying the biblical bases for the church's peace witness.[15] Both the essays and the consultation demonstrate once again that bringing together disciplined biblical scholarship and sensitivity to the churches' differing traditions can lead us to reexamine our divergent traditions in the light of God's word as witnessed by Scripture. For example, consultation participants concluded that the New Testament poses specific problems for both the proponents of the just war tradition and adherents of the peace church tradition. In particular, it poses a major *confessional* problem for proponents of the just war tradition, and a problem of similar scope for the churches of pacifist persuasion.[16] Similarly the biblical scholars and other participants in the consultation concluded that the Old Testament renders problematic any *confessional* reading that claims to ground either a just war or crusade or pacifist position in it, though the problems posed differ in each case.[17]

It is one thing for interchurch consultations to draw on the resources of contemporary biblical scholarship to point to shortcomings

15. See the section entitled "A Biblical Study," in Jeffrey Gros's introduction to this volume (pp. 10-11 in chapter 1); see also the Summary Statement, sections II, III, and IV.

16. See the Summary Statement, IV.

17. See the Summary Statement, III, and Ben C. Ollenburger's essay (chapter 3 above).

or even errors in the divided traditions of scriptural interpretation. It is another matter to move toward a constructive articulation of the church's peace witness that meets the scriptural criterion of apostolicity. In addition to addressing the problems of divided confessional traditions and their use of Scripture, movement toward recognizing the apostolic character of the church's peace witness may also need to address critically the diverse hermeneutical and theological methods that permeate contemporary biblical scholarship and which are to some degree represented in this volume. Otherwise, instead of contributing to the formation of a broader consensus on the apostolic calling of the church to be a community of peace and of peacemaking in the world, we risk replacing traditional confessional divisions over the church's peace witness with reconfigured scholarly divisions.[18]

This volume is thus intended to begin a conversation rather than to state conclusions of a finished debate. It will fulfill its purpose to the degree that it contributes to that ongoing conversation and to the churches' recognition of our common calling to be faithful witnesses in today's world to Christ's ministry of peace.

18. On the promise and the limits of contemporary biblical scholarship for interchurch conversation and unity, see George Lindbeck, "Two Kinds of Ecumenism: Unitive and Interdenominational," *Gregorianum* 70 (1989), 647-60.

Consultation on the Apostolic Faith and the Church's Peace Witness: A Summary Statement

Background

The October 27-29, 1991, consultation in Douglaston, New York, was the second consultation on the apostolic faith and the church's peace witness, sponsored by the Commission on Faith and Order of the National Council of the Churches of Christ in the U.S.A. It continued and built on the deliberations of the first gathering, which was held in March 1990 at Bethany Theological Seminary, Oak Brook, Illinois.

The first consultation focused on peace statements produced by Roman Catholic, Orthodox, Protestant, and historic peace church (HPC) groups in North America during the 1980s. Participants in the March 1990 meeting came with responses to these peace statements. The responses identified points of convergence and divergence among the statements in their use of Scripture, in their theological arguments (including their use of historical, philosophical, or political reasoning), in their primary theological categories (e.g., ecclesiology, christology, creation and its preservation, individual Christian vocation, peace), and in the ecclesial and moral implications of the positions taken.

Participants in the first consultation also served as an initial planning group for the 1991 consultation and commissioned several of their number to complete preparations for it. The group decided that more attention should be given to the biblical bases for the church's peace witness and secondarily to two historical periods that have been crucial for unity and division in Christian peace witness (the period of the early church in the first three centuries, and the time of the appearance of the historic peace churches in the sixteenth, seventeenth, and eighteenth centuries). In preparation for the second consultation, several biblical scholars talked together and wrote papers, which were forwarded to participants prior to the second consultation. The historical studies provided additional background for understanding divergences in the churches' traditions.

Participants in the second consultation discussed these biblical and historical papers and also heard a presentation by Reformed theologian Richard Mouw of Fuller Theological Seminary, Pasadena, California, on dialogue between Reformed and Mennonite theologians on the church's peace witness. Mouw's case study in ecumenical conversation summarized key areas of traditional Anabaptist-Reformed disagreement and noted some signs of hope for further dialogue in the contemporary context.

What follows is a summary statement from consultation participants on common concerns, areas of convergence and divergence, and recommendations for further conversation.

I. Introduction

We acknowledge that those Christian groups historically opposing church involvement with the state and especially with its violent defense have claimed to be doing nothing less than preserving the faith delivered to the apostles. For them, differences among the churches on issues of Christian participation in violence and war stand in the way of confessing a common faith. These divisions are a matter of vital importance, like the church order, sacramental, and creedal differences that have already been widely recognized as separating Christians.

We are aware that movement toward a common expression of the apostolic faith involves much more than resolving a particular ethical issue frequently presumed to have only peripheral theological and confessional significance. Movement toward the Christian unity envisioned in the gospel of Jesus Christ also requires a common understanding of the ecclesiological issues that both inform and derive from the churches' disagreements about what faithfulness in the church's peace witness entails.

II. The Uses of Scripture in North American Church Peace Statements of the 1980s

At the 1991 consultation, with the help of Howard John Loewen's detailed analysis (see chapter 2 in this volume), we noted similarities as well as wide-ranging differences in the use of Scripture in peace statements produced by the historic peace churches and by Roman Catholic, Protestant, and Orthodox churches or their representatives during the 1980s. Similarities and differences were noted with respect to specific Scripture texts cited, hermeneutical assumptions, use of Scripture in theological argument, and ethical and ecclesial implications drawn from or incorporated into the appropriation of Scripture. The statements generally agree that peace is a central theme in Scripture, that it is rooted in some way in the eschatological reign of God, and that Jesus did not resort to violence. They differ in their estimate of the relevance of biblical views of peace, war, and violence for churches in the contemporary context.

We did not come to clear conclusions on the significance of the hermeneutical practices reflected in the churches' peace statements for the churches' *confessional* divergence or convergence. It may be that the statements' shared concern for peacemaking is beginning to inform the churches' appropriation of Scripture in ways that relativize the traditional interpretations that have undergirded confessional divisions along just war and pacifist lines. The fact that all these statements have recently been produced by these groups does seem to indicate that concern for peace witness, which had earlier been left largely to the historic peace churches, has now become important for virtually all Christian groups.

We were left with several questions about the churches' peace statements' use of Scripture. First, to what degree do the peace church, just-peace church, and other traditions sufficiently establish the claim that the positions represented in their statements are based on Scripture or in harmony with Scripture? Conversely, to what degree do they either neglect to make that claim or fail to establish it adequately?

Second, is a new paradigm emerging in the churches' assessment of violence and war to supersede the paradigm that has supported traditional divisions between pacifists and just war adherents? The recent church peace statements appear to share several characteristics that may indicate movement toward a new model: a focus on creating conditions for peace and preventing war, a central concern for nonviolence and finding alternatives to war, a presumption that all (not only national leaders) are responsible for making peace and preventing war, and a concern to learn from rather than to ignore or condemn pacifists.

Third, to what degree do the churches' peace statements present a persuasive call to give a biblical vision of peace priority over understandings of peace in postbiblical traditions? Some of us perceived the churches' statements to be granting a biblical vision that kind of priority, while others were less sure that all the statements have done so or have intended to do so.

Fourth, to what extent does the world situation of the 1990s call for a reassessment of the use of Scripture in the church peace statements of the 1980s? The threat of nuclear holocaust arising from massive confrontation between superpowers of the East and West is no longer an issue demanding the churches' reflection. To what degree did that problem condition the churches' use of Scripture in ways that call for critique and reinterpretation?

III. The Old Testament as a Scriptural Base

Our conversations on the Old Testament as a scriptural base for the church's peace witness were informed by the papers provided by Ben Ollenburger ("Peace and God's Action against Chaos in the Old Testament") and Dianne Bergant ("Yahweh: A Warrior God?"), chapters 3 and 4 in this volume.

We noted that biblical scholars generally, and the biblical scholars contributing to this consultation specifically, differ in their understandings of the relation between *confessional* and scholarly readings of Scripture, as well as on hermeneutical and theological method. Nevertheless, we agreed that it is as difficult to justify Christians' participation in the wars of our nations on the basis of the Old Testament as it is to justify Christians' refusal to participate in any war on the same basis. Or to put the matter in other terms: The Old Testament renders problematic any *confessional* reading that claims to ground a just war or crusade or pacifist position in it, though the ways in which it challenges each of these readings may differ.

Several Old Testament texts and passages related to deliverance, war, peace, and creation figured prominently in the presentations and discussion, including (but not limited to) Exodus 14 and 15; Judges 4

211

and 5; Psalms 24, 68, 89, 104; and Isaiah 17 and 37. Some participants missed sustained attention to the themes of the suffering servant and Cyrus in Isaiah 40–55.

We agreed that affirming the continuity between the Old and New Testaments remains foundational on theological and confessional grounds, as well as for hermeneutical reasons. We also agreed that the Old Testament, in continuity with the New Testament, could provide greater resources than the churches have yet appropriated for the praxis of faithfulness to God in just peacemaking.

IV. The New Testament as a Scriptural Base

It is perhaps ironic that we devoted less time to conversations on the New Testament as a scriptural base for the churches' peace witness than to other aspects of the consultation. Our discussions were informed by Paul Anderson's essay, "Jesus and Peace" (chapter 5 in the present volume), an earlier version of the Richard Jeske paper (now titled "Peace in the New Testament," chapter 6 above), and an essay on Romans 13 by Thomas Hoyt (which was not available for this volume).

We acknowledged that the New Testament unambiguously calls the church to accept and proclaim the gospel of peace, to follow the way of Jesus in loving enemies and rejecting violence, to carry out a ministry of peacemaking and reconciliation, and to practice the justice of God's reign. It therefore poses the major *confessional* problem for just war proponents, to the extent that they seek to justify their position on the basis of Scripture. Simultaneously, it challenges proponents of pacifism, to the extent that they focus narrowly on rejecting Christian participation in war and violence.

The presentations and our discussions covered a wide range of New Testament themes and passages related to peace, war, nonviolence, and reconciliation. Themes given particular prominence included Jesus' temptations, teachings, and example, Christians' discriminating submission to the demands of the state, and their ministry of peace and reconciliation. Particular attention was given to several New Testament texts, including Matthew 5, Mark 10:42-45, John 14:27 and 16:33, Romans 5 and 13, 2 Corinthians 5, Philippians 2, Ephesians 2, and several passages in Revelation.

V. The Historical and Contemporary Appropriation of Scripture in the Churches' Peace Witness

The historical essays by David Hunter (chapter 7: "The Christian Church and the Roman Army in the First Three Centuries") and by Donald Durnbaugh and Charles Brockwell (chapter 8: here titled "The Historic Peace Churches: From Sectarian Origins to Ecumenical Witness") and Richard Mouw's presentation provided the background and basis for discussing the convergence and divergence of several church traditions on Christian participation in war. Most of the conversation centered on Mouw's description and assessment of similarities and differences between the Reformed and the Anabaptist/Mennonite traditions.

We noted factors that make Christian pacifism both difficult and attractive for nonpacifists. For example, the concern to liberate, defend, or preserve the neighbor from oppression, evil, and death — using the sword if necessary — out of love for the neighbor, renders pacifism difficult for nonpacifist Christians. Simultaneously, the desire to be faithful to the New Testament witness and awareness of past abuses of just war rhetoric and practice make Christian pacifism attractive.

Similar considerations make a nonpacifist stance both attractive and difficult for pacifist Christians. The plight of the neighbor in situations of overwhelming evil makes a nonpacifist approach attractive to pacifists concerned for justice. At the same time, awareness of the church's departure from its pre-Augustinian social ethic and the desire to follow Jesus faithfully make any use of violence difficult for the Christian pacifist to accept.

VI. Major Issues Warranting Additional Attention

In the course of the consultation, we noted several questions related to apostolic faith and the church's peace witness that we believe deserve more sustained reflection than we were able to give them:

1. What is the relationship between our primary identity as Christian disciples and members of a transnational church and our identity as citizens of a particular nation and our exercise of power in that society?

2. Should the influence of national loyalty and identity on the churches' peace witness and on their biblical interpretation be understood in positive or negative terms, as constructive or problematic, or both?

3. What is the role of spiritual formation in nurturing, sustaining, and guiding the church's peace witness?

4. Do the changing language and categories in the churches' biblical interpretation regarding peace fundamentally call into question the traditional paradigms that have contributed to or justified divisions between churches?

5. Should our review of historical traditions in our search for Christian unity involve reexamining confessional condemnations by churches teaching just war doctrine of churches rejecting participation in war and violence?

6. According to the non-HPCs, is a Christian pacifist stance (together with participation in war under certain conditions) also compatible with the apostolic faith? Is this still a church-dividing issue for these Christians?

7. According to the HPCs, are churches that accept both Christian pacifism and Christian participation in war under certain conditions acting in harmony with or contrary to the apostolic faith?

VII. Recommendations

1. We recommend to the Working Group on Faith and Order that the study and conversation on the apostolic faith and the church's peace witness be continued during the 1992-95 quadrennium. Although the consultations to date have taken several steps toward clarifying the biblical bases of the church's peace witness, significant work remains to be done, particularly on the New Testament basis for this witness and its continuity with the Old Testament. Further, questions about a possible change in paradigm of churchly and scholarly understandings of peace and the significance of such a change for traditionally church-dividing positions merit further examination, clarification, and response (see VI.4 above). Has there been a paradigm shift? If so, what is its character and what are its implications for significant convergence in the churches' peace witness?

2. We suggest that further attention be given to encouraging and developing recommendations for conversation and reconciliation between the churches whose historic teaching and practice on war and peace have been an occasion for strife, division, condemnation, and persecution.

3. We propose that the Working Group on Faith and Order share the results of this consultation with those in the broader ecumenical conciliar movement seeking a common understanding of what it means to confess the apostolic faith today. We also encourage them to give sustained attention to the apostolic character of the church's peace witness.

Participants in the Consultation

Paul N. Anderson	*Society of Friends*
Charles F. Brockwell, Jr.	*United Methodist Church*
John R. Burkholder	*Mennonite Church*
Justine Darling	*Roman Catholic Church*
Judy Fisher	*Episcopal Church*
Dean Freiday	*Society of Friends*
Barbara Nelson Gingerich	*Mennonite Church*
William E. Gramley	*Moravian Church in America*
Harry Huebner	*Mennonite Church*
Chris Iosso	*Presbyterian Church (U.S.A.)*
Rosemary Jermann	*Roman Catholic Church*
Howard John Loewen	*Mennonite Brethren Church*
Elizabeth Mellen	*Episcopal Church*
Lauree Hersch Meyer	*Church of the Brethren*
Marlin E. Miller	*Mennonite Church*
Richard Mouw	*Presbyterian Church (U.S.A.)*
Ben C. Ollenburger	*Mennonite Church*
Thomas Paxson	*Society of Friends*
John Rempel	*Mennonite Church*
Ben Richmond	*Society of Friends*
Glen Stassen	*Southern Baptist Church*
David Steele	*United Church of Christ*
John Stumme	*Evangelical Lutheran Church in America*

215

Select Bibliography

Denominational Peace Statements, 1980-91

Baptist   "American Baptist Policy Statement on Peace." Adopted by the General Board of the American Baptist Churches, 1985. Available from National Ministries, American Baptist Churches U.S.A., P.O. Box 851, Valley Forge, PA 19482-0851.

Catholic   National Conference of Catholic Bishops. *The Challenge of Peace: God's Promise and Our Response, A Pastoral Letter on War and Peace.* Washington, DC: United States Catholic Conference, 1983.

Episcopal   *To Make Peace: The Reports of the Joint Commissions on Peace of the General Convention of the Episcopal Church.* Cincinnati: Forward Movement Publications, 1988. Available from Office of Peace and Justice, Episcopal Church Center, 815 Second Ave., New York, NY 10017.

Evangelical   *Guidelines: Peace, Freedom, and Security Studies.* National Association of Evangelicals, 1986. Available from

216

National Association of Evangelicals, P.O. Box 28, Wheaton, IL 60189.

Historic Peace Churches

Douglas Gwyn, George Hunsinger, Eugene F. Roop, and John Howard Yoder. *A Declaration on Peace: In God's People the World's Renewal Has Begun. A Contribution to Ecumenical Dialogue Sponsored by Church of the Brethren, Fellowship of Reconciliation, Mennonite Central Committee, and Friends General Conference.* Scottdale, PA: Herald Press, 1991.

Lutheran

Lutheran Church in America Social Statements: Peace and Politics. Adopted by the Twelfth Biennial Convention of the Lutheran Church in America, 1984. Available from Division for Church in Society, Evangelical Lutheran Church in America, 8765 W. Higgins Rd., Chicago, IL 60631.

Methodist

The United Methodist Council of Bishops. *In Defense of Creation: The Nuclear Crisis and a Just Peace.* Nashville: Graded Press, 1986.

Orthodox

"Orthodox Perspectives on Justice and Peace." In *Justice, Peace and the Integrity of Creation: Insights from Orthodoxy,* edited by Gennadios Limouris, 16-27. Geneva: WCC Publications, 1990.

Presbyterian

The United Presbyterian Church in the United States of America. *Peacemaking: The Believers' Calling.* New York: The General Assembly of the United Presbyterian Church in the United States of America, 1980. Available from Office of the General Assembly, 1201 Interchurch Center, 475 Riverside Dr., New York, NY 10115.

Reformed

"Christian Faith and the Nuclear Arms Race: A Reformed Perspective." A Report from the Theological Commission, General Synod, The Reformed Church in America, 1980.

UCC [United The Peace Theology Development Team. *A Just Peace*
Church of *Church*. Edited by Susan B. Thistlethwaite. New York
Christ] (now Cleveland): United Church Press, 1986.

War and Peace in the Bible

Craigie, Peter C. *The Problem of War in the Old Testament*. Grand Rapids: William B. Eerdmans, 1978.
Janzen, Waldemar. *Still in the Image: Essays in Biblical Theology and Anthropology*. Newton, KS: Faith and Life Press, 1982.
Lind, Millard C. *Yahweh Is a Warrior: The Theology of Warfare in Ancient Israel*. Scottdale, PA: Herald Press, 1980.
Mauser, Ulrich. *The Gospel of Peace: A Scriptural Message for Today's World*. Louisville: Westminster/John Knox Press, 1992.
Niditch, Susan. *War in the Hebrew Bible: A Study in the Ethics of Violence*. New York: Oxford University Press, 1993.
Swartley, Willard M., ed. *The Love of Enemy and Nonretaliation in the New Testament*. Louisville: Westminster/John Knox Press, 1992.
von Rad, Gerhard. *Holy War in Ancient Israel*. Translated and edited by Marva J. Dawn. Grand Rapids: William B. Eerdmans, 1991.
Yoder, Perry B. *Shalom: The Bible's Word for Salvation, Justice and Peace*. Newton, KS: Faith and Life Press, 1986.
Yoder, Perry B., and Willard M. Swartley, eds. *The Meaning of Peace: Biblical Studies*. Translated by Walter Sawatsky. Louisville: Westminster/John Knox Press, 1992.

War and Peace in the Early Church

Helgeland, John, Robert J. Daly, and J. Patout Burns. *Christians and the Military: The Early Experience*. Philadelphia: Fortress Press, 1985.
Hornus, Jean-Michel. *It Is Not Lawful for Me to Fight: Early Christian Attitudes toward War, Violence, and the State*. Translated by Alan Kreider and Oliver Coburn. Scottdale, PA: Herald Press, 1980.
Swift, Louis J. *The Early Fathers on War and Military Service*. Message of the Fathers of the Church, 19. Wilmington, DE: Michael Glazier, 1983.
von Harnack, Adolf. *Militia Christi: The Christian Religion and the Military*

in the First Three Centuries. Translated by David McInnes Gracie. Philadelphia: Fortress Press, 1981.

War and Peace in Later Christian History

Bainton, Roland H. *Christian Attitudes toward War and Peace: A Historical Survey and Critical Re-Evaluation.* Nashville: Abingdon Press, 1960.

Brock, Peter. *Freedom from Violence: Sectarian Nonresistance from the Middle Ages to the Great War.* Toronto: University of Toronto Press, 1991.

————. *The Quaker Peace Testimony 1600 to 1914.* Syracuse, NY: Syracuse University Press, 1990.

Holmes, Arthur F., ed. *War and Christian Ethics.* Grand Rapids: Baker Book House, 1975.

Ecumenical Conversation on War and Peace

"Die lutherisch-mennonitischen Gespräche in der Bundesrepublik Deutschland 1989-1992." *Texte aus der VELKD* 53 (1993). Available from the Office of the Lutheran Church, Richard Wagner Str. 26, 30177 Hannover, Germany.

Durnbaugh, Donald F. *On Earth Peace: Discussions on War/Peace Issues between Friends, Mennonites, Brethren and European Churches, 1935-75.* Elgin, IL: The Brethren Press, 1978.

Les Entretiens Luthero-Mennonites: resultats du colloque de Strasbourg, 1981-1984. Avec une préface de Pierre Widmer et une présentation de Marc Lienhard. Montbéliard, France: Les Cahiers de Christ Seul, 1984. Available from 3, route de Grand-Charmont, 25200 Montbéliard, France.

vom Berg, Hans Georg, Henk Kossen, Larry Miller, and Lukas Vischer, eds., *Mennonites and Reformed in Dialogue.* Studies from the World Alliance of Reformed Churches, 7. Geneva: World Alliance of Reformed Churches, 1986.

Index of Scripture References

Index of Scripture References

227